Sadek Hamid is currently a senior researcher at the Oxford Centre for Islamic Studies in the University of Oxford and has written widely about British Muslims, young people and religious activism. He is the editor of *Young British Muslims: Between Rhetoric and Realities* (2016) and co-editor of *Youth Work and Islam: a Leap of Faith for Young People* (2011).

'Sadek Hamid has offered up an excellent, panoramic study of a misunderstood community. Deeply researched and dizzying in its detail, this book will likely stand as a seminal work on British Muslims. More than that, however, Hamid has much to say on Islam's role in public life and what it means to be Muslim. The book is also about that most universal of questions: the search for meaning and identity in an increasingly confusing and uncertain political moment.'

Dr Shadi Hamid, Senior Fellow, Brookings Institution and author of *Islamic Exceptionalism: How the Struggle Over Islam is Reshaping the World*

'It is a pleasure to commend this book by one of the leading scholars of Islam in Britain. Dr Sadek Hamid has the perfect combination of personal biography and experience, allied to academic rigour and attention to detail that makes this a nuanced, timely, well-informed contribution to the debate about Islam in Britain today.'

Prof. Sophie Gilliat-Ray, Professor in Religious and Theological Studies at Cardiff University and author of *Muslims in Britain: An Introduction*

T0348028

'Quite simply breathtaking. A real *tour-de-force* in every sense of the word. Sadek Hamid painstakingly charts and navigates with precision the landscape of British Islam by identifying the major intellectual trends competing, and at times vying, with one another for authority among second- and third-generation Muslim Britons. In so doing, he also introduces the key individuals who have shaped or contributed to the religious currents in what is an engaging tale of religious activism and often inter-group rivalry across Great Britain. This surely will become a primer for understanding the richness, complexities, challenges and fault-lines of Islam in Britain today, and hence, essential reading for policy-makers, students and general readers alike.'

Aftab A. Malik, Global Expert on Muslim Affairs, UN Alliance of Civilizations

'Sadek Hamid's book is absolutely essential reading for anyone who wishes to further their knowledge of the dynamics of Islamic activism in Britain. It rescues Islamism from the rhetoric of terrorism and highlights the essential differences between "Islamicisation" and "radicalisation".'

Prof. Ron Geaves, Honorary Visiting Professor in the School of History, Archaeology and Religion at Cardiff University, author of *Islam in Victorian Britain: The Life and Times of Abdullah Quilliam*

'Dr Hamid has written an invaluable study illuminating and evaluating the changing landscape of Islamic activism in Britain over the last 30 years. He devotes a chapter each to four faces of activism: reformist Islamist, radical pan-Islamist, Salafi and neo-Sufi. Their transnational origins, history, evolution and mutual rivalries are mapped and assessed in a measured, non-sensational and accessible manner. He also explores the extent to which they are positioned to respond appropriately to the experiences and questions of a new, media-savvy generation of British Muslims. Indispensable for policy-makers, academics, students and the general reader.'

Dr Phil Lewis, author of *Young, Muslim and British* and *Islamic Britain* (I.B.Tauris, 2002)

'This well-researched study provides an alternative, altogether insightful perspective of socio-religious trends that continue to influence and shape the landscape of Islamic activism in twenty-first-century Britain. It is unique in that it provides a comprehensive, insider-based account regarding movements that competed to promulgate often similar reforms but from differing standpoints.'

Dr Abdul Haqq Baker, author of *Extremists in Our Midst: Confronting Terror* and former Chairman of Brixton Mosque, London

'The author of this perceptive study provides a sharp analysis of what is happening among the religiously active parts of the new generation of Muslims in Britain. He covers the spectrum from those opting out of or pushing back against the British context to those who are critically and constructively engaging with it. One would wish that people in the media and political debates would read this study before pronouncing.'

Prof. Jørgen S. Nielsen, Professor in Contemporary European Islam. University of Birmingham

'Sadek Hamid in his authoritative and enlightening new book pinpoints how currents in Britain's Islamic reform movement found themselves vulnerable to changes by becoming irrelevant to the majority of young, generally working-class Muslims, effectively abandoning them to face deeply-rooted social and economic problems within their communities and intensifying Islamophobic discourses without.'

Hassan Mahamdallie, Deputy Editor of *Critical Muslim*

'This is a superb book, and I would urge all Muslims involved in activism to read it; for the general reader looking for an account of British Islamic activism in the recent past, there could be no better place to turn to and no surer guide than the author.'

islamicate.co.uk

'Sadek Hamid provides a history of British Islamists which steers well clear of the sensationalist rhetoric of newspapers and right-wing think tanks, and takes the reader up to the modern period.'

onreligion.co.uk

'Sadek Hamid correctly explains that understanding the history of British Muslim activism is a vital precursor to engaging with its present and future. And in *Sufis, Salafis and Islamists*, that recent past is succinctly unpacked, before projections into possible futures are considered. And for such highly-charged subject matter, it's the perfect sober, scholarly primer.'

sociologicalimagination.org

'Whilst in recent years there have been numerous books and studies on the subject, Hamid's contribution stands out for three reasons. First and foremost, this book is a voice from the inside and reflects years of community work in addition to extensive field research. Second, as the author himself attests, the book is a radical departure from other inside voices, notably ex-Islamists who with establishment support have successfully rebranded themselves as "counter-radicalisers." Third, notwithstanding the author's deep and sympathetic affinity with the subject, the book is generally a dispassionate treatment of the issues at stake and is produced to a rigorous academic standard.'

religion.info

'In this well-researched and cogently-argued book, Sadek Hamid seeks to unsettle contemporary suppositions about the "Muslim Question" in Europe. Although limited to the United Kingdom, Hamid's study belies the perception of Islamic activists in Europe as a united front bent upon asserting Muslim values in a secular society. Rather, Hamid shows that Islamic activists have rarely moved beyond the recurrent splits and multifarious disagreements within their own circles.'

fairobserver.com

SUFIS, SALAFIS AND ISLAMISTS

The Contested Ground of British
Islamic Activism

Sadek Hamid

BLOOMSBURY ACADEMIC
LONDON • NEW YORK • OXFORD • NEW DELHI • SYDNEY

BLOOMSBURY ACADEMIC
Bloomsbury Publishing Plc
50 Bedford Square, London, WC1B 3DP, UK
1385 Broadway, New York, NY 10018, USA

BLOOMSBURY, BLOOMSBURY ACADEMIC and the Diana logo are trademarks of
Bloomsbury Publishing Plc

Reprinted by Bloomsbury Academic 2020

ISBN: HB: 978-1-7883-1061-1
PB: 978-1-3501-5262-5
ePDF: 978-0-8577-2710-7
eBook: 978-0-8577-2915-6

Typeset in Garamond Three by OKS Prepress Services, Chennai, India

To find out more about our authors and books visit www.bloomsbury.com
and sign up for our newsletters.

For Hena, Adam, Emaani, Tahani and Muhammad

CONTENTS

ACKNOWLEDGEMENTS

The partial inspiration for this book came from a newsletter article written by pioneering British Muslim journalist Faisal Bodi while he was a student at Manchester University in 1993. Entitled 'The Players', it made an amusing comparison of the characteristics of Islamic activist groups competing for the attention of Muslims in campuses across the UK. The following pages are an attempt to understand how these groups emerged to mobilise second- and third-generation British Muslims into faith-based collective action. I am grateful to Ron Geaves for enabling the doctoral research which this text draws upon; he is an inspiration and a generous mentor. A number of individuals have directly and indirectly helped influenced this book through engaging in discussions with me and providing invitations to share my research at various stages over the years in different publications and at conferences in Britain and abroad. I would like to thank Faisal Bodi for his encouragement, Yahya Birt for the inspiration and collaboration, Tahir Abbas for the opportunities, Sophie Gilliat-Ray for her advice and support and Philip Lewis for his recommendations. Many people have shaped this work by sharing their recollections, especially Aftab Malik, Fuad Nahdi, Abdul-Rehman Malik, Usama Hasan and Atif Imtiaz, who were generous with their time and contributions through many conversations. I also appreciate the input and assistance of a number of academics along the way, in particular Roel Meijer, Malik Badri, Rebekah Tromble, Mazen Hashem, Linda Woodhead, Abdulkader Tayob and Tariq Ramadan. I would also like to express my gratitude to all the people who shared their experiences of Islamic activism: Qassim Afzal, Saddaf Alam, Mansoor

Hussain, Jahangeer Akhtar, Abdul Haqq Baker, Abdurraheem Green, Noman Hanif, Jai Byron, Yasir Rahman, Wakkas Khan, Afzal Khan, Robina Shah, Balal Siddique, Hamid Rashid, Robina Ahmed, Dilwar Hussain, Inayat Bunglawala, Ahtesham Ali, Ibrahim Osi-Efa, Tim Winter, Humera Khan, Abaas Choudury, Luqman Ali, Jahan Mahmood, Sajjid Miah, Laura McDonald, Tahir Haqq and the many other anonymous respondents.

I am grateful to Alex Wright at I.B.Tauris for his enthusiasm in publishing this book, Baillie Card for the helpful editorial support and Keith Devereux, Dan Shutt, Akbar Ahmed for writing the kind foreword, Omar Anchassi, Nasser Kurdy and the anonymous reviewers for their input. Early versions of Chapters 2, 3 and 4 have appeared in 'Islamic Political Radicalism in Britain: The Case of Hizb-ut-Tahrir', in Tahir Abbas (ed.), *Islamic Political Radicalism: A European Comparative*, (Edinburgh University Press, 2007), 'The Attraction of Authentic Islam: Salafism and British Muslim Youth', in Roel Meijer (ed.), *Global Salafism: Islam's New Religious Movement* (Hurst Publishers, 2009) and 'The Rise of the Traditional Islam Network: Neo-Sufism and British Muslim Youth' in Ron Geaves and Theodore Gabriel (eds), *Sufism in Britain* (Bloomsbury, 2013). Needless to say that any misrepresentations or shortcomings are entirely my own.

LIST OF ABBREVIATIONS

AM	Al-Muhajiroun
BMF	British Muslim Forum
BMSD	British Muslims for Secular Democracy
FOSIS	Federation of Student Islamic Societies
HT	Hizb ut-Tahrir
IAS	International Association of Sufism
iERA	Islamic Education and Research Academy
IFE	Islamic Forum of Europe
IPCI	Islamic Propagation Centre International
ISB	Islamic Society of Britain
JI	Jamaat-e-Islami
JIMAS	Jamiyyah Ihya' Minhaj as Sunnah
MAB	Muslim Association of Britain
MB	Muslim Brotherhood
MCB	Muslim Council of Britain
MET	Muslim Education Trust
MSS	Muslim Student Society
MUQ	Minhaj-ul-Quran
OASIS	Organisation of Ahl-al-Sunnah Islamic Societies
TI	Traditional Islam
UKIM	UK Islamic Mission
WAMY	World Assembly of Muslim Youth
YM	Young Muslims (UK)
YMO	Young Muslim Organisation

GLOSSARY OF ARABIC TERMINOLOGY

Adab	Correct Islamic etiquette
Ahl al-Hadith	The people of Prophetic narrations
Ahl al-ra'y	The people of reasoning
Ahl al-Suffa	The people of the Bench
Al-Firqaal-Najiya	The Saved Sect
Ahle-Sunnah wal-Jamaah	The people of the Sunni majority consensus
al-Wala' wal-bara'	Principle of loyalty and disavowal
Al-Wasatiyya	The Middle Path
Amir	Leader
Aqeeda	Creed
Barakah	Spiritual blessing
Batil	Falsehood
Bayyah	Allegiance
Bid'a	Religious innovation
Dar al-Islam	Land of Islam
Dar al-harb	Land of War
Daiyee	Caller to Islam
Dawah	Invitation to Islam
Deen	Religion, way of life
Fitna	Temptation/discord
Fitrah	Primordial nature
Hadith	Recorded traditions of Prophet Muhammad

Halaqah	Study circle
Haraki	Activist movement
Haram	Religiously forbidden
Hidaya	Guidance
Hijab	Head scarf
Hizb	Party/group
Hizbiyyah	Partisanship
Ihya	Revitalisation
Ihsan	Spiritual excellence
Ijazah	Scholarly licence
Ijtihad	Independent legal reasoning
Iman	Faith
Islah	Reform
Istightha	Seeking intercession from the deceased
Jahiliyyah	Pre-Islamic condition of ignorance
Julus	Devotional procession
Kafir	Disbeliever
Kufr	Disbelief
Khilafah	Representative/successor to Prophet Muhammad
Khimar	Outer garment for women
Jamaah	Community
Jihadi	Member of violent ideological movement
Jilbab	Long dress for women
Madhab	School of jurisprudence
Manhaj	Methodology
Maqasid	Purposes and intentions of the Shariah
Marifah	Spiritual gnosis
Mujaddid	Reviver of Islam at the turn of each century
Murid	Disciple of Sufi shaykh
Murtad	Apostate
Mushrif	Teacher
Nahdah	Cultural renaissance
Naqib	Study circle teacher
Nasheed	Religious song
Pir	Spiritual guide
Rafidi	Pejorative Salafi reference to Shi'a Muslims
Sahwa	Awakening

Salaf	First three generations of Muslims after the Prophet Muhammad
Salafiyah	Salafi groups
Sharia	Islamic Law
Shaykh	Scholar/leader
Shirk	Polytheism
Shura	Consultation
Silsilah	Scholarly chain of transmission
Sunnah	Example of the Prophet
Tafsir	Exegesis of the Qur'an
Tajdeed	Religious revival
Takfiri	Excommunicating characteristic of jihadis
Taqlid	Following of a school of jurisprudence
Tarbiyah	Moral education and training
Tariqa	Sufi order
Tassawuf	Sufism
Tawassul	Seeking Divine proximity via intercession of pious individual
Tawhid	Oneness of God
Tazkiyah	Spiritual purification
Ulama	Religious scholar
Ummah	Global religious community
Ustadh	Teacher
Wahhabi	Follower of Muhammad ibn 'Abd al-Wahhab
Wahdat al-wujud	Unity of existence
Wali	Friend/guardian
Zuhd	Worldly detachment

FOREWORD

Dr Sadek Hamid is a bright young scholar whose work provides critical nuance and insight into the British Muslim community and its Islamic currents. As a former activist and community development professional turned academic, he has channeled his intellect, passion and vigor into writing sharp academic studies and developed new programmes for studying Muslim youth work in the UK. With this diverse background, he provides a valuable and unique perspective on British Muslim religious trends, of which all in British society should take careful note.

This work highlights the importance of recognising how immigrants from the Muslim World identify with each other and with broader British society – a crucial factor needed to understanding Islam in the UK. These identities have shifted from generation to generation, whereas many of the first-generation who came in the 1950s and 1960s, socialised on the basis of ethnic identity, the second generation in the 1980s started seeking both a more religious identity and space in which to exercise their faith. This second generation, as Dr Hamid's historical analysis shows, is when Islamic movements in the UK were first founded as a way to balance out the 'non-Islamic influences' in wider society, before eventually developing into faith-based activism. He argues that from the mid-1980s onward, second-generation British Muslims generally identified with four religious orientations: the 'reformist Islamist' Young Muslims UK (YM), the 'radical pan-Islamist movement' Hizb ut-Tahrir (HT), the Salafi-oriented, JIMAS and neo-Sufi 'Traditional Islam' network (TI). These movements were especially attractive to young Muslims for a number of reasons. For one, they saw it as the way to be a 'good Muslim'; many activists were responding to a sense of struggle between Islam and the 'Other', as well as those who articulated the need for a strong British Islamic identity. The divisions between Muslim and non-Muslim Britons were clearly having a strong impact on the community at large and were frequently channeled into these faith-based movements.

Going into the third generation though, Dr Hamid explains how Islamic group dynamics have vastly shifted. No longer are the Islamic groups formal, hierarchal socio-political movements, but rather more decentralised, web-based political movements. He finds that some of the core factors here have included the rapid pace of growth in the British Muslim community, the securitisation of integration discourses and new communication technologies that exposed young people to new sources of religious introduction, among others. His study also demonstrates that divides between Muslim and non-Muslim Britons still exist; despite several decades of settlement and interaction, Muslim Britons are still struggling to find acceptance in modern British society.

Ultimately, in order to build bridges in British society and throughout the West, it is going to take work on both sides of the gap. Much as I have found in my work studying Muslim communities in the West, he finds a troubling lack of transparency and intellectualism within these trends. Muslim societies need to once again engage with *ilm* or knowledge and start focusing on sophisticated intellectual and philosophical ideas. But British society has a responsibility too. It needs to return to its humanist roots and engage with Muslim communities to address issues of inequality and discrimination to build stronger relations between communities. In a time when many in the UK and across Europe are grappling to learn more about their Muslim neighbours, Dr Hamid's poignant work can serve as a guide to policy makers, students and everyday citizens alike in learning more about their Muslim neighbours.

Professor Akbar S. Ahmed
Ibn Khaldun Chair of Islamic Studies
American University
Washington

INTRODUCTION

Islam's future is quite literally in the hands of its youth.[1]

Peter Mandaville

There is a widespread perception that Muslims in Britain have become more religiously observant and visible.[2] This is arguably substantiated by the increased number of mosques in major cities, daily news stories about Muslims, religious conservatism and radicalisation.[3] Mirroring similar developments among Muslim communities in Europe and North America, many British-born Muslims appear to be more attentive to public displays of prayer, overtly religious forms of dress and expressions of solidarity for transnational Muslim causes. However, is this perception true? If so, how did this occur, should it be considered a problem and why does it matter to debates about Islam in Britain? In the following pages, I will offer an explanation by telling the largely unwritten story of how a set of global Islamic trends competed to shape the religiosity of second- and third-generation Muslim Britons. Contemporary Islamic activism in the UK cannot be understood without reference to the contestations between these trends, and is important for what it tells us about how religion influences social change and the implications for wider social, policy and political questions in relation to British Muslim communities.

From the mid-1980s onwards, many second-generation British Muslims who wanted to take their faith seriously and participate in collective religious activism were drawn to four dominant religious orientations; the reformist Islamist Young Muslims UK (YM), the Salafi-oriented JIMAS (Jamiyyah Ihya' Minhaj as Sunnah – the Society to Revive the Way of the Messenger), the radical pan-Islamist movement Hizb ut-Tahrir and the neo-Sufi 'Traditional Islam' network, which emerged during the mid-1990s.[4] The descriptors 'Islamists' and 'Salafis' have gained wide currency in recent years, with little appreciation for the diverse meanings that these terms encompass. Instead, they are most often used interchangeably to discredit politically active Muslim individuals or institutions. In fact, Islamism is a broad spectrum of movements that all share a desire to have religious values inform their culture, economics and politics. Hizb ut-Tahrir, for example, is a transnational Islamist movement that calls for the establishment of a supranational Islamic state. Salafis are known for adhering to literalist interpretations of Islam and insistence on matters of correct doctrine, while Sufis tend to focus on the spiritual dimensions of faith and practice. Just as there are various denominations within Christianity, theological distinctions matter to people inside Muslim communities and these important religious differences should be recognised outside of them.

Much of the analyses of British Muslim communities over the last ten years has adopted a problem-centred approach and produced crisis-driven publications that focus upon terrorism, extremism, religio-cultural differences or social unrest.[5] Many commentators, politicians and elements of the media continue to express alarm about assertive Muslim identities and the threat of 'Radical Islam', but fail to distinguish differences between the two.

Since the London bombings of 2005, successive governments and commentators have searched for 'Moderate Muslims' and tried to isolate those considered 'Extremists'. These remain highly contentious terms and are energetically challenged by British Muslims, who see this language as evidence of a sustained effort to engineer compliance with specific government policies. A number of right-wing think-tanks in Britain, journalists such as Melanie Phillips, Douglas Murray and Andrew Gilligan, and politicians such as Michael Gove, have described Islamist and Salafi-oriented forms of religiosity as dangerous and could lead to the Islamisation of Britain.[6] Similar to Islamophobic networks in the US,[7] a cluster of writers and individuals associated with London-based think-tanks such as the Centre for Social Cohesion, Policy Exchange, the Henry Jackson Society and the Quilliam Foundation have produced numerous reports articulating their opposition to Islamism and highlighting its potential to infiltrate institutions and dominate the representation of Muslims in Britain.[8] For instance, in early 2015 the journalist John Ware produced a report for the BBC *Panorama* documentary programme which suggested that a 'Battle for British Islam' was taking place, a kind of culture war which presents a stark choice between those who promote a form of Islam 'in sync with British values', and 'non-violent extremists' who provide mood music for violent radicalisation.[9] This measuring of moderation and integration is even apparent in more serious studies of British Muslims.[10] The reduction of the intricate diversity of a faith community into moderates and extremists perpetuates the hostile politicised discourses which gained currency after the 9/11 terrorist attacks. Resorting to a rhetorical binary of 'Good Muslim' and 'Bad Muslim' reinforces prejudice, instead of providing meaningful explanations for the complex religious identities and experiences of Britain's second largest religious minority.

This deliberate avoidance or ignorance of nuance underscores the importance of trying to decode and contextualise religious activism among British Muslims. Understandable fears about violent radicalisation have skewed public discussion about these communities. After the '7/7' London bombings of 2005, young British Muslims came under unprecedented public scrutiny, such that juxtaposing 'Muslim' and 'youth' tended to trigger automatic associations with criminality and religious extremism. Since then, a growing body of scholarly literature, as well as journalistic accounts, have attempted to explain why some young people from Muslim backgrounds have been drawn to religiously inspired terrorism.[11] Whilst this is an important task, securitised perspectives often fail to fully grasp the wider context of Islamic activism, particularly its complex religious diversity and how international religious paradigms have 'travelled' and been transformed in the UK. Most of these studies also obscure the fact that the vast majority of young British Muslims participating in faith-based activism do so peacefully, in heterogeneous religious communities that are to a great extent unknown to outsiders. Equally, they are often unaware of the deep concern within Muslim communities about the misappropriation of Islamic symbolism by a vocal minority, and are unable to hear the passionate debates about social marginalisation, civilisational decline and the importance of transmitting Islamic values to future generations.[12]

Except for fragmented references in a handful of academic texts, populist British Muslim memoirs and journalistic treatments, the genesis and evolution of these specific trends is not well known.[13] Perhaps the two most widely read among these writings is Muslim intellectual Ziauddin Sardar's *Desperately Seeking Paradise: Journeys of a Sceptical Muslim*, which provided autobiographical reflections of his encounters with some of the main Islamic trends in the 1970s and early 1980s. However, Mohamed Mahbub 'Ed' Husain's controversial *The Islamist: Why I joined radical Islam in Britain, what I saw inside and why I left* has arguably exercised the greatest influence upon establishment perceptions of Islamic activism in the UK. Whilst his account contained some genuine insights about the inner workings of a number of British Islamist groups during the 1990s, it has drawn almost universal criticism within Muslim communities for being a politically motivated polemic.[14] In fact Husain, and his fellow traveller Maajid Nawaz, contributed to the simplistic usages of the concept of Islamism in British media and government circles.

In an effort to advance an understanding of British Islamic activism, this book explains how four distinct Muslim tendencies became national trends that exercised a tangible impact upon Islamic identity formation and catalysed the various forms of Islamic activism visible in Britain today. Understanding their role is also salient, as they assumed informal religious authority and defined the parameters for those aspiring to become devout Muslims. Crucially, they reflect wider global patterns whereby formal religious authority in Muslim majority societies has broken down and the new types of informal popular religious leadership in the West have been created.[15] The focus of *Sufis, Salafis and Islamists* is the visible minority of Muslim activists who embraced Islam as their primary identity marker. I critically examine the subject of Islamic activism as an academic and former activist, well-positioned to explain what happened within activist circles over a period of three decades. However, this is not another sensationalist 'ex-radical Muslim' account, but rather my attempt to fairly contextualise each of these four trends and their evolution in Britain. This book draws upon my own formal empirical study, and reflections from informal conversations with hundreds of people who have engaged in different variants of Islamic activism.[16]

A great deal of the complex Islamic activist scene we see today is led by people who are either former members of these trends, or have been influenced by them. I offer insider perspectives from people who joined these groups, what they intended to achieve, their internal group dynamics, the impact of external social changes and also consider whether there are links between religious activism and violent radicalisation. I will trace their origins from the mid-1980s, their rise to prominence in the 1990s and their transformation in the 2000s to the present decade. Overall, I will attempt to explicate the rise of visible Muslim religiosity by arguing that youth (re)Islamisation, where it occurred, was largely due to the work of these activist trends and that they continue to exert an influence on modes of personal and collective faith commitment.

A British *Ummah*

Muslims in Britain are a diverse tapestry, reflecting various strands from across the world. They comprise a population of nearly three million people, about 70 per cent of whom are from South Asian backgrounds alongside those from Arab, African, Persian and South East Asian heritage. Nearly 50 per cent are the children or grandchildren of the first generation settlers of the 1960s and 1970s who became adults in the late 1980s and early 1990s. The Islamic tradition, while containing a core normative set of beliefs and practices like other faiths, possesses a rich internal diversity of different theological currents, schools of jurisprudence and philosophical and spiritual trends developed over time and space. Contemporary theological trends in British Muslim communities were transmitted to Britain with the early communities of the 1960s and 1970s. These differences are complicated by differences in migration history, settlement patterns, nationality, ethnicity, kinship networks, class, geography, political allegiances and religious observance. Most South Asian British Muslims are from Sunni theological backgrounds that consist of a range of sectarian traditions.[17] Within this, four major religious traditions predominate; the devotionalist Barelwi Sufi tradition, the scripturally-oriented reform of the Deobandis, the Islamist Jamaat-e-Islami (JI) inspired institutions and the *Ahl al-Hadith* (people of Prophetic narrations) mosque network.[18] However, not all British Muslims necessarily define themselves according to their faith. Many in the first generation identified themselves in terms of the country of origin, ethnicity or acquired nationality. Like members of other faith traditions, some Muslims are devout, others are not. A few possess highly politicised religious identities, while others are observant of their religion but have no interest in politics. It is also possible to find people that consider themselves Muslims culturally but hold anti-religious or even atheistic sentiments.[19]

During the early 1980s, most people of Muslim heritage were starting to move from ethnic self-identification to describe themselves primarily as Muslim.[20] This gradual transition was expressed through communal concerns around securing halal meat, places of worship and how to ensure the transmission of religious values to their children. Among the key areas for the development of a faith-based identity was in education. Those of an activist inclination realised that their children were spending most of their day at school, and that after-school religious education provision in mosques were inadequate to balance the 'non-Islamic influences' of the state education system. They responded by creating institutions such as the Pakistani JI-influenced UK Islamic Mission (UKIM), founded in 1963, the Middle Eastern Muslim Brotherhood (MB)-inspired Muslim Students Society (MSS), created in 1962, and the Federation of Student Islamic Societies (FOSIS) in 1963. As Islamist institutions with clear ideological goals, they wanted to create a network of like-minded activist organisations that would cater for the children of the first-generation settlers and overseas students in the 1960s.

UKIM was intended to provide members and supporters of the JI with a base to continue spreading the ideas of JI founder Sayyid Abul A'la Mawdudi (1903–79). JI-inspired institutions such as the Muslim Education Trust (MET), created in 1966, and the Islamic Foundation in 1973, were at the forefront of efforts to provide religious education resources to compensate for the absence of Islamic religious instruction in the state sector, whilst at the same time promoting the ideological perspectives of the JI and MB. In the 1970s UKIM established the first Muslim youth movement, and were involved in the creation of the Young Muslims UK (YM) in the mid-1980s. The Bengali membership of UKIM formed separate organisations in the late 1970s, leading to the creation of Dawatul-Islam and the Islamic Forum of Europe (IFE), and its youth wing the Young Muslim Organisation (YMO), in 1978. In addition, the Union of Muslim Organisations

(UMO) was established in 1970, which attempted to act as a national interlocutor for Muslim political and civic concerns to government, and could be viewed as a predecessor to the Muslim Council of Britain (MCB) launched in the mid-1990s.

Explicit faith-based activism became more visible in the mid-1980s, when some of these bodies entered the public sphere. They questioned aspects of the national curriculum in relation to the content of school lessons and how they impacted on Muslim children. Localised campaigns to withdraw children from Christian-based assemblies, sex education classes, music lessons, mixed gender physical education and requests for the provision of halal meat became sources of debate and resistance. These later developed into active nationally coordinated operations sparked by a number of conflicts between Muslim parents and local schools in the late 1980s. For instance, allegations of racism made against a Bradford headmaster, the suspension of two sisters for wearing the *hijab* (head scarf) at a school in Manchester and calls for a greater parity between funding for Muslim schools and Christian and Jewish schools, became high profile flash points between school authorities and Muslim communities who felt that their religious rights were being denied. As a result, Muslims increasingly campaigned under the banner of their faith separately from Black anti-racist platforms that challenged discrimination against minorities but ignored religion in their work. These issues, over time, penetrated the communal consciousness of Muslims as they began to appreciate the power of faith-based collective action.[21]

Learning to be Muslim

For most Muslim children, the basis of their religious identity acquisition is developed in their formative years by inculcating their 'Muslimness' through the familial space, peer group contact and attendance in after-school classes in the mosque. The level of understanding gained by children in mosques is affected by the effectiveness of teaching pedagogies in these institutions. Traditional South Asian mosques are often criticised for failing to impart religious teaching in a meaningful way because of the use of rote-learning methods in mother tongue languages and corporal punishment, which was common in many mosques in the 1970s and 1980s. These two approaches in particular highlight the linguistic, intellectual and cultural disconnect between the religious leadership in many Muslim communities and the young people they sought to educate. Furthermore, the increasingly secular cultural milieu of modern Britain, and the lack of accessible places to learn about Islam, were additional factors for the emergence of religious revival groups. Until the mid-1980s, very little was being done to provide Muslim children with religious education in the English language. For most first-generation Muslims, Islam was an aspect of their ethnic identity, and faith adherence was more to do with participating in communal life and less about personal religiosity.

It was not until the 'Rushdie Affair' that significant numbers of second-generation Muslims seriously began to consider what their faith meant to them. The controversy had iconic importance for this generation, which was coming to terms with its religion, ethnic cultures and position within British society. Though most people in Muslim communities did not read the book, the incident politicised them and it became a 'wake-up call' for many young people. Up to that point, religion had not played a prominent role in most young Muslims' lives and, as one young Muslim journalist reflected: 'It was Salman Rushdie who made us realise, as a community, that we were primarily Muslims.'[22]

On a macro level, many Muslim-majority societies across the world were impacted by the rise of Islamic revivalist sentiment in the 1970s and 1980s. There were various global political shifts that had repercussions for Muslims in Britain. The first one to have consequence in the UK was the 1979 revolution in Iran, and its subsequent competition with Saudi Arabia for influence among Muslim communities through its financial support for institutions and mosque construction.[23] In addition, the impact of international political crisis events in the 1990s, such as the first Gulf War and conflicts in Bosnia and Chechnya, became critical landmarks that had traumatic effects upon many young Muslims, causing them to ask why it was happening and why most non-Muslims did not seem to care. These events raised other questions about what their faith meant to them and encouraged them to identify with advocates of *ummah* – a global religious community. As Islam is a community-oriented religion, those seeking religious identities sought out like-minded others to share their experiences. Islamic revitalisation groups provided opportunities to express what French scholar Olivier Roy called a globalised 'deterritorialised' Islamic identity, that is to say a decultured, universal Islam which expressed varieties of a born-again religiousity that transcended ethnicity, culture and space.

Spectrum of Islamic praxis

The British Islamic activist landscape today is populated by a spectrum of religious orientations and organisations, which include: Sufis, Salafis, Islamists, anti-Islamists, post-Islamists, Jihadists, and civil society service-based initiatives. Defining Muslim faith-based activism is contentious as so many competing terms attempt to capture the essence of this phenomenon. Specialists continue to debate the utility of appellations such as Fundamentalism, Islamism or Political Islam, knowing that the activists themselves do not always accept these labels. These terms are also often accompanied with qualifiers such as 'radical', 'militant', 'conservative' and defined within specific analytical frameworks in response to particular modes of historical, social and political inquiry. Similarly, theological descriptors such as *Salafi*, *Wahhabi*, *Jihadi*, and *Takfiri* are not only political doctrines but also living theological traditions that are interpreted, contested and evolve over time. I prefer to use Islamic activism to describe Muslim faith-based religious collective action as it accommodates the various manifestations of religious reform movements recognisable in the Western academic tradition and is elastic enough to encompass the meanings of the Arabic terms *dawah*, *ihya*, *nahdah*, *islah* and *tajdeed*, which correspond to invitation, revitalisation, renaissance, reform and revival. These are definitions and strategies used by the activists themselves and include religious trends that are non-political and sometimes opposed to politicised trends. The Islamic activist impulse, in its essence, is driven by the desire to reform lapsed Muslims and invite non-Muslims to Islam.

The many different typologies that claim to distinguish between these trends are useful to the extent of providing approximate conceptual maps of theological and political differences between different groups, but are not rigid categories which possess predicative power. Most recognised classifications adopt versions of a tripartite split that organise Islamic activism into ideological responses to the 'Western colonial encounter', 'traditionalism/fundamentalism' and 'modernism'/'secularism'.

Scholars such as John Esposito have analysed them according to what he calls 'attitudes towards modernisation and Islamic socio-political change' and identifies 'conservative', 'neo-traditionalist', 'Islamic reformist' and 'secularist' attitudes.[24] Historian John Voll treated them as 'styles of action' in Islamic history and categorised them as 'adaptationist', 'conservative' and 'fundamentalist'.[25] With his six major tendencies model, Muslim academic Tariq Ramadan produced perhaps the most comprehensive categorisation of Muslim global activist trends so far.[26] These are grouped as 'Scholastic Traditionalism', 'Salafi Literalism', 'Salafi Reformism', 'Salafi Political reformism', 'Liberal' or 'Rationalist' Reformism and Sufism. I have summarised his schema with relevant British examples, as follows:

Scholastic Traditionalism has a distinct approach to the two primary sources of religious knowledge – the Qur'an and Sunnah (personal example of the Prophet Muhammad).* It is characterised by a strict, often exclusive adherence to one of the main schools of jurisprudence – either one of four Sunni schools of jurisprudence (Hanafi, Maliki, Shafi'i, Hanbali) or two Shi'a schools (Zaydi, Ja'fari) – and the meanings of the Qur'an and Sunnah are mediated through recognised scholars from a given school, who allow a limited scope for interpretation. Scholastic traditionalists focus on acts of worship, increasing personal piety and dress codes, and rely mainly on the legal opinion of scholars codified between the eighth and eleventh centuries. There is little room for *ijtihad* (independent reasoning), which is often seen as baseless and an unacceptable modernisation and generally avoid social or political participation.

In the UK this trend is best represented by the Barelwi and Deobandi schools. Each sharply criticises how the other understands the nature of the Prophet Muhammad. Generally speaking, Barelwis are mainly concerned with devotional matters and promote attendance at gatherings that praise the Prophet. The British Muslim Forum (BMF) acts as the main umbrella organisation for the various Barelwi groups and perhaps the most active organisation within this current is Minhaj-ul-Quran (MUQ), a reformist Barelwi movement, originating in Pakistan, founded by the scholar Tahir-ul-Qadri. The other main example are the Deobandis, who derive their name from the Islamic reform work initiated in the late nineteenth century in Deoband, India. This movement was developed as a reaction to British colonialism and is distinct from the Barelwis for their disinterest in what they consider as excessive reverence of the Prophet and shrine culture. They are also known for their strict adherence in following a madhab (school of jurisprudence) and focus on Islamic education. From their headquarters in Bury, north-west England, the Deobandis have an extensive network of religious institutions and centres of learning throughout the UK.

Salafi Literalism adherents perceive themselves to be following the *Salaf* – the first three generations of companions of the Prophet. They are distinguished for their insistence on referring to the Qur'an and 'authentic' Hadith texts to evidence correct belief, religious action, dress code and social behaviour. Their understanding of the text in its literal form has a constraining force and cannot be subjected to interpretations that allow *bid'a* (religious innovation) and, unlike the scholastic traditionalists, generally reject the mediation of the schools of jurisprudence. Most avoid social involvement with spaces that are considered non-Islamic and function as isolationist communities trying to protect themselves from Western cultural influences. Salafi groups in Britain are inspired by and are in constant communication with Salafi scholars based in Saudi Arabia, Jordan, and Yemen and have split into several factions. JIMAS, created in 1984, was the most prominent early representative of this trend before rupturing into different orientations in the mid-1990s.

Salafi Reformism shares with Salafi Literalists the desire to refer back to the Salaf and bypass the boundaries of the juridical schools. In contrast to the literalists, they adopt a reading of sacred scripture based upon the *maqasid* (purposes and intention) of the Shariah, believe that contextualised *ijtihad* is necessary and are eager to engage with the socio-political challenges of the day. They would like to achieve pan-Islamic unity and have expressed the desire to recreate a caliphate. Most Salafi reformist groups grew out of the inspiration of late nineteenth century and early twentieth century Islamic thinkers and in Britain include groups such as the Young Muslims, Young Muslims Organisation, Islamic Forum of Europe, Dawatul Islam and the Muslim Association of Britain.

Political Literalist Salafism has grown out of the political repression that exists in parts of the Muslim world. They want to trigger radical social and political transformation with a literalist reading of the texts.

They tend to take oppositional stances towards government in Muslim lands and are preoccupied with capturing state power and reinstating a caliphate. They also see themselves as resisting Western imperialism and are opposed to the idea of integration within Western societies. The most prominent examples here are Hizb ut-Tahrir (HT), Supporters of Sharia and the offshoots of Al-Muhajiroun (AM). In Britain, HT attempts to mobilise public opinion so it becomes favourable to their mission to re-establish their vision of a caliphate. Al-Muhajiroun was founded by the former leader of HT in the UK – Omar Bakri Muhammad – and has gone through a number of reincarnations such as 'Al-Ghuraba', the 'Saviour Sect' and 'Islam4UK'. The now defunct Supporters of Sharia (SOS), founded by Abu Hamza, can also be placed in this category.[27] The SOS, AM and its offshoots are notable for their religious extremism, intolerance towards other Muslim groups, intention to establish the caliphate in the UK and open incitement of British Muslims to violence.

Sufism encompasses a broad range of different trends with diverse origins and representations. The primary texts of Qur'an and Hadith (recorded traditions of Prophet Muhammad) are the ultimate point of reference, in addition to the works of well-known Sufi scholars. Sufi circles lay emphasis on the inward life and call to spiritual purification and seeking closeness to God. There are various historical Sufi orders that are represented by their own shaykhs or representatives and network of disciples. They can both shun and promote social involvement depending upon the particular trend. The most significant historical *turuq* (Sufi orders) in the UK are the Naqshbandi, Chistiyya, and Qadiri orders. The Barelwis would also fit into this category as they see themselves as connected with the historical orders. The modern trans-Atlantic neo-Sufi trend, which is known as 'Traditional Islam', is discussed in detail in Chapter 4.

'Liberal' or 'Rationalist' Reformism trends emerged out of the colonial period and are intellectually indebted to the European Enlightenment. Essentially a secularising outlook, they insist that the Qur'an and Hadith cannot be primary reference points in regulating the behavioural norms and expect Muslims to assimilate into Western culture. In Britain this trend is exemplified by organisations such as British Muslims for Secular Democracy (BMSD), founded by a small group of British Muslims writers, academics and professionals, and the controversial Quilliam Foundation (QF). The Quilliam Foundation, which brands itself as 'the world's first counter-extremism think tank', was created by two ex-members of HT.[28] This trend also included the now defunct Sufi Muslim Council (SMC), which attempted to cast itself as the voice of moderate Sufi Islam in the UK.[29] All three organisations have been vocal against Islamist and Salafi trends.

Although all these six tendencies are visible in the UK and have different levels of influence, it is the Sufis and different versions of Salafism (literalist, reformist and political) – the latter two usually referred to as Islamists, which have most impacted religious activism within British Muslim communities. Another more concise way of understanding how these trends differ is to distinguish them according to their strategies of dealing with non-Muslim society, or what could be called *participation orientations*. 'Conservative Isolationist' trends like the Salafis focus on maintaining religious identity, creating institutions that continue to transmit their values and tend to engage wider society only when they want to demand their rights. 'Integrationist' trends like YM/ISB, YMO/ IFE and MAB are generally keen to participate in wider society. A third approach, exemplified by HT and the offshoots of the Al-Muhajiroun organisation, are both isolationist and confrontational, and rationalise their presence in Britain by promoting their own political agendas.

It is also important to acknowledge that although South Asian and Middle Eastern Salafi reformist movements have dominated the British activist scene, there are other important Islamic trends that have constituencies which are not well known outside their sectarian or ethnic membership bases. These include for instance, the followers of Shi'a organisations like Al-Khoei Foundation, the Dawoodi Bohra, Ismaili Shi'as communities and the community in Norwich who follow the teachings of Scottish convert Shaykh Abdal Qadir al-Murabit. There are also organisations inspired by the Turkish Muslim scholar Fethullah Gulen and a variety of African and South East Asian Islamic associations active in their localities. My specific interest in this book are the four dominant currents and hence precludes analysis of other important trends that deserve separate attention such as the Barelwi trends and young scholars and activists from Deobandi institutions. I have also only selected Sunni movements and have intentionally left out important Shi'a organisations and other well-established trends that may be active at a local level. The disproportionate coverage given to trends that work with South Asian Muslim communities reflects the current demographic majority, though I have attempted as much as possible to include a diversity of Muslim voices and backgrounds. The synoptic presentation of the ideas of these groups here are not intended as definitive histories of the four trends but as an integrated, analytical narrative.

The structure of this book follows a similar pattern for the next four chapters. The first chapter contextualises reformist thought by making reference to its intellectual genealogy and key ideas of Islamic reformism. It then touches upon the influence of figures who provided the conceptual foundations of YM and provides an overview of the first ten years – arguably its most influential period – and an account of the tensions which led to its demise. Chapter 2, delineates the main features and history of the British branch of the transnation movement HT. This chapter outlines its historical foundation, British modes of operation and how it distinguished itself as major force within the UK Islamic activist scene. Chapter 3 provides a survey of the emergence and establishment of Salafi trends within Muslim communities in the UK. It highlights some of the main conceptual characteristics of Salafism then goes on to describe the development, evolution and diversification of British Salafism after the creation of JIMAS and how it competed against YM and HT. Chapter 4 provides an outline of historical understandings of the Sufi tradition and then describes how it became established in British Muslim communities. It provides an introduction to the so-called 'Traditional Islam' network by delineating its main contours, how it differs from existing ethnic/transnational Sufi orders and why it emerged in the British scene. Chapter 5, links together the four broad narratives by looking at the popular discourses that they have produced. It does this by applying set analytical tools from Social Movement Theory to show how these discourses helped to recruit people into the different trends. Chapter 6 describes how the four trends deal with social change and the shift in rhetoric caused by the repercussions of international events and new developments within Muslim communities. Chapter 7 summarises the main themes, makes an assessment of the impact of each trend, highlights new patterns of activism and leads to the concluding chapter, which identifies some potential challenges for those working in the activist scene.

CHAPTER 1

'TAKING ISLAM TO THE PEOPLE': THE YOUNG MUSLIMS UK

> The day will then come when Britain will give up all 'isms' and
> established religions, and submit to the will of the Creator. That
> day Britain will become Islamic. Let that be your goal.[1]
>
> Khurram Murad

The 1990s were the defining period for British-born Islamic activists and
perhaps the most intense for its micro-identity politics. The decade was
also notable for the forms of global Muslim solidarity that emerged during
various international political crises. This growing Muslim consciousness
was vividly expressed in the coordinated outrage that followed the
publication of Salman Rushdie's novel *The Satanic Verses* in 1988: attempts
by British Muslims to have the book banned, the intervention of Iran's
religious leadership and the violent demonstrations that took place in
some Muslim-majority states. The Rushdie Affair became the first event
to capture the imagination of a generation of young Muslims coming to
terms with their multi-layered identities and became a personal turning
point for some. The internationalisation of this incident also triggered
greater interest in the politics taking place within Muslim communities
and in wider society. This youth politicisation was accelerated further by a
series of international confrontations involving Muslims beginning with
the first Gulf War in 1991, the Bosnian tragedy between 1993–5, the
Chechen conflict in 1994, the Kosovan crisis in 1998 and unresolved
political disputes in Palestine and Kashmir. While youth activists from

Muslim backgrounds joined leftist organisations in the 1970s to challenge discrimination and address internationalist causes, those who came of age in the late 1980s saw these events from the perspective of their faith, articulated their concerns in religious terms and called on others to do the same. At the forefront of this shift was the Young Muslims UK, one of the first British Muslim youth organisations to successfully establish a national following. It inspired a generation of activists, but struggled with its internal commitment to two different and often diverging goals that seeded ideological disagreements within its leadership and caused its eventual decline.

Revival and Reform

The feature that distinguished traditional forms of religiosity associated with the first generation of Muslims migrating to Britain in the 1960s and religious institutions created by reformist activists is the idea of *dawah* – invitation to Islam which may be given to either to non-Muslims or Muslims. To fellow Muslims, *dawah* is intended to remind them of their religious obligations and bring about religious social reform. The idea of *tajdeed* (revival) and *islah* (reform) are Qur'anic concepts, the former refers to the religious mission of various divinely inspired Messengers to their societies, while the latter is exemplified by a well-known tradition of the Prophet Muhammad which informs believers that 'God will send for the *ummah* at the advent of every one hundred years a person (or persons) who will restore/reform the deen'.[2] This implies that periodically an individual or a group of people will revive and restore the centrality of the Qur'an and Sunnah of the Prophet in the everyday lives of Muslims.

The origins of modern reformist thought corresponded with the apex of Western military and commercial power and a sense of crisis which gripped Muslim societies in the nineteenth century. While some Muslim intelligentsia advocated a rapid, wholesale embrace of Western ideas about science, progress, art, politics and economic models, other conservative elements rejected change and resisted by retreating into their own mental and physical enclaves. Reformist scholars, intellectuals and statesmen advocated responses in different ways to these changing realities, whilst retaining their loyalty to Islam. The contemporary Islamic resurgence is credited to a series of Salafi reformist religious thinkers that emerged in the Middle East and Indian subcontinent in the late nineteenth century to the early and mid-twentieth century. The writings and activism of Jamal al-Din al-Afghani (1838–97), Muhammad Abduh (1849–1905), Rashid Rida (1865–1935), 'Abd al-Hamid bin Badis (1889–1940), Hasan al-Banna (1906–49), Sayyid Abul A'la Mawdudi (1903–79), Malik Bennabi (1905–73), Sayyid Qutb (1906–66), Syed Abul Hasan Nadwi, (1914–99), Yusuf al-Qaradawi (*b.* 1926), Rachid Ghannouchi (*b.* 1941), Khurshid Ahmad (*b.* 1932) and Khurram Murad (1932–96), though differing in their perspectives all had significant influence far beyond their countries of origin.[3] They provided critiques on what they thought were the causes of Muslim civilisational decline, sought political liberation from colonisation and mobilised Islamic sentiment. Some focused their efforts intellectually while others pursued social reform movements that generated a wide spectrum of social, political, economic and cultural trends drawing inspiration from Islam. Most called for a peaceful, gradual reform of Muslim societies, including educational and scientific development, while a minority advocated violent revolutionary change. Some, such as as Sayyid Qutb, who was executed in Egypt in 1966, were sympathetic to revolutionary militancy.[4] Others, like Rachid Ghannou-chi, a key figure of the current Ennahda movement in Tunisia, advocates gradualist politics and democratic participation.[5] Despite many differences in emphasis and priorities, they all shared a concern for preserving Islamic values from what they saw as the irresistible forces of Western modernity. Collectively referred to as Islamists, they are recognised for their deployment of signs and symbols 'that (re)construct repertoires and frames of reference from Islamic traditions'.[6] They are best exemplified by the *Ikhwan al-Muslimun*, otherwise known as the Muslim Brotherhood (MB) in the Middle East, Jamaat-e-Islami (JI) in the Indian subcontinent, Ennahda of Tunisia, Party for Justice (PJD) in Morocco, Parti Islam Se-Malaysia (PAS) party in Malaysia. In the past, most Islamist movements indicated a desire to capture state power and apply Islamic law in its totality, but in recent times the majority advocate a pragmatic, gradualist vision which works for representation at governmental levels so as to influence policy and legislation. Most now generally accept the nation-state, democratic norms, function with the constitutional frameworks of the countries' attempt to reconcile tradition with modernity and selectively borrow from the West.

This reformism is Salafi in character in that it is based upon the idea that reform can only take place if Muslims not only re-centre the primacy of the Qur'an and Sunnah as their religious reference points but also revive *ijtihad* as a principle in solving new societal challenges. The two populist movements which defined reformism as a political project were the Muslim Brotherhood in Egypt founded by Hasan al-Banna in 1928 and Sayyid Abul A'la Mawdudi's Jamaat-e-Islami, created in India in 1941.[7] Although formed independently, they shared a set of common assumptions and goals combining anti-colonialism, religious revivalism, opposition to secular governments and have inspired similar movements throughout Muslim majority societies and organisations in the West. During the twentieth century both experienced successes and failures but remain potent forces. The diffusion of the modern reformist ideas pioneered by these two movements has had a global impact on Islamic activism, particularly in the creation of Islamic institutions in the West. Professor of Islamic Studies Marcia Hermansen, observing the conceptual basis of Islamist revivalist movements in the US, noted:

> An ideological premise of internationalist identity Islam is that this 'true' Islam is apparently floating above everything cultural. It is pristine and unassailable, politically it had established a utopian state where everyone was happy and honest, and that this state should be re-imposed on humanity today and it will make a better world. Internationalist Muslim revivalist movements such as Jamaat-i Islami and Muslim Brotherhood [. . .] have encouraged this concept of a 'cultureless' Islam around the world. These revivalists have been able to dominate Muslim organizations and mosques because of their commitment, pre-existing networks, external material support, and defined ideological agenda.[8]

Islamist reformism is a symbolic framework that encompasses identity, education, culture, socio-economics and politics. It was in many ways an ideologisation of faith, developed as an intellectual response to Western ideological currents that were gaining popularity in Muslim societies at the time. The ideas and writings of Hasan al-Banna, Sayyid Abul A'la Mawdudi, Sayyid Qutb and Yusuf al-Qaradawi, migrated with members of the Jamaa'ti/Ikhwani traditions as they settled in Britain in the 1960s.[9] Largely centred on the notion that 'Islam is a complete way of life', Mawdudi and Qutb in particular theorised the interconnectivity between personal faith and practical life – which for them required converting religious beliefs into dynamic social action. This conceptualisation of Islam as an active force in human affairs propelled the spirit of reformist organisations. Among its key themes was the self-perception of reformists being leaders of an 'Islamic awakening' who would promote 'Islamic social justice' in British Society. The influential work of these two thinkers formed part of the essential reading for the workers of the 'Islamic Movement' in Britain, as reformists like to call themselves. The ultimate goal of this Islamist movement, to 'establish the supremacy of Islam' in Britain, naturally alarmed critical observers anxious about the implications of such slogans and the track record of their antecedents in the Middle East and Indian subcontinent. However, while the fears of a grand Islamist entryist strategy to infiltrate and conquer Europe animated a growing number of journalistic and securitised writings about these movements, closer scrutiny of their actual capacity and achievements in Muslim communities demonstrated a failure to deliver most of their founding mission statements, let alone Islamise a continent.[10]

Building the Foundations

In Britain, the activist trends that appeared in the 1980s were led by Salafis and Islamists who were primarily interested in re-Islamising Muslim youth. This trend was established by the early generation of migrant settlers in the 1960s, who belonged to such organisations as the MB-inspired Muslim Student Society and the JI influenced UKIM, which was formed in 1962. UKIM was effective in creating a network of mosques in most British cities and towns with significant Muslim populations and together these two groups shaped the discourse of a generation of pre-eminent Islamist-oriented organisations and insti-tutions, such as the World Assembly of Muslim Youth (WAMY), FOSIS, the Muslim Educational Trust, Islamic Foundation and Dawatul Islam. UKIM's ideational stance reflected Mawdudi's vision of Islam for Britain, which desired the creation of an Islamic social order. Like their counterparts in JI, UKIM – with its network of mosques – was concerned with training 'a righteous community' that would provide a dynamic nucleus for the Islamisation of society. Most of the personnel of

UKIM were members of JI or people sympathetic to the ideas of Mawdudi. It had a small number of *ulama* (religious scholars), but no thinkers or strategists. Indeed, up until the late 1990s they were still looking to Pakistan's JI for direction and intellectual leadership. One of the most influential JI figures to support the work of UKIM was Khurram Murad, who was born in Bhopal, India and was a civil engineer by profession. He joined JI as a teenager and rapidly rose through the movement to become a leader of its student wing, the Jamiat-e-Talaba, in Pakistan in 1952–3. He developed a reputation for being an inspiring and effective organiser and was selected to become president of the East Pakistan branch of the movement before its separation into Bangladesh. He later became well known as a close disciple and translator of Mawdudi's work and was the author of over 50 books in Urdu and English. Murad gained recognition as one of the most important reformist strategists in the late twentieth century and was a pioneer of the view that Muslims should be permanent settlers and transmitters of *dawah* to the West. His thoughts were articulated in three influential publications: *Islamic Movement in the West: Reflections on Some Issues, Da'wah among Non-Muslims in the West: Some Conceptual and Methodological Aspects* and *Muslim Youth in the West: Towards a New Education Strategy.*[11] The supreme goal of this 'Movement' was intended to be:

> an organised struggle to change the existing society into an Islamic Society based upon the Qur'an and the Sunnah and make Islam, which is a code for entire life, supreme and dominant, especially in the socio-political spheres [...] the movement in the West should reaffirm and re-emphasize the concept of total change and supremacy of Islam in the Western society as its ultimate objective and allocate to it the highest priority [...] it shall not be realised unless the struggle is made by the locals. For it is only they who have the power to change the society into an Islamic society.[12]

Khurrum Murad, familiar with the intellectual and social realities of Western societies, departed from his mentors approach and instead advocated an organic Islamisation by both intellectual exchange and face-to-face interaction between Muslims and non-Muslims. Murad argued that:

We do not invite people to a 'new' religion; we invite them to the oldest religion, indeed to their 'own' religion, the religion of living in total surrender to their Creator, in accordance with the guidance brought by all His Messengers. Indeed, if I am not misunderstood, we may be bold enough to say that we do not invite anyone to change his 'religion', to transfer his allegiance to a rival religion. For, by our own admission, Islam is not a new or rival religion among the many competing for human allegiance; it is the natural and primordial religion. All nature lives in submission to its Creator; all Messengers from Adam to Muhammad brought the same religion.[13]

This is because Islam is believed to be a continuation and culmination of 'the same truth [...] brought by all the earlier Messengers [...] coming to Islam is like going back to one's own roots in nature, and in history'.[14] These ideas reflect normative understandings of the missionary nature of Islamic teaching and its relationship with Abrahamic traditions. Accordingly, to convert to Islam is to return to ones original religion and hence many new Muslims refer to themselves as 'reverts'. This perspective is widely established in Islamic activist communities today and can be credited to figures like Murad, who along with Palestinian-American thinker Ismail Raji al-Faruqi (1921–86), were the most prolific theorists of *dawah* in the West and frequently invited to speak and advise Islamic organisations in Britain, America and South Africa.[15] To implement Murad's vision required an effective movement of British-born Muslims well acquainted with Western culture and able to communicate in an idiom that Muslim youth and non-Muslims would understand. He knew that young people would be instrumental in this process and this required the creation of an effective Islamic youth movement.

Made in Britain

After its inception, UKIM tried to persuade young people to transmit its ideology and by 1965 was offering scholarships to promising students who could 'establish Islam in Britain'. Prior to the formation of YM, the earliest attempt at developing an Islamic youth forum in Britain can be traced back to the activities of the Islamic Youth Movement (IYM) in the mid-1970s. The IYM was created in Bradford by UKIM, in the hope that its youth cohort would one day take over as leaders of the organisation. They seconded one of its members, Ahmed Jamal, to develop youth work among children who attended after-school religious education. By working in local schools, he was able to recruit a small core of individuals to form a youth network. The work of the IYM focused on developing recreational activities, camping trips and regular weekly meetings where they studied the works of reformist ideologues. In 1976 the IYM published a magazine called *The Movement*, though by the end of the 1970s it had collapsed due to members of the organisation moving on to adult life responsibilities and having little spare time. Efforts to create a national youth organisation continued until the early 1980s and was given fresh impetus by Khurram Murad, who is credited as the spiritual father of Young Muslims UK. Under his guidance, in 1982 a small group of young men close to UKIM were chosen to form the executive committee for a new national Islamic youth movement. After receiving training from Murad, they launched the Young Muslims UK at a convention in Bradford on 4 December 1984.[16] This was followed up by a series of members meetings in Leicester in the spring of 1985 and the first public conference in Birmingham later that year.

I would suggest that YM has gone through three phases and has produced three generations of activists. The first phase was from its establishment in 1984 to its gradual distancing from UKIM in the late 1980s. The second was its expansion and internal crises during the mid-1990s and most recent was its relaunch and gradual withering away as an organisation from 2002 to the present. The Young Muslims was originally constitutionally linked to UKIM and in its earliest days grew under the close supervision of its members. However, some in the leadership of the first generation were uncomfortable with UKIM's ethos and ideological influences. According to prominent founding member and later UKIM president, Afzal Khan, some in the YM *shura* (executive committee), such as Dr Munir Ahmed, were more impressed by the MB and the perception that it was Islamically more authentic as it had 'Arabic speakers' – the language of the Qur'an – rather than the Urdu-speaking UKIM membership.[17] This observation is supported by the increase in references towards the MB's brand of Islamism seen in the pages of its publications, choice of conference speakers and teachers of its 'study circles' from the early 1990s. As word spread about these study circles YM activities began to draw larger audiences, as it was one of the very few organisations at the time to discuss Islam in the English language. They were able to capture the attention of many religiously-minded young people because of their conscious decision to move away 'from the often narrow, sectarian, ethnic, linguistic and cultural biases of some parents and elders'.[18] This helped the organisation to experience rapid growth and by February 1986 over 200 members attended the member's convention in Glasgow to witness the election of YM's second national president Abdul Hamid Qureshi.[19] In the autumn of 1987, YM broke more new ground by holding their first national camp for young Muslim women, which resulted in the formation of the YM 'Sisters Section'. It was the first national youth organisation to actively involve young women, which was unique in this period, and enabled young Muslim women to discuss issues and address problems in spaces free from the constraining aspects of their parental cultures. Importantly, it allowed them to engage with religious reference points that challenged patriarchial religious interpretations, empowered them with arguments from within an Islamic framework and created a community of female Muslim activists. For former member Robina Shah, YM appealed to her because:

> YM was the first group I met. It was open and there was sense of spiritual sisterhood in the national events. There was something attractive about the structure, unlike HT who was aggressive and all they did was talk about politics and with the Salafis, it was all visual and stringent and they came across as a 'finger pointing' movement.[20]

She also believed that YM helped build confidence in young women by drawing upon their skills and talents. Most early members were students and were given the organisational freedom to develop new ways of engaging young Muslims. This paid off as membership continued to grow and by 1988 the YM had reached a new high point in its activism through the introduction of regular large national camps. The first was held in Wolverhampton, when Zahid Pervez was elected as the next national president.[21] These events grew in popularity and the major camps consistently attracted over 1,000 young people. The profile of YM's work in Muslim communities began to become more noticeable after the Rushdie Affair, which helped draw a second wave of recruits, like Atif Imtiaz who became a prominent member of the 1990s generation.[22] Within a few years, YM had a presence in every major town and city with a significant Muslim population and spread to create vibrant branches in Bradford, Birmingham, London, Leicester and Glasgow. Its work also expanded through the distribution of its newsletter, *Trends*, which later turned into an innovative glossy colour magazine, containing features about Islamist movements, religious practice and articles exploring the challenges of maintaining a Muslim identity in Britain.

A common feature among Islamist movements is their tendency to be totalising, closed ideological entities which believe they can address all of life's complexities and ambiguities. 'Islam is a complete and comprehensive way of life (*deen*) and it offers guidance for all spheres of life: personal, interpersonal, spiritual, physical, communal, penal, judicial, economic, political etc', reads a quote from YM 'manifesto' document *Striving for Revival*, written by Atif Imtiaz.[23] For Inayat Bunglawala, a former spokesman for the MCB and YM member of the 1990s generation, the differences between the different trends 'didn't really sink in until Atif's booklet helped us distinguish between HT and JIMAS'.[24] The short tract was meant to be a summary of YM's values and goals, as well as statement of difference to other revivalist trends. As a youth movement, YM was loosely modelled on JI pyramidal hierarchies, with an overall *Amir* (president), *shura* (executive committee), branch presidents, two levels of membership – 'Module One', committed 'Module Two' members – and sympathisers who had membership potential. There was also the figure of the *naqib* (study circle teacher). The *naqib* often doubled up as the branch president and had to report back to a regional president or directly to the national *shura*. The committed members were taught in the closed 'Module Two' study circles where they were meant to emulate a set of six characteristics: Godliness, Comprehensiveness and Balance, Pragmatism and Gradualism, Construction, Universality and Collectivity. This list of attributes were ideals that members were meant to embody and would help to distinguish them from other Islamic organisations. In reality there were more similarities than differences as YM members were taught that Islam was an ideology and holistic system, using vocabulary very similar to Hizb ut-Tahrir. Practically, they were delivered in small discussion groups that would study an English translation of the Qur'an, sayings of the Prophet and weekly homework given on the works of Islamist thinkers. This process relied upon peer learning, an approach facilitated by people who were slightly older or of the same age.

If an individual attending their open activities was receptive to YM's message, they were encouraged to join the organisation on the proviso that they committed to the following personal duties: *dawah*, *jamaah* (collective work) *tarbiyah* (moral development), *tazkiyah* (spiritual purification) and *riyaayah* (social welfare activities). Income was generated for the organisation by the requirement of Module Two members to pay a monthly standing order and by the sale of *Trends* magazine, audio lectures and fundraising at the large annual camps. These activities and sustained contact with the organisation shaped the religious mindset of its young members, who were usually between 13–21 years of age. It succeeded in providing religiously inclined young British Muslims the opportunity to learn about their religion in a way that was relevant and offered opportunities to develop transferable skills such as journalism, public speaking and teaching. For Inayat Bunglawala, 'YM was a training ground that allowed us to make our own mistakes. We very much saw ourselves as British, whose future was here and we had to make it work here.'[25] The mid-1990s executive committee also started experimenting with new ways of drawing in new members and started to hold study circles in people's houses and increasingly in colleges and some universities. This development was supported by UKIM's national network of mosques, often providing the space for these meetings as well as sending their sons and daughters to become involved. Other innovative approaches included the introduction of *nasheeds* (religious songs), widescale circulation of audio taped lectures and invitations to well known international Muslim speakers such as Jamal Badawi, Ahmed Deedat and Yusuf Islam. A national camp in August 1991 attracted over 3,000 people, which was the biggest event of of its kind at the time. These large summer thematic conferences became 'must-go-to' events for young people and their mobilisation spurred competition with rival Islamic tendencies such as HT and JIMAS. At the beginning of 1992, Mahmud al-Rashid became the next president of the organisation.[26] This was during the period that YM began to strengthen its connections with leading international Islamist organisations, through organised visits to France and Egypt, where they were hosted by leading members of the Muslim Brotherhood. People such as early Brotherhood member Mahmoud Abu-Saud (1911–93) were invited to speak to YM members at their training camps, as was leader of the Tunisian Islamic Movement, Rachid Ghannouchi, who at the time was exiled in Britain. In 1993, members flew out to Sudan as guests of Islamist ideologue Hassan al-Turabi and other trips were organised to meet the Refah Party in Turkey, Jamaat-e-Islami in Pakistan and PAS party in Malaysia. These visits helped to reinforce the idea that YM was part of a global Islamic movement which was leading the re-Islamisation of Muslim societies.

A central stand of YM's re-Islamisation strategy was the attempt to provide a counter-culture for Muslim youth. This was done by the production of a range of religiously inspired media and recreational alternatives to popular secular youth activities. YM members became instrumental in acquiring and running annual Ramadan radio stations in cities where they had a significant membership, such as Glasgow, Bradford and London. From 1993–4, YM's popularity peaked due to a series of successful campaigns centred on the genocide of Muslims in Bosnia and ongoing conflicts in Palestine and Kashmir. This helped to establish its national profile and develop its reputation for innovating special projects and large-scale events. Led at this point by new national leader Ahtesham Ali, it was able to create a dynamic national movement of English-speaking young men and women who were seen as future Muslim leaders. Now crackling with a dedicated new second generation of members, it was able to cash in on Spike Lee's *Malcolm X* film by exploring the Muslim dimension of his life in *Trends* magazine, selling religiously themed T-shirts and cassette recordings of charismatic African-American convert Imam Siraj Wahhaj speakers' tours. Imam Wahhaj, a widely respected figure within American Muslim communities, was frequently invited to speak at various British Islamic organisations between 1993 and 2000. YM also experimented with other outreach strategies, which included the publishing of a translation of the Qur'an in modern English and encouragement of its membership to do regular community work with charitable and voluntary organisations.

Doubt and Disintegration

Towards the middle of the 1990s these achievements would slowly unravel. Behind the apparently successful public image of YM, a number of internal tensions were precipitating a crisis within the organisation. Though the YM claimed to be cultivating a British Muslim identity, a latent friction over religious reference points divided its leadership and caused confusion among its membership. At the top, executive members were increasingly polarised around those who inclined towards the work of JI and others that were attracted to the approach of the MB. This was partially due to the fact that some of YM's senior study circle teachers were members of the MB, a movement that carried a great deal of prestige among international Islamist circles. The tilt towards the MB was also accelerated by certain individuals secretly recruiting members to join the MB-oriented Muslim Association of Britain (MAB). Another factor for the fragmentation was the unease some YM executive members felt towards the Islamic Society of Britain (ISB), which a number of individuals felt was not a proper Islamist movement and that it was unfair to expect members to transfer to it when they became too old to remain in YM.

The ISB was conceived in 1990 as a national English-speaking platform where all Islamist movement organisations could work together. The membership originally consisted of personnel from UKIM, first generation YM members, Bengali Islamists from the IFE and Dawatul Islam. However, the appetite for unified work dwindled very early on and people retreated back into their own organisations, leaving it to be managed by the first generation of YM members such as Farooq Murad and Munir Ahmed. According to Atif Imtiaz, who became national leader of YM in the mid-1990s, a number of people in YM's executive felt that members of ISB had become prematurely middle-aged in their outlook, losing their dynamism, and that the structural relationship between YM and ISB was not working properly. He began to have misgivings about YM's methods, in particular the idea of *bayyah* (giving oath) to the president which led him to question other organisational ideas. He was also unhappy with other things – which he listed as 'YM's "pick and mix" approach to the four schools of Islamic law; a lack of intellectual depth, shallow understanding of modernity, absence of spirituality, failure to offer a coherent strategy for the UK and frustration with his previous teachers'.[27] Imtiaz cited personality clashes between certain individuals in YM and ISB as aggravating the situation further, which led him to experience a personal existential crisis of sorts.

Other executive members also began to voice intellectual and spiritual disillusionment with YM, tensions which came to a head in 1997 when Imtiaz resigned as president of YM. While pursuing postgraduate studies, Imtiaz began to seriously consider the neo-Sufi discourses of American TI scholars Nuh Ha Mim Keller and Hamza Yusuf, went to study Arabic in Jordan and became a *murid* (spiritual disciple) of Keller before returning to the UK.[28] During this turbulent time, senior figures from JI and MB, unsuccessfully tried to reconcile the various factions by forming a *hidaya* (guidance) council and creating a 'vision document' to redirect the organisation out of the period of uncertainty. Imtiaz's successor, Mahbub Gani, also later resigned in 1998, creating another crisis from which the organisation never fully recovered. Gani defected to the MAB because he felt more at home in its MB-inspired atmosphere but later also left that organisation after becoming disenchanted. This resulted in the virtual collapse of YM. A small number of the YM executive went off to form a UKIM youth wing because they were more comfortable within its JI ethos, some left to join MAB, while others floated around ISB waiting to see what would happen next. This organisational rupture impacted the Islamic activist landscape for a few years as many individuals were switching from one group to the other.

Former national president of FOSIS in the mid-2000s, Wakkas Khan, provides a case study that is typical of the trajectory of many young Islamic activists and their fleeting association with YM in the late 1990s and early 2000s. Khan became actively committed to Islamic activism through his participation as a child in the Muslim Youth Foundation in Manchester in the late 1980s. In his late teens, he grew disillusioned with this Islamic youth centre and went through a period of associating with local members of HT.[29] He later returned to the centre but remained relatively passive. However, this changed when he went to university and became active in the Islamic Student Society. Members of YM encouraged him to join their organisation in 1999, but he was turned off by the dismal state of the organisation as it was not long after the resignation of Gani. As he became more active, Khan gained a position on the national executive of FOSIS and was eventually elected as national president in the mid-2000s. By this point he had moved on to MAB and remained a member, even though he spent most of his time representing FOSIS in the wider body of student politics. After qualifying as a dentist and realising the limitations of Islamic activist organisations, he reoriented his focus and today spends his spare time supporting Muslim and non-Muslim civil society organisations.

After the decline of YM in the late 1990s, it took a number of years to salvage the remains of the organisation and its status only improved after the former national president, Ahtesham Ali, was reinstated as leader. The group then went through a process of restructuring and soul searching in a rapidly changing Islamic landscape. From 1998–2005, YM had a relatively low profile and was barely visible outside a few larger cities where, historically, it had a strong presence. The partial rehabilitation of YM did not fully occur until after 2002, when it was reinvented as a lighter, associational youth group type organisation. Its public work concentrated on organising Islamic concerts and camps in a handful of the major cities with large Muslim communities. YM was forced to go through another major facelift after the events of 7/7, which was in part motivated by its flagging profile and the fact that its previous website chat room was being used by extremists to promote Jihadist messages.[30] The YM's sympathy for Islamist perspectives continued publicly until just after the 7/7 bombings, when media interest in Islamist organisations spiked. At that time, on its website YM had a number of articles that would be considered problematic in the post-7/7 era, such as pieces that extolled the virtues of jihad and encouraged the boycotting of the *kafirs* (disbelievers). Their website up to that point included articles from the key early figures of the MB and JI, which is unsurprising given that they provided the ideological inspiration for YM. This passage is representative of the material that was available:

Jihad, beloved brother, is a powerful, invigorating yearning for Islam's might and glory, an intense, overwhelming desire for Islam's golden days, its strength and its pride, which makes you cry when looking at the weakness of Muslims today and the humiliating tragedies crushing them to death painfully everywhere. Jihad, beloved brother, is to turn your back on those who turn their back on their Faith, and to boycott those who openly wage war against Allah and His Messenger, so you should not have any dealings, or socialising or relationships of any kind [...] when the might of Islam is under threat, its pride is blemished, and the bugle calls for Muslims to rise and restore to Islam its power and glory.[31]

Other pieces included articles on the 'evils of atheism and secularism' and a piece in the current affairs section entitled 'Israel Simply Has No Right to Exist'. These examples are characteristic of the mixed messages transmitted by the organisation up to that point. The militant tone and references to movements and theological concepts such as *batil* (falsehood) and *shirk* (polytheism) indicated the competitive environment that YM was operating in compared to HT and JIMAS. Nadeem Malik, a former member of YM and a vice president of ISB, claimed he was unaware of the material on YM's website and stated that 'I'm not going to pretend otherwise and I'm not going to justify anything that's on there [...] but if it is on there it's a very small part of a much bigger structure that is very much against those views.'[32] This comment reflected either a disingenuous response or the incompetence of the ISB leadership for failing to have oversight of the content of its youth wing's website and conflicting ideological inspirations. To contextualise the persistence of such views, it must be noted that the literature of most activist organisations during this time was saturated with the rhetoric of jihad and criticism of Israel. YM, like most Islamic organisations, reflected the mood of Muslims towards the issue of Israel/Palestine and Kashmir and therefore was reluctant to speak out against the more extreme messages that were being pushed by the other groups. In the days after 7/7, the vocabulary and religious references from the Islamist ideologues were permanently removed from YM's publicity materials and website.

Other 'Young Muslims'

An interesting parallel group to YM is the Young Muslim Organisation (YMO), which was founded in 1978 in East London. Like its peer, YMO caters for and is run by young people, although nearly all of its members are of Bangladeshi origin. YMO's reformist work includes religious education, recreation and the tackling of specific social problems within their communities. Though it claims to be a national movement with branches in Oldham, Birmingham and other locations, YMO is in reality a Tower Hamlets based organisation. They also have a separate young women's movement called Muslimaat and both are organisationally linked to the Bengali Jamaat-e-Islami inspired IFE, which is based at the East London Mosque. Practically, the main difference between the YM and

YMO was the latter's more conservative interpretation of Islamic law. YMO also paid greater attention to formal youth work and has members that went on to train as professional youth and community workers. In the East London borough of Tower Hamlets they have successfully helped raise educational achievement by encouraging members to become teachers and governors who work with high schools, colleges and universities. Comparing the characteristics of people in both youth organisations in the 1990s, some observers noted that many YMO members seemed to display an inferiority complex towards their counterparts in YM. This is perhaps because most of members of YM were generally more educated then the membership of YMO at that time. The relationship between the two worsened when YM encroached upon YMO's territory in East London in the late 1990s, even though they both drew upon almost identical Islamist references and scholarship.

Evaluting this situation, it could be said that the Islamist Muslim youth groups were selling the same goods but with different labels in competing stores. Both the YMO and YM, and the MAB youth wing at times, have tried to recruit the same people and they collectively saw HT as their main threat. To appreciate the intensity of the broader competition in youth activism between YM, HT and JIMAS in the 1990s, it is helpful to understand the wider context. All three trends were struggling for recruits and influence within communities, colleges and university campuses. While YM was fighting a 'hot war' with HT in university campuses, it was simultaneously fighting a 'cold war' with JIMAS in communities.[33] The groups clashed with each other over membership as well as with other ideological orientations like the extremist groupings such as Supporters of Shariah (SOS), Al-Muhajiroun and its offshoots the 'Saviour Sect' and 'Al-Ghuraba'. At the core of this contestation was a battle over the meanings of fundamental Islamic concepts, which were prioritised differently by each group. For reformist youth groups like YM and YMO, *the* cause was *dawah*, while HT was only interested in telling people about the importance of re-establishing a caliphate. The Salafi groups emphasised the need for correct *aqeeda* (creed) and avoidance of *bid'a* (innovation). They influenced one another and selectively co-opted each other's ideas and methods. This inter-group rivalry was dramatically altered with the emergence of the neo-Sufi 'Traditional Islam' networks, which is discussed in greater detail in Chapter 4.

The YM, YMO and MAB youth wing parallels the youth projects set up by other reformist Islamist movements in other European countries, such as the MB-influenced UOIF (Union des Organisations Islamiques de France) in France and Turkish Islamist-inspired Milli Gorus in Germany. Similar patterns can be identified in the USA with the Islamic Society of North America's (ISNA) youth group, the Muslim Youth in North America (MYNA), the Islamic Circle of North America (ICNA) Young Muslim group, the youth wing of the Muslim American Society (MAS) and the Young Muslims Canada. They all share reformist Islamist reference points and have similar goals in trying to institutionalise the maintenance of religious values among young people and the creation of elite youth leaderships who will participate in the public sphere. Membership of the YM provided spaces for young people to learn about their faith in the English language and develop strong friendship networks. These informal networks offered opportunities to develop an Islamic identity, create communities of shared meaning and contribute to the construction of a British Muslim cultural identity by pioneering 'halal alternatives' in sports, music, recreation, camps and leadership training. The YM enabled young people to learn about their faith in a deculturalised, unmediated way. They were at the forefront of the articulation of a new religious identity discourse that attempted to reconcile the demands of faith, family and British society. At the same time, YM aspired to be part of an international Islamic reformist movement, an ambivalence which eventually divided the loyalties of its senior leadership and led to an organisation crisis and decline which it has not recovered from since. The next chapter profiles one of its most potent competitors – Hizb ut-Tahrir.

CHAPTER 2

'KHILAFAH COMING SOON': THE RISE AND FALL OF HIZB UT-TAHRIR IN BRITAIN

The aim of Hizb ut-Tahrir is to resume the Islamic way of life and to convey the Islamic *Da'wah* to the world. This objective means bringing the Muslims back to living an Islamic way of life in *Dar al-Islam* (land of Islam) and in an Islamic society such that all of life's affairs in society are administered according to the Shari'ah [...] under the shade of the Islamic State.[1]

Hizb ut-Tahrir

The second trend to impact British Muslim communities in the 1990s originated in Palestine in the aftermath of the creation of Israel and competition between variants of Arab nationalism. Hizb ut-Tahrir – party of liberation – was founded in Jerusalam by Palestinian scholar Taqiuddin al-Nabhani (1909–77). Proclaiming Islam as its ideology, he stated that the aim of the party was to restore the political unity of the Muslim world by re-establishment of the *khilafah*, or pan-Islamic state.[2] After an unsuccessful attempt to register as a legal political party in Jordan on 17 November 1952, the group was subsequently banned by Jordan for its anti-Arab nationalist stance and radical Islamic rhetoric. In Britain, Hizb ut-Tahrir (HT) is not specifically a Muslim youth movement, but draws most of its membership and popularity from younger people and students.[3] The group is credited with (re-)introducing the concept of *khilafah* into popular Muslim discourse and first came to public attention in 1988 after one of its leaflets entitled 'The Islamic Rule on Hijacking Airplanes' was passed on to the Attorney General by the Board of Deputies of British Jews. It later gained media attention in the build up to its 1994 international conference at a Wembley Arena. Members of HT had already spread alarm within Muslim communities for their confrontational tactics and apparently increasing popularity among young people. HT in Britain was for a time the most well-known Islamic activist youth trend, famous not only for its rhetoric against 'The West' and Israel, but also equally notorious for its aggressive tactics against other Muslim activist groups and publicity-seeking stunts such as vandalising public spaces with their red coloured 'Khilafah Coming Soon' stickers.

In Arabic, the term *khilafah* implies successor and vice-agent, lieutenant, substitute, proxy, or deputy.[4] In the Qur'an, it is used in reference to the idea of human responsibility for acting as God's trustees on Earth. The concept of *khilafah*, or caliphate, for most Muslims is associated with nostalgic memories of the unified state governed by the *al-khilafah al-rashida* – the rightly-guided four successors to the Prophet between 632–61. Historically it refers to the pan-Islamic polity of smaller states that made up the Muslim empires that spanned the seventh to early twentieth centuries. This includes the periods ruled by the Umayyads (661–750), Abbasids (750–1258), the Fatimid dynasties (909–1171) and later the Ottoman Empire (1299–1924). For most Islamic activists, memories of the *khilafah* evoke images of a lost, powerful and culturally superior Islamic civilisation. Calls for the creation of a *khilafah*, are in many ways a religiously infused postcolonial discourse of empowerment, which energises an activist mobilisation that combines faith-based language 'with political aspirations, creating in the process powerful emotional and moral commitments as well as legal responsibilities'.[5] Memories of the historical caliphate act as the repository of utopic pan-Islamic aspirations of unity, power and glory. However, as some scholars have pointed out 'although the old imagery can be supported by selective historical references, in reality the caliph's rule was often challenged by ambitious governors aspiring for autonomy independent of central authority'.[6] As political scientist Abdelwahab El-Affendi points out in his influential *Who Needs an Islamic State?* modern debates on the Islamic state were conducted against the background of two unprecedented and interconnected developments:

The first was the advent of the colonial era, which saw the bulk of Muslim lands subjected to invasion and control by alien powers. The second, which was a corollary of the first, was the collapse of the caliphate and the conversion of Islam into a stateless religion for the first time in its history.[7]

It has been noted, 'while some Muslims may retain the nostalgic memory of the caliphate [. . .] very few are currently working on making the dream come true [. . .] substantial numbers of Muslims are loath to see the flag of a caliphate raised in Muslim capitals, even though some of them may long for the application of *shari'a* in their countries.'[8] Despite this, the appeal to re-create a caliphate, remains a powerful slogan that resonates among certain people in Muslim majority societies. This sentiment is complicated by the self-proclaimed jihadists, Islamic State (IS), and is regarded as illegitimate by most Muslims. Before the emergence of IS, the quest to recreate a contemporary Islamic state was most notably linked to the political project of the Hizb ut-Tahrir movement. Its stated central focus is the re-establishment of a supra-national polity that would re-unite Muslims across modern nation state borders into a community of believers, who could then liberate themselves from the forces of Western hegemony. HT literature presents the Khilafah in ahistorical, idealised terms, which has caused many to criticise the movement's utopianism. In the words of Olivier Roy, HT's conceptualisation of this institution is 'without any historical or geographical consideration, as if the caliphate was some sort of dream, an Islamist utopia in competition to the West's dystopia'.[9] Indeed, this has worked to its advantage, enabling it to constitute the caliphate as an emotional category that has nothing to do with geography, states or borders. Its formulation of Islamic rule claims to be based upon the governance models of the first four caliphs, but is also influenced by Western political vocabulary, a fact which becomes clear after a close reading of the ideas of its founder Taqiuddin al-Nabhani.[10]

A Radical Thinker

Taqiuddin al-Nabhani was born in Haifa, Northern Palestine, in 1909. He came from a scholarly background and continued the family tradition by studying at the prestigious Al-Azhar University in Cairo,

Egypt, for his undergraduate studies. Upon returning to Palestine he was employed as a religious studies high school teacher, but left as he believed that the curriculum was corrupted by Western influences. He later secured a post as a judge in an Islamic court during a time when the Middle East was still adjusting to the creation of Israel and increasing Arab Nationalist sentiment in the region. Al-Nabhani was initially attracted to pan-Arabist, Baathist ideology, as evidenced in his book *Inqadh Filastin* (*Saving Palestine*) in which he wrote a history of Palestine in the nineteenth and twentieth centuries. His early work led al-Nabhani to conclude that Western colonialism was responsible for the loss of Muslim power, in particluar the spread of nationalism which made Muslims vulnerable to European imperialism. His solution was to agitate for a United Arab States that would consist of the following territories: Iraq, Syria (to include Syria, Jordan, Lebanon and Palestine), northern Arabia (Hijaz and Najd), southern Arabia (Yemen and Hadramawt), North Africa (Morocco, Algeria and Tunisia) and Egypt– Sudan–Libya. When this political union was achieved, the Arabs would be able to focus their resources upon liberating Palestine. However, in al-Nabhani's view, the main obstacle was the persistence of Western hegemony and a lack of political will among Arab governments. To overcome this he concluded that there would need to be a revolution in the minds of Muslims in the region. This was the first indication of his belief in the efficacy of 'revolutionary vanguardism', which he borrowed from Marxist-Leninist political thought. However, al-Nabhani soon became disillusioned with Arab Nationalism after his attempts to rally Arab leaders were ignored. Undeterred, he continued to search for ways to arrest what he saw as the cultural and political degeneration of Arab nations. This spurred al-Nabhani to his next phase as a pan-Islamist. In August 1950 he sent a letter to members of the Cultural Summit of the Arab League in Egypt. This document argued that the primary duty and achievement of the Arabs was Islamic civilisation and that only the political unification and revival of the Muslim *ummah* would restore its former glory. This message also fell on deaf ears and became the precursor to his creating HT. The vision for his new project was to:

> Engender an intellectual revolution by supplanting the erroneous beliefs that have arisen due to the Ummah's state of decline and colonialist contamination with its own ideology. This ideology is

construed as a correct representation of a 'pristine' Islam cleansed of all distortion.[11]

His literary output now focused on Islamic apologetics and developing his ideas into a coherent system of thought. He produced books such as *Nidham al-Islam* (*The System of Islam*), which he hoped would help Muslims to reaffirm their faith as well as reach out to sceptical minds. Its content, typical of his later publications, emphasised the rational foundations of Islam and offered logical proofs for the belief in God, Prophecy and the divine provenance of the Qur'an. This was then followed by critiques of the prevalent ideologies of the day, in particular; nationalism, socialism, communism and capitalism. To his mind, communism contradicted human nature and appealed to the animal instincts of fear, misery and hunger, while capitalism separated religion from everyday life.[12] He contended that only Islam was in harmony with human nature and based on reason. HT's unique strategic difference to comparable Islamist movements lay in the subordination of all other concerns to the goal of re-establishing a modern Islamic state. Al-Nabhani believed it was a crime against Islam to digress from the task of establishing the caliphate and often maligned political rivals, particularly the Muslim Brotherhood whom he accused of abandoning this fundamental tenet and pursuing projects that only provided temporal solutions. Distancing himself from the approach of the Brotherhood, he believed theological discussions on morality and charity were inane and did not alter the fundamental pillars of society:

> Moral behaviour is part of obedience to God in Islam; a call to morals wrongly implies that Islam is merely a moral message. Moreover, one need not be a Muslim to be a moral person; and by the same token one may be Muslim who does not observe ritual but otherwise conducts himself morally. So Muslims committed to reviving Islam should not stray down the path of moral reform movements for they will not fundamentally change the situation.[13]

He insisted that 'Islam will not return by constructing mosques or preserving morality' because these are partial solutions that distract

Muslims from the true objective, which is to re-establish Islamic government.[14] Downplaying the role of morality caused HT to become heavily criticised by fellow Muslims for some of its unorthodox views on matters of theology and law, in particular for holding a number of problematic religious legal verdicts considerd alien to Islamic norms. For instance, aspects of basic religious practice could be held in abeyance until the caliphate is reinstituted, or that it was permissible for Muslims to 'kiss strangers as long as it is done without carnal appetite'.[15] This is in addition to bizarre policy positions such as campaigning for Saddam Hussein to assume the role of Caliph outside the Iraqi Embassy during the first Gulf War, despite the fact that Saddam was persecuting HT members in Iraq.

The Liberating Party

The urgency of restoring a caliphate was based upon al-Nabhani's particular reading of Islam and the role of the human intellect. For al-Nabhani, a correct understanding of the world was only possible by careful rational thinking filtered through Divine revelation, which would enable the solving of earthly problems. He attempted a systematic re-interpretation of the canonical textual sources of Islam, reconstructing them into a distinct ideological worldview with a coherent, detailed series of systems that were supposed to be superior to 'man-made' ideologies. For him, the work of HT was a re-imagining of the mission of the Prophet and therefore participating in its goal was inferred as a religious duty for all Muslims. Despite his efforts, obvious contradictions and capitulations weakened the internal coherence of his ideas, as evidenced by partially naming his movement a *hizb*, political party as understood in the Western lexicon. His recasting of Islam into modern ideological categories is suggestive of apologetics to target non-Muslim audiences and demonstrate that Islam can meet the requirements of the modern world. Interestingly, rejecting the main features of modernity did not rule out coveting products of Western scientific knowledge and technology. Anticipating this obvious descrepancy, al-Nabhani made a distinction between what he understood as civilisation and its material culture. This seperation was meant to allow Muslims to borrow from Western scientific knowledge but not its civilisational motifs such as secularism, democracy and human rights. Al-Nabhani's various writings, particularly his book *The Political Order in Islam*, articulates a vision of a model future Islamic state intended to make democratic models of governance less attractive. The future polity would be a utopic homeland able to present the teachings of Islam in such a compelling way that non-Muslims would automatically want to convert to Islam and join the much happier and prosperous Muslim citizenery. According to this logic, to know Islam is enough to want to embrace it and live within its political project. Another unique feature of Hizb ut-Tahrir's strategy was the presentation of a detailed vision of what a future caliphate would look like – to the extent of producing diagrams to elaborate its organisational structures. This explicit framework appealed to some people looking for a manifestation of a modern Islamic state which combines faith, rule of law, accountability and social justice.

As a political organisation HT was modelled on the Syrian Ba'ath party dream of a unified nation based upon Arab Socialism. It adapted vanguard movement structures that utilised secretive communication mechanisms and transformed them through religious filters. Known for its extremely disciplined workers, they functioned within a pyramidal organisational structure under a highly centralised leadership that maintained strict ideological homogeneity and direction. HT has always had a clear party hierachy with an international *Amir*, followed by three layers consisting of national level leadership, local committees at town/city level and the leader of a local level study circle. It ensured ideological conformity and discipline by informal modes of social control and punishment. Al-Nabhani advocated a methodology for reaching its ultimate goal in three stages. The first was what he called the 'culturing stage', meant to instil a select number of individuals with the party's goals and methods. The second 'interaction stage' attempts to 'intellectually' persuade the Muslim masses to embrace the party message and work towards the establishment of its Islamic state.[16] Finally, after sufficiently mobilising public opinion, influential figures and infiltrating the military, it would enter the 'revolutionary stage', and replace existing governments so that it could implement its social, economic and political paradigms. In practice HT was unsuccessful in gaining legal recognition and was forced to remain as an underground movement after opening cells in Lebanon, Kuwait and Iraq. The organisation remains proscribed in many Muslim states.

Challenging Disbelief

The most significant thinker in HT after al-Nabhani was his successor Abdul Qadeem Zallum (1924–2003). Zallum continued al-Nabhani's stream of thought by arguing that there was a perpetual intellectual and physical struggle between Islam and *kufr* (disbelief):

> The fierce struggle between the Islamic thoughts and the *Kufr* thoughts and between the Muslims and the *Kuffar*, has been intense ever since the dawn of Islam. When the Messenger of Allah was sent, the struggle was only an intellectual one, and was not associated with any material struggle.[17]

In activist circles, HT became equally well known for making frequent denunciations of Muslim leaders from discredited regimes, calling them *kafirs*, as well as other Islamically oriented parties. For instance, in 1996 a particularly harsh judgement was made of the Turkish Islamist Refah Party leader, Necmettin Erbakan:

> As for the loss of Erbakan in this life, it will occur when he executes all what the seculars demand of him, and then they will throw him in the middle of the road, without any regret or sympathy for him. This will not take long. As for his loss in the hereafter, this will occur when he is thrown in hell fire for his apostasy and deviation from the Deen of Allah.[18]

This condemnatory language appears to extend to ordinary people as well. In one of its documents it states 'whoever does not rule by whatever Allah has revealed, denying Allah's right to legislate, as is the case with those who believe in democracy, is a *Kaafir*'.[19] According to a particular chilling interpretation of Islamic law, those who apostate from Islam can theoretically be subjected to genocide. Abdul Qadeem Zallum wrote in his book *How the Khilafah was Destroyed* that 'it is imperative to put back this issue in its rightful place and consider it to be a vital issue, by killing every apostate, even if they numbered millions'.[20] However, whilst such sentiments are extremely disturbing, HT has not yet been associated with any acts of violence. This language was also intended to make its message stand out in a competitive religious field dominated by the more successful **MB** movement. The same types of controversial rhetorical postures were applied when the movement gained a following in the UK.

The early Hizb in Britain

In the early 1980s, Hizb ut-Tahrir was going through a period of persecution in a number of Middle Eastern states, forcing some of the members to seek political asylum in Europe. These circumstances enabled them to observe the political environment on the continent and to provide intelligence useful to their activities in Muslim countries and the eventual decision to set up HT cells in the West. I agree with the assertion made by researchers such as Ahmed and Stuart that the British branch of HT has gone through four distinct stages; foundation (1986–96), retreat (1996–2001), post-9/11 (2001–5) and post-7/7 (2005–present).[21] In the foundational stage, two members of HT, Welsh-Yemeni Abdul Kareem Hassan and Palestinian Fuad Hussain, are believed to have established the first UK branch in 1986. Initially activities were limited to small study circles that tried to recruit overseas students and professionals who would carry on HT's message when they returned home. Up to that point, HT had not yet developed a coherent strategy for Britain and only offered fortnightly public events. As British-born Muslims slowly started to show interest and eventually joined the organisation, they began widening its work to different cities. Though its membership reflected the predominantly South Asian demographic of the Muslim population, Syrian-born Omar Bakri was chosen to lead the British branch around the time of the first Gulf War in 1991. Sometimes referred to by his full name Omar Bakri Muhammad, he was associated with a number of Islamic organisations in his native land, including the Muslim Brotherhood. He travelled to Lebanon in 1979, where he apparently joined HT, then went to Egypt to study at Al-Azhar University in the early 1980s. He claims to have left the university after disagreements with his teachers, whereupon he moved to Saudi Arabia to establish HT cells. After becoming embroiled in a dispute with the Kuwaiti members of HT, he decided to migrate to Europe and in 1986 successfully secured political asylum in Britain. He was then approached by the German HT leader, Tawfiq Amer, and offered leadership of the British branch.

As *Amir* of HT in Britain, Omar Bakri was supported by three key figures: Farid Kassim, Jamal Harwood and Anjem Choudary. Farid Kassim, a former atheist and member of the Socialist Workers Party, was introduced to HT's ideas by overseas students whilst he was at Nottingham University. He developed a reputation for being an aggressive proponent of HT's ideas and spoke regularly at Muslim student societies and communities across the UK. Harwood, an economist by training, joined HT after he converted to Islam in 1987 and was promoted as a 'white trophy Muslim', to demonstrate the effectiveness of the party's ideas. In 1989, Harwood helped set up *Al-Khilafah* Publications to translate al-Nabhani's main works for English audiences and supplemented it with the *Al-Fajr* magazine, which commented on current affairs. The third member, Anjem Choudary, was a lawyer who would eventually succeed his mentor and rose to notoriety in the mid-2000s after he became leader of the extreme Al-Muhajiroun group. Under Bakri's leadership, other activists became alarmed by HT's ability to recruit hundreds of members from around the UK, most of whom were male and female college and university students.

Doing the *Dawah*

HT in Britain considered itself to be in stage two of its methodology, interested only in creating a disciplined intellectual leadership able to demonstrate to Muslims and non-Muslims alike that Islam is *the* ideological alternative to 'man-made' systems of thought. Its recruitment techniques ranged from one-to-one targeting, public programmes and pamphleteering on its regular themes of the ideological struggle between Islam and the forces of Kufr, the self-sufficiency of Islam and condemnations of pro-Western Muslim regimes. Their message was disseminated in distinct A4-paper sized leaflets produced for two audiences: one exclusively for HT members and the other for the general public. Omar Bakri was perceptive in choosing to identify issues that other Islamic groups at the time were not discussing and focused on university students as they held the greatest potential for intellectual enquiry and mobilisation. In the early years his outreach strategies were simple, setting up stalls outside universities with Farid Kassim, where he would exploit what he called the 'Bobby and Abdullah syndrome'.[22] This referred to the fact that some Muslim young people struggled to balance their religio-cultural values with the British dimensions of their identities. In practice, exprienced members targeted both male and female students, offering leaflets after Friday congregational prayers, hosting stalls at fresher's university events, dinners, demonstrations and conferences. Their verbal dialogue would start with discussions around social and political issues and would inevitably lead to the importance of re-establishing the *khilafah*. They followed Bakri's approach and would identify topical issues and concerns affecting young people, capturing their attention and giving the impression that their message could solve their problems. A lynchpin of HT strategy was to create a socio-psychological dissonance between the idea of being both a British citizen and Muslim. Interested newcomers were then invited to an open *halaqah* (study circle), screened for a period of time and if judged suitable, then introduced to its closed study circles. These study sessions were attended by both newer recruits as well as older members and were lead by a *mushrif* (instructor). As one member explained:

> The *Halaqah* is designed to culture the *daris* (novice), building them with the correct thoughts and ideas about Islam [...] so, take a simple example, a Muslim drinks alchohol, this is a corrupt action. So, if you want to change that action then you need to address the corrupt thoughts that motivate that action, like freedom.[23]

Fully committed members were then taught a specific syllabus of the party's core texts, which included: *Systems of Islam, Concepts of Hizb ut-Tahrir* and *Structuring of the Party*. Interestingly, in the book *The Concepts of Islam*, HT ideology is compared with the Muslim Brotherhood and Jamaat-e-Islami, but judged inferior. Acquiring full membership took place after intense immersion in party ideas and literature that could take between six months to three years depending on the ability and commitment of the individual. Acceptance as a full member was dependent upon the completion of the group's foundational texts and taking of an oath of allegiance to the party. This intense experience of learning and socialisation among like-minded peers from similar backgrounds had the effect of forging new individual and collective identities. HT grew in popularity in the early 1990s as it appeared to articulate a convincing theo-political analysis and provide a unique response to the issues and concerns shared by conscientious Muslims, especially in the realm of politics. Young British Muslims searching for satisfying religious identities were drawn to HT's ideology for a number of reasons. It simultaneously tackled three dimensions to their life experiences: it addressed their desire for a strong internal identity, addressed their external social circumstances and provided a connection to an idealised past and promises of future greatness. Furthermore, it was able to offer compelling explanations for the socio-political problems facing Muslim societies, as well as convincing reasons to point the blame at Western powers. For some it was the first Islamic group that provided them with a persuasive explanation for their marginalised condition in British society; for others it offered an interpretation of Islam that appeared more rigorous than what they were taught at home or in the mosque. For some young people the group appeared to offer an attractive ideological alternative to the stifling inward-looking politics of their parents' generation. Overall, it was a message of empowerment and helped to create a sense of community and mission that was reinforced through event attendance, magazines, books and websites.

Members of HT became recognisable by their sartorial choices, cultivating a distinct look for young women, who most often wore specific *hijab* styles, and men who sported designer stubble and causal blazers. As one ex-member admitted 'we even had a very specific dress code that was chosen by the Amir of HT. The leadership made it mandatory for all members to wear the jilbab {a loose dress], Khimar [headscarf] and socks.'[24] Indeed, many young people were attracted to HT entirely because of their particular stylish image, communication skills and ostensible possession of religious knowledge. Another former female member explained that HT stood out among activist groups 'because that was the only articulation that was really out there, I had bumped into HT because they were talking politically, and there was no political narrative amongst the Muslims {at the time]'.[25] Many people found HT discourse to contain the conceptual vocabulary to resist the perception of a Western war against Islam. Revealingly, ex-members have agreed about how their psychological attraction to HT's message was a result of their personal insecurities, giving them a feeling of empowerment after feeling powerless or neglected. As one male ex-member explained:

HT filled a void for the young intellectually frustrated youth who had been told that Islam is the truth, that they must pray and fast by people who couldn't explain why. By HT 'proving' that Freedom, Democracy and Capitalism are defective, and that we Muslims are better than those kafirs are, it restored some of the loss of faith in the relevance of the religion. Muslims believe in Islam but needed to know that their belief was the superior belief, which made them feel superior again. Constant harping back to the glory days of the Caliphate and emphasising its restoration, as the solution to all things seemed very alluring.[26]

The appeal to the past as a guide to the present is a powerful rhetorical device that forms a central strategy of Islamic groups who want to attract new members and inspire them to action. Their emotional sloganeering appealed to youthful angst and a desire to be given a clear direction in life with pre-packaged answers to difficult questions. Kirstine Sinclair, in her research on HT in Britain, observed the important role of emotion in recruitment as the organisation offered:

> [...] a palette of emotions: purpose, direction, confidence, exclusiveness and importance. These emotions are tied closely to Hizb ut-Tahrir's history and the prevailing self-understanding: the organisation understands itself as important and central to future societal and regime changes in the Muslim world.[27]

Membership also fulfilled the need for acceptance, providing a comforting balm to those bruised by racism, Islamphobia and other forms of rejection. According to veteran community activist Humera Khan, a founding member of the An-Nisa Society, 'HT and similar groups functioned as alternate families. Omar Bakri was going to alienated young people from socially deprived, alienated, dysfunctional families and became a father figure to them.'[28]

HT Divided by Two

During Omar Bakri's time in charge, HT managed to cause alarm within Muslim communities for their confrontational tactics and rising popularity amongst young people. Pioneering what has been dubbed 'pamphlet Islam', by producing large numbers of leaflets on different topics, it often created problems for other Islamic activists operating on college and university campuses, which occasionally resulted in the closure of designated prayer rooms at some universities and problems for the mainstream student associations. The central leadership of HT in the Middle East blamed Bakri for a series of controversial stunts aimed at generating maximum publicity for the group. They grew unhappy with his aggressive strategies and media exposure, which they felt distracted focus away from the party message, and forced him to resign in February 1996. Current leaders insist that Omar Bakri's period as leader was an 'aberration'. According to HT spokesman Taji Mustafa, Bakri was ejected from HT due to his refusal to curtail media activity in the UK and because of sensitive disclosures to the Arabic magazine *Al-Majallah* in 1995. The international leadership was frustrated that he and not the party's ideas had become the foci of public interest. In 1996, Abdul Qadeem Zallum expelled Bakri, whereas Bakri claims to have resigned. Whatever the case, Bakri later argued that HT had violated Islamic law in his view by constricting the demands of the Shariah in areas such as; where to establish the caliphate, separating law from belief and not accepting jihad as an individual duty. During the Bakri era, HT became well established in Britain and created a presence in over 50 universities across the UK. Following Bakri's departure members of HT in Britain went through a confusing and difficult time, made worse by a faction who created a second HT in Britain. According to Bakri:

> [...] after my departure from HT in 1996, the old internal disputes arose again and this time around caused an official split in the party [...] The Zalloumis became HT Camp 1 and the followers of Abu Rami, the so-called Nakithoun (renegades), became known as HT Camp 2.[29]

The latter group claimed to be the most authentic by accusing the first of straying away from the founders' original message and methods. However, in 1997 the second group conceded its failure in the UK and instead reverted to focusing its efforts to establishing the caliphate in countries such as Pakistan. Omar Bakri went on to lead the Al-Muhajiroun group (AM), a shortened version of Jamaat al-Muhajiroun, a front name for HT, which he created in 1983 while exiled in Saudi

Arabia. The AM group retained many of HT's aims and methods and Bakri was able to take a significant number of HT members with him to the new organisation. To distinguish themselves from their former colleagues Bakri claimed to have adopted a Salafi *aqeeda* (creed).[30] There were also three critical differences of strategy separating his new group from HT, which in essence was around priorities. First, even though they both believed in re-establishing the caliphate by *coup d'état*, HT limited this project to the Muslim world while AM argued that it included Britain. Second, HT disassociated itself from the *takfiri* jihadism of al-Qaeda, which AM supported. Third, AM adopted a high profile style of moral correction, which led to an increasingly confrontational attitude to other Muslim groups and the British government. During this period, Bakri drew closer to rival radical preachers such as Abu Hamza and worked with him to create the short-lived Islamic Council of Britain, which was meant to rival the Muslim Council of Britain.

Growing Up and Moving On

For most its youthful members, joining HT was a phase that they went through while at college or university. As they grew older they either withdrew from the activist scene, joined more moderate groups or in some cases formed their own initiatives influenced by HT ideology. The message of HT eventually failed to convince its own members, as it did not achieve the all-important objective of re-establishing the caliphate. Disillusioned, most members 'grow up and out' of the movement upon entering adult life. As one female ex-member explained:

> It has now transpired that they are all talk and no action. For example, when I first joined I heard talk of Pakistan being penetrated through the military and it would be overtaken very soon, this was about ten years ago now. The message becomes boring and tiresome, there appears to be no action although people are led to believe that things are moving forward but they never do.[31]

Another ex-member stated that 'HT talks a good game but they don't do anything [...] Muslims are being killed and sisters being raped and HT say wait for the Khilafah; this is rubbish.'[32] The most common reason for leaving the organisation was growing older and becoming more religiously literate and dissatisfied with the one-issue agenda. People left HT because:

> They read more about Islamic history and Islam in general and realise that like any other political group, HT paint a picture of the past and present based on selective information. Once people start looking into these areas for themselves in an objective sense they can no longer hold to HT's parochial view.[33]

The movement was successful in shaping British Muslim public opinion during the early 1990s but failed to gain widespread support for its ideas even though it attracted thousands of people to its major events.[34] Still, HT's plea for a united caliphate will continue to resonate with some Muslims unhappy with an unequal globalised international system dominated by Western powers. As others have observed, 'the Caliphate is a vision that reflects this deep quest for an imagined unity of all Muslims under one flag [. . .] the notion of a universal Muslim *umma* where the bonds of faith override any other tribal, ethnic, linguistic, or civic identity'.[35] The movement seems to thrive on its pariah status and achieved a degree of success in mobilising certain Muslim young people alienated from society. On the other hand it offered little that is constructive, beyond vague general prescriptions about the superiority of Islamic systems and did not have much to say about the pressing social issues affecting British Muslim communities at the grass roots. Its political radicalism derived from its revolutionary message calling for the overthrow of Muslim governments, which in turn reinforces a 'group-think' mentality about the righteousness of its cause. It had an uncompromising ideology and methodology, which put it at odds not only with secular governments but also with fellow Muslims. After decades of effort, the movement's failure to capture state power anywhere in the world even prompted a lament by its founder: 'People in this region – and Muslims in particular – still persist in thinking slowly, spontaneous invitation and rapid perception still elude them.'[36]

In Britain they went through cycles of growth and decline, with their popularity peaking in the mid-1990s after they capitalised on the changing national socio-economic environment, worsening conditions in Muslim countries and a general increase in religio-political consciousness within communities. HT appealed to a section among young people frustrated with what they saw as the inaction of traditional authority in their communities and the ineffectiveness of other Islamic groups. In contrast to its main rival, YM, which targeted a similar audience, HT seemed to hold an advantage over YM for its apparent intellectual sophistication and radical political analysis. HT, like YM, had the ability to attract young people alienated from mosques and traditional activities. It offered a platform for the establishment of a strong collective identity embedded in Islamic reference points and unlike its competitor offered a detailed plan of what a future caliphate would look like. The next chapter looks at the Salafis, the third player in the competition for the hearts and minds of young British Muslims.

CHAPTER 3

'RETURNING TO THE QUR'AN AND SUNNAH': THE SALAFI *DAWAH*

The Salafi Da'wah [. . .] is that of the Qur'an and the Sunnah. [It is] the Religion of Islam – pure and free from any additions, deletions or alterations. It means adherence to the Path of the Messenger [. . .] and of the Faithful Believers (as-Salaf us-Saalih). As-Salaf is a collective term referring to the Pious Pioneers in Islam and all those who follow in their footsteps in belief, actions and morals.[1]

JIMAS

By the 1990s, the Islamic activist scene in Britain became dominated by the struggle between YM, HT and the Salafis. A significant factor in favour of the Salafi perspective was the perception that its adherents had greater religious knowledge. They claimed superiority over the misguided 'clean shaven kids' from YM and HT, because they were practising a more rigorous, authentic version of Islam rooted in the Qur'an and 'authentic Hadith'. For Salafis, the *dawah* efforts of YM and HT were shunned because they were premised upon an incorrect *manhaj* (methodology), contained *bid'a* and lacked religious scholars among them. Competition between the groups became so intense in this period that it acquired a tribal character, resembling the rivalry and loyalty between football supporters. Towards the mid-1990s, Salafism as a religious paradigm became well established nationally through a network of mosques, publications, media and a large body of literature which later became available on the internet. British Salafism was largely popularised through the activism of one organisation but later became diversified into various splinter groups and tendencies. Salafis are not like Islamists in that they do not organise themselves into hierachial organisations but belong to a socio-religious current with clusters of scholars, students and followers. Most are publicly apolitical, believing doctrinal and ritual authenticity will ensure the preservation of Muslim identity in the midst of secularised Muslim and non-Muslim societies.

The Pious Predecessors

The term 'Salafi', or *Salafiyah*, denotes the era of the 'Salaf' or *al-Salaf al-Salih* – the 'pious predecessors' and is understood to apply to the first three generations of Muslims. The reverence for these early Muslims is based upon their chronological proximity to the Prophetic period and they were noted for their exemplary piety and involvement in the early territorial expansion of Muslim power, which led some prominent theologians to suggest a causal relationship between the faith of the 'pious forefathers' and their subsequent political and economic success.[2] They are honoured in textual proofs, such as the famous hadith, which states 'The people of my generation are the best, then those who follow them, and then those who follow the latter.'[3] Another reason for their prototypical significance is the inference suggested in another well-known saying of the Prophet who explained to his companions that, 'Indeed those who came before you from the People of the Book split-up into seventy-two sects and indeed this nation will split-up into seventy-three sects, seventy-two are in the Fire and one in Paradise: they are the Main Body (*al-jama'ah*).'[4] That 'saved group' (*al-firqaal-najiya*) who escape the fires of Hell are implied to mean those who follow the first three generations of Muslims.

Salafi epithets have been present in Islamic texts from at least the twelfth century. 'Being a "Salafi" in the medieval period meant abiding by the doctrine of the forefathers (*madhab al-Salaf*) in matters of dogma and theology.'[5] Some scholars trace modern Salafism to the influence of the famous shaykh Ibn Taymiyyah (1263–1328); others go back even further to the ideas of the juridical and theological debates in the ninth century between the so-called *ahl al-ra'y* and *ahl al-Hadīth* (respectively, people of reasoning and people of Prophetic traditions).[6]

The term 'Salafi' has also been used to describe the modernising reformist movements of the late nineteenth and early twentieth century reformist thinkers Jamal al-Din al-Afghani, Muhammad 'Abduh and Rashid Rida.[7] As indicated earlier, these reformists were convinced the only way Muslims could reverse their civilisational decline was by returning to the unmediated teachings of the Prophet and the spirit of the Salaf. They argued that when Muslims rediscovered this ideal and mastered the technological and political tools of modernity they could reclaim their position on the stage of world history. The Salafi reformism of these figures:

> endorsed a return to the ways of the pious forefathers as a means of resisting European imperialism [...] these movements promoted political activism more than religious purification, and Salafis today are unlikely to identify with these reformers. Indeed, many Salafis condemn these activists as modernist and misguided in their preoccupation with political objectives.[8]

While al-Afghani and his successors were focused on the need for Islam to respond to an external threat, contemporary Salafis have concentrated their energies on the correction of religious belief and practice from within Muslim societies. Salafi as a descriptor is often interchanged with the term 'Wahhabi', derived from the name of the eighteenth century reformer Muhammad ibn 'Abd al-Wahhab (1703–92). Abd al-Wahhab and his followers, were noted for their violent puritanical zeal to purge the Arabian Peninsula from cultural traditions, which they believed were polytheistic practices that had re-emerged in the region.[9] Salafis themseleves reject 'Wahhabi' as a designation, claiming they follow the *Salaf al-Salih* and do not venerate the eighteenth century reformer.[10] Historian Roel Meijer writes that:

> Wahhabism's contribution to Salafism lay in its strengthening of a xenophobic attitude towards foreigners and its sectarianism towards non-Wahhabi Muslims. On the basis of the principle of loyalty and disavowal (*al-wala' wal-bara'*) Muslims were called upon to distance themselves from Muslims who did not adhere to Wahhabism. A true believer could only express his belief and sincerity of his faith by demonstrating open enmity towards 'idolaters'.[11]

There are other important distinctions between Wahhabis and Salafis: for example the Wahhabis tend to be adherents of the Hanbali school of Islamic law, unlike Salafis who generally dislike the idea of following madhabs as they claim that this is *taqlid* – blind imitation – and have little time for *ijtihad*, relying instead on the primary sources of the Qur'an and Hadith. Islamic scholar Khaled Abou El-Fadl suggests that Salafis attempted to cope with the onset of Western modernity by taking refuge in 'apologetics [that nurtured] "pietist fictions" about the Islamic traditions' and one that 'eschewed any critical evaluation of Islamic doctrines and celebrated the presumed perfection of Islam', contributing to 'a sense of intellectual self-sufficiency that often descended into moral arrogance'.[12] According to El-Fadl, the two streams of thought converged when Wahhabism co-opted the language and symbols of Salafism and the two became indistinguishable.[13] Historian Bernard Haykel argues:

> The Salafi imagination reconstructs the early Muslims' sartorial, linguistic, cultural and ethical habits and insists on being exactly like them [...] Salafis spend most of their time learning about Islam and refer to themselves as 'students of religious knowledge.' They are centrally concerned with religious education, because only by understanding the complexities of Islam can a Muslim fulfil his or her duty to God. From this perspective, Muslims must master the commands of God, as outlined in the sources, to ensure that they are following the straight path and have not deviated from the purity of the Prophetic model, necessary to protect *tawhid*.[14]

Moreover, as political scientist Peter Mandaville notes, Salafi frameworks function to provide 'certainty and order in a turbulent world where individual identities – and particularly those with multiple affiliations viewed as (potentially) mutually exclusive – are apt to get lost in the maelstrom of competing cultural and political discourses vying for allegiance and consumption'.[15] Indeed this certitude is one of the primary attractions of the Salafi outlook, further intensifying their self-perception of being the repositories and guardians of Islamic orthopraxy. For them, doctrinal clarity and moral fortification are the conditional basis of collective transformation.

Protectors of 'Pure Islam'

The defining feature of Salafism is the insistence on correct, 'pure' belief and action. The desire for religious hygiene is articulated in discourses about purity of belief, body and social interactions. This is manifested in a 'continous state of boundary maintenance' between Muslims and non-Muslims and 'pure and impure Muslims'.[16] The idea of theological purity – encapsulated in the slogan of 'returning to the Qur'an and Sunnah' – is one of the most well known of catchphrases in the linguistic repertoire of Salafis and indirectly hints at the impurity/deficiency of non-Salafi Muslims. This simple, seductive phrase, underlined the importance of referring directly back to the two sources of authority – the Qur'an and Hadith. This bears a resembalance with some forms of Protestant literalism which insist upon the clarity of scripture accessible to lay readers. However, for all the talk of returning to the texts, Salafis defer to and constantly reference the senior scholars of Saudi Arabia such as the late Abdul Aziz Ibn Baz (1910–99), Muhammad ibn al'Uthaymeen (1925–2001) Muhammad Nasiruddin al-Albani (1914–99) and current Salafi scholars such as Saleh al-Fawzan (*b*. 1933) to bolster their claims of authenticity and silence those with an inferior command of scholastic frames of reference.

Epistemologically, Salafis resist the possibility of subjective knowledge, textual ambiguity, metaphor and dismiss the validity of interpretations of the Qur'an and Hadith outside of a narrow cluster of Salafi scholars. Theologically, they draw upon *athari* (narrations) for their *aqeeda* and loosely follow the legal school of the early jurist Ahmad ibn Hanbal (780–855 CE), which is noted for its textual literalism and avoidance of theological, philosophical and speculative meanings of the Qur'an and attributes of God.[17] Methodologically, Salafism relies upon literalist scripturalism, alternating between a set of binary opposites: *tawhid* (oneness of God) as opposed to *shirk* (polytheism), loyalty to the Prophetic Sunnah in matters of religious ritual as opposed to *bid'a*, and rejection of most of Muslim intellectual history, let alone the by-products of modernity such as rationality, the humanities or liberalism, which are also considered a *bid'a* capable of contaminating Islam. In their particular theological schema, these concepts take on a critical importance, as *tawhid* connotes the doctrine that God alone has the right to be worshipped and that Muslims must protect themselves from *shirk*. This was developed further by some scholars into three categories of *tawhid*: the Oneness of Lordship (*tawhid al-rububiyya*), the Oneness of Godship (*tawhid al-uluhiyya*) and the Oneness of the Names and Attributes (*tawhid al-asma' wa-l-sifat*). Salafis distinguish themselves from most other Muslims by taking an uncompromising position on these creedal matters and frequently condemn fellow believers for compromising *tawhid*.

In the area of ritual practice, nothing is more important than adopting the Prophetic Sunnah. Following the Sunnah can only be achived by relying on the authentic Hadith that record his behaviour. Salafi confidence in the authenticity of their ritual practices rests on the rigorous authentication methodology of the famous Albanian Hadith scholar Muhammad Nasiruddin al-Albani. Linked with the idea of following the Sunnah is constant vigilance against *bid'a*, which for them is an ever-present threat to the true Prophetic example. They blame Muslims historically for allowing newly converted peoples to retain vernacular customs that allowed syncretism and all manner of religious innovations to challenge the integrity of the Sunnah. Therefore, as Olivier Roy argues, modern Salafis seek a 'deculturation' of Islam as practised by the majority of Muslims by removing its folk customs and de-linking it from national and regional cultural additions by 'arguing that a strict constructionist interpretation of the Qur'an and Sunnah is sufficient to guide Muslims for all time and through all contingencies, and that these sources are perspicuous'.[18] Alongside these beliefs, they feel that Muslims should practise *al-wala' wal-bara* towards non-Muslims and therefore not develop any kind of friendships with people who are regarded as disbelivers. Most Salafis condemn Shi'as and Sufis. The Shi'as are regarded as unbelievers, who they call *rafidis* (rejectionists), for aspects of their theology and refusal to recognise the political legitimacy of the first three caliphs. They also consider Sufism as innovation and practices such as celebrating *milad* (the Prophet's birthday), performing *tawassul* (seeking closeness to God by petitioning a deceased pious person) and *istightha* (asking those in the grave for assistance) as infested with *bid'a*, *shirk* and grave worshipping.

Salafism comes to Britain

Salafi approaches to Islam were introduced into the UK in the early 1980s through the increased global influence of Saudi Arabian religious perspectives. This resulted in the propagation of Wahhabi/Salafi discourses through the financing of mosques and institutions by the Saudi state and private donations. A relatively small but growing number of mosques are Salafi-oriented, such as the Green Lane Mosque and the Salafi Institute in Birmingham, Brixton Mosque and Masjid Tawhid in London, The Islamic Centre in Luton and Makki Masjid, Masjid Furqan and Masjid Sunnah in Manchester.[19] While they make up a small number of the approximately 1,600 mosques in Britain, their influence is increasing disproportionally due to their effective distribution of literature, activism and a strong media and internet presence. The organisation that became instrumental in spreading Salafism in the early 1990s was JIMAS, which was formed in 1984, the same year as YM.[20] Its long-time leader Manwar Ali, aka 'Abu Muntasir', is considered by some to be the 'Father of Salafi *dawah* in the UK'. He is credited for helping to spread Salafism among Muslim youth through his countless speeches at study circles, mosques, community centres and universities across the country. Abu Muntasir's leadership brought the organisation to national prominence and attracted individuals such as Usama Hasan, Surkheel 'Abu Aaliyah' Sharif and converts such as Abdurraheem Green and Abdul Haqq Baker, who would in the future become high-profile Salafi figures.[21]

Abu Muntasir's teenage years reflected the common tensions experienced by second generation British Muslims seeking to reconcile their religious upbringing with the influences of majority non-Muslim society. Having decided to dedicate himself to a committed religious identity, he set out to learn about Islam on his own from English sources. The discrepancies between what he understood from textual ideals and what he saw practised in Muslim communities, motivated him to deepen his knowledge and share it with others. In time he started to challenge traditional Barelwi and Deobandi imams and was sometimes physically ejected from their mosques. Abu Muntasir then became involved with the HISAM organisation (Harakat Islah al-Shabab al-Muslimin – Movement to Reform the Muslim Youth), which was ideologically close to the *Ahl al-Hadith* trend.[22] Muhammad Abdul Karim Saqib, Director of the Al-Hijrah Muslim Girls School in Birmingham, originally led the organisation and Abu Muntasir later assumed the HISAM leadership. Disputes between Saqib and Abu Muntasir led him to form JIMAS, a split that represented the first significant moment in the growth of British Salafism.

The 'Salafi Manhaj'

In the beginning, JIMAS was keen to distinguish themselves from their co-religionists by iterating their conceptual and methodological separateness. Visually this was done via dress forms; male members of JIMAS became conspicuous for combining a Saudi-style headdress, army fatigues and boots. Many Salafis adopted a patronymic, prefixing 'Abu' and 'Umm' (Father or Mother) before the name of their eldest child. They also had a tendency to impose their understandings of ritual worship on other Muslims, such as insisting that people's feet should touch while standing next to one another in congregational prayer, or sometimes praying with their shoes on in mosques because they believed it was a Sunnah. These identity markers became expressions of difference that reinforced the perception of Salafis as being arrogant towards non-Salafi Muslims and implications that they were the saved sect. By deliberately challenging established religious norms, Salafis thought they were teaching non-Salafi Muslims the correct understanding of Sunnah and removing *bid'a*. This attitude led to Salafis becoming involved in various disputes with other Muslim currents in Britain, particularly South Asian Barelwi Muslims, Deobandis and members of YM and HT. Strident, unremitting Salafi critiques frequently caused tensions between friends, family members and other Islamic organisations. JIMAS Salafis claimed to represent 'pristine Islam', and were able to attract young people otherwise unreceptive to what became known as 'cultural Islam'. This approach is illustrated in an early JIMAS publication, *A Brief Introduction to the Salafi Dawah*, which explained what the Salafi manhaj stood for. Published in 1993, it demarcates the theological and methodological framework of early British Salafi thought. Stylistically it is characteristically minimalist, referencing only the Qur'an and Hadith or the views of Salafi scholars. Most Muslims reading this booklet would find little to disagree with in the sense that the reference points contain Qur'anic guidelines and Prophetic admonitions that are normative aspects of Muslim belief and praxis. As Bernard Haykel points out:

[The] attraction to Salafism lies in the form of authority that it promotes, and reproduces, as well as the particular hermeneutics it advocates. It is not Salafism's so-called 'de-territorialised' and 'fundamentalist' qualities, nor the 'globalised' condition of modern life, that make Salafism particularly attractive. Rather, it is Salafism's claims to religious certainty that explain a good deal of its appeal, and its seemingly limitless ability to cite scripture to back these up.[23]

He goes on to contend that 'Salafis, unlike other Muslims, rely exclusively on sound proof-texts from revelation as the basis for their views, and they adduce the relevant verses or traditions every time they issue a judgement or opinion [...] The claims to greater certainty of God's law through a hyper-textual methodology are a trademark of the Salafis.'[24] It is this form of authority which makes Salafism attractive in conditions of uncertainty, fluidity and crisis. Factors that are in plentiful supply in many contemporary Muslim majority states as well as Muslim communities in the West. Influential researcher on Islamic activism, Quintan Wiktorowicz, explains a distinguishing feature of Salafi hermeneutics to be the minimisation or elimination of the role of the human intellect in interpreting the text:

> [...] the application of human intellect and logic to the original sources ('rationalism' in the Salafi lexicon). Salafis operate as though the Qur'an and hadith are self-explanatory: if the scholar has enough training and knowledge, then the vast majority of derived rulings are clear and indisputable. As a result, there is no need to apply human systems of logic. The scholars are, in a sense, reduced to the archeology of divine texts: their function is to simply unearth the truth that lies somewhere in the Qur'an and Sunna. In this understanding, there is really no such thing as interpretation – the sources either sanction or prohibit particular beliefs, choices and behavior; there is a single truth, as revealed by the Qur'an and the Prophet Muhammad; and there is no room for interpretive differences or religious pluralism.[25]

Among other influential publications that JIMAS published in this period was a translation of al-Albani's famous book *The Prophet's Prayer Described*. This helped to draw attention to Salafi perspectives and was followed by number of texts translated by converts such as Dawud Burbank and Jamal Zarabozo. Another particularly influential publication was *The Fundamentals of Tawheed* by Bilal Philips, a widely read text outside traditional Salafi-inclined readership which continues to be read today. The spread of Salafism in Britain was further accelerated by the mass circulation of a Saudi government funded translation of the Qur'an, returning graduates from its universities, and lifestyle magazines like *Al-Jumuah*. People found in Salafi perspectives an approach to religious commitment that seemed to be intellectually rigorous, evidence-based and free of the corruption of folkloric religion or the 'wishy washy' alternatives offered by YM or the hyper-politicisation of HT. Compared to YM and HT, Salafis seemed to be taking their religion more seriously. The Salafi trend mainly attracted young second-generation male and female South Asian Muslims, in addition to a significant number of black and white converts. Well-known preacher Abdurraheem Green epitomises the appeal by saying: 'Salafi thinking was powerful because it exposed the discrepancies between religion and culture'[26] while Abdul Haqq Baker insists that Salafism represents 'simplicity, clarity, connectivity and a chain of authenticity to early orthodoxy, that is to say the Qur'an and Hadith'.[27] When younger Muslims and converts become convinced, adopting a Salafi identity becomes a straightforward process of exchanging and rerouting religious symbols and acquiring membership of a de-ethnicised supranational identity.

Salafisms

Salafis across the world are by no means a unified religious trend and display a number of internal divisions and scholarly points of view. The divergences stem from the different perspectives on how to respond to modernity and the socio-political challenges facing Muslims. This sometimes pits different factions against each other over what constitutes the correct manhaj. The hugely influential Salafi scholar Nasiruddin al-Albani, for example, argued that Muslims should shun participation or affiliation with any type of formal group, political parties or even civic organisations, as he believed they led to division. Disputes over correct manhaj form the most obvious dividing line between contemporary Salafis internationally and these debates became visible among British Salafis when they began fragmenting in the mid-1990s. Quintan Wiktorowicz developed a useful typology in differentiating three main global Salafi trends; 'purists', 'politicos' and 'jihadis'.[28] All three tendencies share the same Salafi positions in matters of theology but differ in their analysis of problems in the Muslim world and how they should be solved. Within this classification, the purists or 'Scholastic Salafis', are known for their loyalty to the principles of the Salafi *aqeeda* and the Saudi state and resist attempts to challenge the authority of ruling Muslim governments. They prioritise personal reform and the correction of Muslim belief and ritual practice and became known as 'Madkhalis', i.e. those who follow Saudi scholar Rabee' al-Madkhali (*b.* 1931). They justified their quietism by arguing that any form of political activism is *haram* (forbidden) because it can lead to *fitna* (temptation/discord) and that Muslims are required by Islam to be obedient to the rulers even if they are unjust. They are ridiculed by their enemies for being obsessed with the application of minor details concerning Islamic law whilst neglecting wider socio-political issues. The 'politicos', or *harakis* (activists), while agreeing on the importance of the Salafi creed, argue that the Salafi manhaj had to take into consideration the complex and changing social-political realities taking place in the world and have incorporated the political reformist methodologies of the Muslim Brotherhood. In contrast, jihadist-Salafis are often called *takfiris* for their habit of excommunicating fellow Muslims, violent action against 'apostate governments' and attempts to engage Western governments in a perpetual jihad. They are recognised by their impatience with the status quo and use violence to affect change.

Emergence of the 'Super Salafis'

These currents had a direct impact on splitting the Salafi scene in the UK. The growth of British Salafism reached a critical juncture in 1995 when tensions that had been simmering between factions inside JIMAS eventually caused the organisation to rupture and left an ideological and methodological split that remains to this day. Ever since the first Gulf War in 1991, Salafi scholars were divided over the presence of US troops in a land which is considered to be the spiritual heart of Islam. The origins of this fracture started within the Kingdom of Saudi Arabia, when some younger scholars began questioning why the rulers had invited the Americans to fight another Muslim country and, worse still, establish military bases on sacred territory. These dissenting scholars, led by Salman al-Awdah and Safar al-Hawali, the so-called *Sahwa* (Awakening) Shaykhs, were intellectually influenced by the reformist ideas of the Muslim Brotherhood and gained prominence through their critiques of the Saudi government. Abu Muntasir had made links with the Salafi politicos in Saudi Arabia, while influential Abdul Wahid (aka Abu Khadeejah), opposed the politicised orientation of Abu Muntasir. He challenged Abu Muntasir, who was sympathetic to the Sahwa movement, and this led to the fragmentation of JIMAS in 1995–6. Despite attempts by senior figures within the Salafi community to mend the rift, it became irreconcilable and Abu Khadeejah and others broke away to form their own organisations. In Abu Khadeejah's view, the split was due to Abu Muntasir's leading JIMAS away from the true Salafi way:

> Throughout the second half of 1995 Abu Muntasir travelled around the Salafi communities in the UK promoting the ideas of Sayyid Qutb and al-Maududi, mentioning them and praising them in circles. This actually added to his own unravelling due to the fact that many Salafis had already been made aware through the efforts of the likes of Dawood Burbank, Amjad Rafiq, Abu Sufyaan, Bilaal Davis and myself (amongst others) that these ideas were alien to Salafiyyah.[29]

The specific trigger seems to have been the invitation given to two members of Kashmiri jihadist group, Lashkar-e-Taiba, to speak at the JIMAS conference in 1995. According to Usama Hasan, a senior member of the JIMAS executive at the time, the split would have happened anyway and these divisions were inevitable. He believes that the organisation had become so large that diverse currents which were pursuing their own interests would have broken away sooner or later.[30] These apolitical purists went on to establish Salafi Publications, the Salafi Institute in Birmingham and websites linked to Salafi.com. They became known for their increasingly intolerant attitude to former colleagues as well as their vindictiveness towards other Muslim groups. They installed a sort of purist inquisition that began to label other Salafi Muslims as religious innovators. This paralleled developments in America, where a similarly bitter schism took place.[31] For example, the Salafitalk.com website, one of the mirror sites of Salafi publications, warns new visitors on its website that:

Any attempts at propagating false and deviant ideas will result in posts deleted and being banned from the board. This includes the ideas of the Khawaarij, Shi'ah, Qadariyyah, Murji'ah, Mu'tazilah, Jahmiyyah, Ash'ariyyah, Soofiyyah, Ahl ul-Kalaam, or any of their contemporary representatives.[32]

Salafi publication websites have libraries of articles and PDF files that classify what and who 'true Salafis' are, as well as singling out Salafis who should not be trusted. They include papers pointing out the 'deviant' nature of many well-known groups, popular Islamic preachers and scholars. This led the purists to initiate a policy of boycotting other Salafis who did not meet their criteria. The name-calling was a tactic in the power struggles to delegitimise the credentials of fellow Salafis. Due to the harsh condemnation of other Salafis for their alleged adulterations of true Salafi belief and methodology, Abu Khadeejah and his colleagues were labelled 'Super Salafis', 'Saudi Salafis', or 'Madkhalis' by other Salafis and Islamic activists. This resulted in a form of theological McCarthyism, producing blacklists and character assassination which continue to divide British Salafis. This practice of vilification also had severe consequences for personal relationships between members and their families, sometimes leading to divorces and what became known as 'Salafi Burnout', a term that describes a dramatic loss of faith and a steep decline of religious practice.[33] An example of the disdain purists have for fellow Salafis can be gleaned from an entry on a web discussion group on Salafitalk.net. Writing in a post about 'Giving Da'wah to the innovators, its nature, conditions, and context', Abu Khadeejah lists people who have failed to be authentically Salafi:

> we took issue and oppose Bilal Philips with his open attachments to the likes of Ali Tamimi, Zarabozo, JIMAS and others known for their *hizbiyyah* and deviation, and going to the platforms of the likes of these people – all of whom are known to be amongst the Harakiyyoon, upon the manhaj of Safar and Salman and Abdur-Rahmaan Abdul-Khaaliq and others.[34]

Bemoaning this situation, Bilal Philips wrote an article rebutting accusations made about him by Abu Khadeejah, writing that:

The path of true guidance, i.e. Salafiyah, was never intended to be an exclusive club, in which certain individuals can grant membership and confiscate it from whomsoever they please. This attitude is similar to the very *hizbiyyah* (factionalism) which our brothers are trying to fight [...]. As I see it, there are some elements in our midst who are masquerading as Salafees who really do need to be exposed. However, a vocal minority among our English-speaking and Arab Salafee brothers with limited knowledge have highjacked this legitimate need and gone overboard with it. They have taken it upon themselves to act as the ultimate judges of common Muslims and students of knowledge. They claim to have the criterion by which they can justly expel whoever they please out of the realm of Salafiyyah. Much valuable time is dedicated to slandering those who have been already labelled, or to searching for the past or present mistakes of those on the current hit list. Furthermore, if anyone disagrees with them on any issue, they issue severe warnings to him and if he doesn't fall in line, they then proceed to warn against him also, and attribute their actions to the Salafee manhaj.[35]

The details of actual differences between various protagonists are a labyrinth of theological argument, claims and counter-claims, accusations and rebuttals, which can be sampled by a visit to their main websites.[36] On these sites fellow Salafis were accused of 'Hizbiyyah', 'Qutbiyyah', or of being 'Suroori' and 'Kharijites'. Hizbiyyah would imply that the individual/faction was influenced by movements like the Muslim Brotherhood, that Qutbiyyah/Qutbists were followers of the Ikhwani ideologue Sayyid Qutb and Suroois were followers of Muhammad Suroor, who was a prominent Arab Salafi figure based in the UK for two decades until the late 1990s. Khajirite is a reference to the earliest sect in Muslim history, during the reign of the fourth caliph Ali bin Abi Talib, who were known for their religious extremism and tendency to excommunicate fellow Muslims.

During this tense period the majority of Salafis did not only have to defend themselves against the inquisitional practises of the Super Salafis, but also had to cope with the emergence of a Salafi jihadist trend, represented by people like Jamaican convert Abdullah el-Faisal. He caused anxiety among both JIMAS and the Saudi Salafis because of his perceived superior religious knowledge. El-Faisal was a graduate of Imam Muhammad Ibn Saud University, Saudi Arabia and served for a short time as the Imam at Brixton mosque in the early 1990s, before he was removed. He became known for his fiery speeches with themes that condemmed the Saudi religious establishment. He produced well-known lectures such as *The Devil's Deception of the Saudi Salafis*, declaring the UK as *dar al-harb* (land of war) and encouraging people to steal from rich Gulf Arab tourists. His rhetoric presented a major problem to British Salafis of all persuasions, causing some to orientate towards jihadism. Jihadism is the most extreme end of the activist spectrum and has various specific characteristics. Jihadist thinking presumes a binary division of the world into belief and non-belief. In this black and white world view, Muslim and non-Muslim states are in a permanent state of war until Islam attains global supremacy. The concept of jihad is intepreted as an obligation on all Muslims, and *takfir* is pronounced on Muslims who disagree with their position. This rejectionist trend accuses authoritarian Muslim rulers of relapsing into a state of *jahiliyah* (religious ignorance) or becoming *murtad* (apostate). Jihadists support the idea of attacking the 'far enemy', that is engaging in combat with the US and its Western allies, rather than the 'near enemy' of corrupt Muslim regimes.[37] It justifies suicide bombing as tactic of asymmetric warfare and condones the killing of innocents, including other Muslims, as collateral damage. El-Faisal's message was reinforced by the antics of the notorious Abu Hamza and Omar Bakri. What distinguishes this trend from the purists and politicos was their open incitement of British Muslims to violence and calls to attack British interests abroad.[38]

To put the intra-Salafi divisons in context, it is worth noting that sectarian conflicts have been present among Muslims since very early on in history, beginning with the Khawaarij and the emergence of the Shi'a, and there have been many modern examples, such as the ensuing polemics between Sufi-oriented Barelwis and Shariah-minded Deobandis. This latter internal Muslim argument began in the late nineteenth century and transposed to the UK in the mid-twentieth century. Whilst the prevalence of Salafi perspectives was growing in part as a protest to the more traditional, 'devotional Islam' prevalent in South Asian Muslim communities, the Barelwi tradition was in danger of being completely discarded by second-generation Muslims. Influential Sufi scholars such as Muhammad Hisham Kabbani attempted to respond to

Salafi polemics against Sufism by taking on the doctrinal objections head-on and using the same primary textual sources to defend their interpretations of theology and ritual practise. Kabbani's seven-volume *Encyclopaedia of Islamic Doctrine* was among the major publications produced to offer a scholarly rebuttal to the Salafi anti-Sufi literature. As Ron Geaves observed, this approach was part of a broader set of strategies deployed by Sufi traditionalist communities to counter the appeal of Salafi and reformist groups. They realised that in order to appeal to young people they would need to:

(i) win the loyalty of British-born Muslims who are alienated from ethnic and religious divisions brought by their parents from their place of origin; (ii) to develop a systematic doctrinal challenge based upon the Qur'an and Hadith that counteracts the teachings of the reform movements; (iii) to develop an educational system in Britain that rivals the *dar al-ulums* (seminaries) established by the reform movements, and (iv) develop organisational structures that compare with tight-knit movements found amongst the reformers.[39]

In practice this resulted in Sufis organising more activities and producing literature aimed at recapturing younger members of the community. The Minhaj-ul-Quran movement, led by the Pakistani scholar Tahir ul-Qadri, while retaining traditional Sufi motifs, imitated reformist movements in their structures and operational modes in order to be more appealing to young British Muslims. Their activism led to the establishment of centres that provided Islamic education, launched websites as well as issuing *The Revival* magazine, which resembled YM's *Trends*. Among Deobandi communities, the relationship with Salafi discourse was more complex, as they had historically shared elements of the Salafi critique of Barelwis. They also criticised the Barelwi fixation on the metaphysical and spiritual qualities of the Prophet Muhammad, shrine culture and associated rites, but differed sharply with the Salafis over their disinterest in following the schools of Islamic law and privileging the study of Hadith over *fiqh*. The Deobandis similarly felt the need to reach out to younger Muslims by also offering large one- and two-day conferences, which for the first time had speeches in English, and also turned to electronic and print media to disseminate their messages. The leadership among both of these theological trends realised the need to adapt and become relevant as their young were more attracted to Salafi and reformist currents.

Sufis v Salafis

Salafism in the UK was only significantly challenged by the arrival of a different form of Sufism, popularised by charismatic American convert scholar Hamza Yusuf. He dazzled audiences with his knowledge of Islam and seemingly polymathic command of subjects as diverse as philosophy, medicine, music and politics. Prominent Salafis at the time, though privately in awe of his learning, publicly dismissed him as a Sufi. The 'Traditional Islam' trend, an intellectual, activist form of classical Sufism, became popular for many young Muslims across the sectarian and ideological spectrum. This trend represented a modern, highly articulate, scholarly alternative that emphasised respect for traditional scholarship as represented in the four juristic legal traditions and recognition of *tassawuf* (Sufism) as being a valid part of the Islamic tradition. In effect it appropriated some of the authority from the Salafi scholars, which resulted in reducing the aura of knowledgeability of British Salafis, and offered a broader, granular understanding of Islam. The impact of Hamza Yusuf's message was reinforced and echoed by two other prominent traditionalist scholars: the British academic Tim Winter (aka Abdal-Hakim Murad), a Cambridge University lecturer in Islamic Studies, and the American Sufi Shaykh Nuh Keller, based in Jordan. They deconstructed the claims to textual orthodoxy of the Salafis and critiqued the politicised readings of Islam found in the literature of Islamists. The consequence of this Sufi counter-response was the emboldening of the Barelwis and Deobandis, who had until then been dominated by the Islamists and Salafis. Both Yusuf and his colleagues were crucial in broadening the understandings of Islam away from the narrow sectarianism that had hampered young British Muslims until then. Behind the scenes a significant number of younger prominent members of both the Salafi and Islamists trends became interested in the alternative perspectives of the two figures. A telling effect was the fact that JIMAS started to invite Sufi speakers to address their annual summer conferences.[40]

Salafis gained influence within British Muslim communities by claiming to return to the primary texts of Islam and rejected what they considered alien religious beliefs and practices. Embracing Salafi identities was ultimately an attempt by Muslim young people to learn and practise their religion. Salafism provided certainty, clear group identity and an individually empowering approach to the sources of the religion with a compelling evidence base. It allowed for an adoption of a 'rationalised Islam', one which was 'stripped of the niceties and ambiguities of juristic reasoning, the complexities of theology and the subtleties of Sufism'.[41] They were successful in winning some Muslim youth and converts over to their point of view through their activism, image and truth claims. The next chapter examines the impact of the fourth main actor, the Sufism of the 'Traditional Islam' network and some of its interactions with the other currents.

CHAPTER 4

SUFISM STRIKES BACK: EMERGENCE OF THE 'TRADITIONAL ISLAM' NETWORK

Traditional Islam is the 'plumb line', the trunk of the Islamic tree, if you prefer, whose roots are firmly buried in the soil of Prophethood. Over time, tributaries sprout from the 'plumb line' and eventually die out, but the line continues because ours is a tradition based on isnad – sound, authentic, reliable transmission of sacred knowledge.[1]

Hamza Yusuf

The popularity of Salafi and Islamist perspectives within British Muslim communities grew, in part, as a reaction against conservative, quietest religious traditions prevalent in South Asian Muslim communities. The Barelwi-Sufi tradition in particular was in danger of being abandoned by second generation South Asian British Muslims, but was rejuvenated by the same globalisation of ideas and operational modes utilised by their competitors. The success of this trend can be credited to a network of influential Western Sufi figures that provided a counter-response to Salafi polemics against Sufism. Using the same primary textual sources to defend their interpretations, they offered a substantive challenge to Salafi and Islamist dominance in the activist arena and as a result were able to win over the hearts and minds of many young British Muslims from rival trends. In order to appreciate the deep differences between Sufis, Salafis and Islamists, I now sketch some historical features of the Sufi tradition and its establishment in Britain.

A Reality with a Name

The words 'Sufi' and 'Sufism' are terms adopted from Arabic which can be identified in texts dating from the tenth and eleventh centuries to describe devotees of a particular type of Muslim piety. As adjectives they are said to have their etymological origins in the original word *tassawuf*, derived from the word *suf* (wool).[2] The other most frequent interpretation suggests they acquired their meaning from an expression used to describe a group of impoverished early Muslims that gathered in the Prophet's mosque – the *Ahl al-Suffa* (The People of the Bench). It is also sometimes described as the 'psycho-spiritual aspect of Islam', a phrase used to layer three levels of religion – *islam* (submission), *iman* (faith) and *ihsan* (spiritual excellence) described in a famous Hadith of the Prophet.[3] It is the third realm that particularly interests aspiring Sufis. The path to *ihsan* is achieved by the performance of ritual practices and adopting a life of renunciation to facilitate higher states of God consciousness.

Historically, Sufism has manifested into two main streams.[4] The first is 'Sober' Sufism, an orthopraxy concerned with personal introspection and *tazkiyat'l nafs* (purification of the soul), God consciousness and living frugally. The other, a so-called 'Drunken' or 'Ecstatic' Sufism of those who appeared intoxicated after reciting formulas that invoke God, recited poetry that seemed to celebrate wine drinking or people preoccupied with *fana* (spiritual union with the Divine). The later quest for esotericism and mysticism is best exemplified by figures such as Ibn al-Arabi (*d.* 1240 CE), or more controversially by Persian mystic Mansur al-Hallaj (*d.* 922 CE), who in an ecstatic state uttered his infamous statement *ana'al Haq* ('I am the truth', i.e. God), which cost him his life after he was judged a heretic. The tension between the two understandings of Sufism appears to run throughout Muslim history as professor of Islamic studies, William A. Graham points out:

> Their divergences have often been a source of conflict and tension in the Ummah. The 'ulama' have been the guardians of what

Hodgson has called 'shari'ah-mindedness,' or the shar'i Muslim vision of life lived according to the dictates of the Shari'ah, or Muslim 'law.' Typically they have been wary of Sufi excesses and critical of antinomian strains in Sufism, just as many Sufis have been critical of what they perceive in shar'ia piety as superficiality and lack of sufficient stress on inward spirituality.[5]

The debate between the two positions essentially focused on what constitutes orthodox belief and whether certain ritualistic practices are sanctioned in the Shariah. Proponents in favour of Sufism argue that it appeared at the very beginning of early Muslim history in the personal example of the Prophet Muhammad, whose austere lifestyle and performance of demanding supererogatory acts of worship vindicate these practices. They explain that early believers pursing the interior path of spiritual purification and closeness to God, were not trying to create a separate sect called 'Sufism', but focusing on the aspects of Islam that emphasised personal piety. Modern Sufi scholars such as Seyyed Hossein Nasr have argued that *tassawuf* is actually the essence and heart of Islam, contending that Sufism was taught as a normative part of Islamic tradition and was accepted across the centuries in contradistinction to more recent expressions of the modernist, Salafi or Islamist kind.[6] They also declared that the misconduct of those that claim to be Sufis were excesses, an aberration that should not be used to judge the whole tradition. However, his view appears to suggest a defensiveness to critiques by Salafi and Islamists intent on challenging its place within Islam.[7]

Rejecters of Sufism dispute this link with Islamic teachings, remain unconvinced of its historical legitimacy and attack the origins of Sufi thought by pointing to Hindu, Greek and Christian theological influences, which at times produced syncretic theologies and practices alien to the faith. These critical narratives continue to associate Sufism with the adoption of non-Islamic cultural traditions which dilute an original, pure Islam. In the late nineteenth and twentieth century, modernist thinkers, particularly Sayyid Ahmad Khan and Ameer Ali in the Indian Subcontinent and leading Salafi reformists Muhammad 'Abduh and Rashid Rida, became the most vocal critics of Sufism, blaming its widespread prevalence as a major factor in the decline of Muslim civilisation. Opponents also dismiss the specific Sufi vocabulary and liturgical practices such as ecstatic dancing, singing with musical instruments and entrancement. Defenders of these Sufi practices have provided justifications and argue its validity using scriptural and analogical reasoning.[8] Other objections include the claim made by some Sufis of having risen to the state of being *wali* (friend) of God and thus no longer needing to follow the Shariah, extreme *zuhd* (worldly detachment) or adopting a life of peripatetic asceticism. In India, these *Qalandars*, as they came to be known, resembled wandering Hindu Sadhus more than they did Muslims.

Other critical sources of disagreement were the accusations that some Sufis did not understand the boundaries of the relationship between the Creator and the creation. These limits were infamously breached by Mansur al-Hallaj. His defenders claim his statements were uttered in an ecstatic state and were not in a literal anthropomorphic sense, rather a metaphoric expression of total annihilation of his self in the pursuit of the love of God. Opponents of Sufism also disliked the practice of taking an oath of allegiance to a spiritual master, which they believed produced a slavish Shaykh-*murid* relationship that allowed popular practices like graveside veneration. Critics of these forms of Sufism have emerged periodically throughout Muslim history. For example the renowned scholar Abu Hamid Muhammad al-Ghazali (1058–1111), known for his works on spirituality, attempted to purge Islamic philosophy from Greek and Hellenistic influence. Later, the formidable jurist Ibn Taymiyyah, hero to modern Salafis, was noted for his intense dislike of the shrine culture that became associated with popular Sufism, even though he was a member of a Qadiri Sufi order.[9] Other famous efforts to reform Sufism were made by two prominent Indian scholars Ahmad Sirhindi (1564–1624) and Shah Wali Allah (1703–62). Sirhindi considered himself to be a *mujadid* (a reviver of Islam at the turn of every century), who stated his life mission was to expose and correct the erroneous ideas and practices of 'every section of society masses, scholars, Sufis and statesmen'.[10] Shah Wali Allah was concerned that exposure to Hinduism and the spread of Ibn al-Arabi's theosophical concept of *wahdat al-wujud* ('unity of existence') blurred the boundaries between God and the world, compromising Islamic orthodoxy.[11] Interestingly, a number of Western Orientalists also accused Sufism for accelerating the decline of Islamic civilisation and for being incompatible with Islamic teachings. W. Montgomery Watt, for instance, believed that:

> Sufism is a blend of various thoughts and philosophies. By intermingling a few traces of Islamic teachings with it, in particular the teachings of Neo-Platonists [...] Greek pantheism became an integral part of Sufi doctrine.[12]

Reynold A. Nicholson argued that the reason Muslims were suspicious of certain Sufi practices was because of the influence of Christian monasticism from Syria[13] and A.J. Arberry also blamed the 'cult of miracles', which led 'incredulous masses allowing themselves to be duped by "impostors"', to contribute to the general decay in intellectual life and increasing superstition and ignorance.[14] Other critics accuse Sufis of being indifferent to the decaying condition of some Muslim societies and for colluding with European rulers during the colonial period. While this criticism may hold true in certain places, it clearly did not apply in others such as Russia, Algeria and Sudan, where the resistance to colonial foreign occupation was led by different Sufi orders.

Summarising the historical development of Sufism, Ron Geaves describes the passing of three stages: 'Asceticism', 'From Fear to Love' and the 'Fully Developed Doctrine of Sufism'.[15] The ascetic phase occurred within the period of the first century of Islam, after a rapid expansion of the Islamic Empire. In this period certain Muslims became anxious about the creeping worldliness of Muslim cultures and became concerned at the corruption in the Umayyad and Abbasid dynasties. Disgusted by this situation, these Sufis sought to protect their faith in the face of earthly temptations by withdrawing from everyday life. Not only did they renounce their interest in the world, they also desired to 'escape the horrors of judgement' by devotion to the ideal of *tasjid* (renunciation), which became a central concept in the teachings of ascetics and remains so throughout the history of Sufism. The next phase, beginning in the eigthth century, is noted for the emergence of Sufis who stressed a change of emphasis from fear to love, which is best illustrated by the life and writings of three noted Sufi teachers; Rabi'a al-Adawiyyah (713–801), al-Muhasibi (781–857) and Dhu'l-Nun (796–859). All three utilised the language of love to describe how they felt about the Divine and were renowned for urging Muslims to seek nearness to God. The last period, from the ninth century onwards, saw Sufism as a distinct perspective within Islam with its own developed doctrinal and methodological approaches.

In the following thousand years, Sufism became a part of Islamic orthodoxy and embedded in most Muslim societies through the efforts of itinerant Sufi preachers and different *turuq* (Sufi orders). The most influential were the Shadhili *tariqa* in North Africa and the Middle East, the Naqshbandia in Turkey and Asia, Chisti and Qadri in the Indian subcontinent, Tijjania in West Africa and Nimatullah in Iran. There are also a number of non-traditional Sufi groups that emerged in the West in the early and mid-twentieth century, prominent among them were the followers of Inayat Khan (1882–1927), Idris Shah (1924–96) and quasi-Sufi organisations such as the International Association of Sufism (IAS). The first significant Sufi communities to arrive in Britain were the Yemeni and Somali sailors who formed the earliest permanent settled Muslim communities in Britain in the late nineteenth century.[16] The Yemenis were specifically from the Hadramawt region of the country, known for its connection to the Bani Alawi *tariqa* and the Shaykhs associated with it. In the early days of the community's formation, the Alawi Shaykhs preferred to teach as individuals and did not create an organised structure. One of the most influential among these early Sufi teachers, who moved to Britain in 1936, was Shaykh Abdullah Ali al-Hakimi (1900–54). Also during this time, the ideas of Inayat Khan and Idris Shah and their 'universal Sufism' were also in circulation and were helped by the migration of some of his American followers to the UK. However, Sufism did not become established until Muslims arrived and settled in significant numbers after World War II, bringing with them Naqshbandi, Mevlevi and Tijjania Sufi traditions from Turkey, Asia and Africa.

British Sufi Trends

The transmission of South Asian Sufi *tariqas* such as the Qadri and Chisti, which are popular in Pakistan, India and Bangladesh, occurred mainly in the 1960s. Principal among these was the Barelwi school, which derives its inspiration from nineteenth century Indian Sufi reformer Ahmed Riza Khan (1856–1921).[17] Born in the Bareilly district of the North Indian state of Uttar Pradesh, Khan taught his followers to consider themselves as the *Ahl a-Sunnah wal-Jamaah* (people of the Sunni majority consensus) rather than Barelwis, to ensure their inclusion within global Sunni orthodoxy. This boundary marking was also used to delegitimise the theological authenticity of followers of the Deobandi school and members of the Jamaat-e-Islami. Barelwi Sufis perhaps constitute the largest number of South Asian British Muslims and can be distinguished by their particular understanding of the nature of the Prophet Muhammad and popular devotional practices.[18] They are also known for extolling the miraculous qualities of pious deceased Muslims, grave visitation to seek spiritual intercession, celebrating the Prophet's birthday, *julus* (processions), *urs*, (death anniversaries), wearing *ta'wiz* (healing amulets) and the veneration of sacred relics. However, unlike the older established Qadri, Shadhili and Naqshbandi *tariqas*, Barelwis do not have one united organisation in Britain and instead draw allegiance to individual *pirs* (spiritual leaders) in their own locales. Ethnic and political rivalries have hampered attempts at creating unity among Barelwis, made more difficult by strong loyalties to a family shaykh or a particular deceased saint. This lack of centralisation was realised to be a disadvantage compared to the more organised non-Sufi groupings and eventually led to the formation of the British Muslim Forum (BMF) in the 2000s. Prominent among British Pakistani Sufis was the Naqshbandi leader, Sufi Abdullah Khan (1923–2015), who was based at the Ghamkol Sharif Mosque in Birmingham and Qadri *tariqa* representative, and Pir Maroof Hussain Shah (*b.* 1936), who resides in Bradford. Both men are well known and have a following across the UK.[19] Though elderly figures, their sermons and writings have attracted younger second- and third-generation British-born Muslims, as well as a number of white and African-Caribbean converts.

Founded in 1981 in Pakistan by its leader Tahir ul-Qadri (*b.* 1951), the Minhaj-ul-Quran (MUQ) is also sympathetic to Sufism. The UK headquarters of the MUQ are in Forest Gate, East London, and the organisation also has active branches in Manchester, Oldham and other cities with significant Pakistani Muslim communities. Among Bengalis, the figure of Abdul Latif Chowdhury (1913–2008), aka 'Fultali', was the best known among devotionally oriented Muslims from the Sylhet district of Bangladesh. Though based in his native country, he made well-attended annual visits to the UK to preach and raise money for his projects. Among the transnational Sufi orders, the Haqqani Naqshbandis have a following among ethnic Turkish-Cypriot communities, some South Asians and a number of converts. The order is named after its leader Shaykh Muhammad Nazim Adil al-Haqqani (1922–2014) who started visiting Britain regularly in the early 1970s.

Like Sufi Abdullah and Pir Maroof, he attracted followers through his exemplary piety and spiritual presence. Al-Haqqani's son-in-law, Hisham Kabbani, is considered ambassador for the Tariqa in the West. He moved to the US in the late 1990s to establish the order and also regularly visits Britain. Another branch of the Naqshbandis can be found in the Hijazi Naqshbandis, based in Nuneaton, which continues the legacy of Pir Abdul Wahab Siddiqi (1942–94). The eldest son, Faiz-ul-Aqtab Siddiqi, along with his brothers have made their *tariqa* unique in Britain for being the first Sufi order to have its deceased founder buried in Britain. This *tariqa* has a modest but growing following, helped by the profile of Fiaz-ul-Aqtab Siddiqi, who regularly participates in public debates about Shariah law. Other influential globally networked British Sufi orders include the Murabitun community, which coalesced around the Scottish convert Abdul Qadir as-Sufi (Ian Dallas) in Norwich in the early 1970s. He joined the Darqawi order in the early 1960s and went on to establish communities of followers in Britain, Spain, Mexico and South Africa. He is well known for his works: *Root Islamic Education* and *Jihad: A Ground Plan* and some of his students, such as Aisha Bewley and Yasin Dutton, are scholarly figures in their own right. His followers were distinct for their campaigning for the return of the gold and silver dinar as the standardised currency among Muslims.

Emergence of the Anglo-American 'Traditional Islam' Network

Due to the influential interventions of a group of convert scholars and the shifting dynamic within rival Islamic trends, the mid-1990s proved to be the turning point in the fortunes of Sufism among younger Muslims in Britain. As indicated earlier, existing Sufi orders had a limited appeal to the second generation, who saw them as a folkloric legacy of their parents' generation. The inability of the older traditional South Asian Muslim communities to respond to the needs of young British Muslims deeply entrenched sectarian divisions and the inadequacies of Islamist and Salafi trends left a gap for a new approach to religion. This vacuum came to be occupied by those identifying themselves as 'Traditionalists' or what I call the Traditional Islam (TI) network. The establishment of this neo-traditional Sufi trend was catalysed by the private and public work of a group of individuals whose efforts converged in the year 1995. The interventions of three people in particular initially helped to publicly define the TI scene: American convert scholars Nuh Keller and Hamza Yusuf and British Abdal-Hakim Murad. Within the UK, Fuad Nahdi, Ibrahim Osi-Efa, Masud Khan and Aftab Malik were critical in supporting and promoting TI perspectives. In America, Zaid Shakir and Umar Faruq Abd-Allah are important figures, whilst Nazim Baksh, Faraz Rabbani and Abdul Rehman-Malik were the pioneers in Canada. The TI network was also linked early on to some of the most well known Sunni scholars in the Muslim world such as the late Shaykh Sayyid Ramadan al-Buti (1929–2013), Muhammad al-Yaqoubi and Muhammad al-Ninowy from Syria, Habib Ali al-Jifri from Yemen and Shaykh Abdallah Bin Bayyah of Mauritania. According to TI adherent Abaas Choudury:

> In the 1990s Traditional Islam looked very different to how it is today and very few effective organisations and programmes were created to channel this thought to the community. In the late 1990s there was an emergence of efforts, which were almost like a breath of fresh air for those who had grown tired and weary of local mosque debates.[20]

TI insider Aftab Malik, in his book *The Broken Chain: Reflections upon the Neglect of a Tradition*, illustrates the elasticity of the phrase 'Traditional Islam', when he suggested that it:

> means different things to different people depending on the context. The usage implied [...] is the legacy of the juristic, theological and spiritual interpretive communities that forms around the third century and continues to develop and be codified onto tenth century, Hijri. These interpretive communities developed a particular set of paradigms, symbolism, and linguistic specificity that constitute what we now call, orthodoxy, 'mainstream' Islam, otherwise known as the *Ahl al-Sunna wa al-Jama'a*. Characteristically of all traditionalists scholars is the *isnad* that links him or her with scholars of a prior generation and so on until this chain links back to the time of the Salaf and ultimately to the Prophet of mercy himself.[21]

This is a useful summation of how most adherents of the TI network understand the role of tradition within Islam and highlights its core themes. This traditionalism also distinguishes itself from the better known Sufi currents by the way it engaged with the experiences and challenges facing Western Muslims. Its emergence and growth reflect a transnational coalescence of peoples, institutions, friendships, networks, and real and virtual spaces, scholars and students that agree on a consensus of priorities rather than a formal organisation entity. The Sufism of the South Asian elders, with its major nodal points in cities such as Birmingham, Bradford and London, was felt to be isolationist and often territorial. Among the reasons for the success of the 'Sufi fightback' in Britain was their appeal to tradition and orthodoxy, ideas that hold great methodological and rhetorical value. This perspective resembles the efforts to reform Sufism by neo-traditional scholars in the eighteenth and nineteenth centuries, as the Sufism in this period was seen as to be 'shorn of its ecstatic and metaphysical characteristics and assuming in their place the features of orthodoxy'.[22] Importantly, this auto-reforming impulse 'has for centuries remained the fundamental principle of validating the transmission of religious knowledge [...] and is the basis on which institutionalised Sufism, with its lineage of masters and disciples, rests'.[23]

Prior to the emergence of the TI network in 1995 a number of individuals, such as journalist and former publisher of *Q-News* magazine, Fuad Nahdi, were quietly laying the foundations. One of the other most important people behind the scenes was Liverpool-based Ibrahim Osi-Efa, founder of several Islamic initiatives such as the Ibn Abbas Institute and Greensville Trust. Osi-Efa is of Nigerian-Muslim heritage and initially became a black political activist in his teens in the early 1980s. Identifying with the African-American racial consciousness movement, his interest in Malcolm X eventually led him to rediscover the religious dimension of his identity. Between 1991 and 1992 he became interested in Islamic approaches to social activism and started to attend the activities of the Liverpool branch of YM. At first, he was attracted by their religious education work and political activism, but soon became dissatisfied with what he considered its 'watered down, superficial teachings'.[24] He started searching elsewhere for more spirituality and realism and then encountered JIMAS. After spending time with them, he felt that they also lacked spirituality and Islamic manners. At this point, he sought advice from American Imam Siraj Wahhaj, who as mentioned earlier was frequently invited to the UK by YM. Wahhaj encouraged Osi-Efa to 'do his own thing' and motivated him to initiate a number of projects that would be instrumental in developing the infrastructure for the British TI network. First he set up the Al-Muslimoon organisation in 1992, which was envisioned as a holistic organisation that would provide Islamic, Arabic, health and martial arts education and training. This later became known as the Ibn Abbas Institute for Human Development. By 1994, Osi-Efa felt he had reached the limit of his own capacity to educate people in Islamic studies and realised that a command of Arabic was the key to furthering his own development. He initially travelled to Sudan to study and upon returning organised two month-long Arabic classes in liaison with Dr Mawil Izzi Dien, an academic who at the time was Director of the MB-influenced L'Institut Européen des Sciences Humaines in Château-Chinon, France. It was during this period that Osi-Efa was introduced to Hamza Yusuf, who he invited to Britain to teach for a month in Liverpool. At the time, Hamza Yusuf's profile was ascending in the US, so Osi-Efa believed that British Muslims could also benefit from listening to Yusuf and arranged for him to speak at a major IFE conference in August 1995.

The Californian Shaykh

Now recognised as one of the most influential Muslim scholars in the Western world, Hamza Yusuf converted to Islam in 1977 and then spent many years studying classical Arabic and Islamic law in the UAE, Algeria and Mauritania. He is known to be a passionate advocate of classical Islamic teaching methodologies, is co-founder of the Zaytuna College and translator of classical texts such as *Purification of the Heart Signs: Symptoms and Cures of the Spiritual Diseases of the Heart*, and *The Creed of Imam al-Tahawi*. After his British 'debut' at the IFE conference, he rapidly gained a reputation within British Muslim communities for being a powerful orator with flawless Arabic, deep Islamic learning and the ability to engage young people. A telegenic figure, he almost single-handedly altered the content of Islamic discourse in British activist circles by popularising interest in the acquisition of classical Arabic, traditional Islamic learning methodologies and the importance of spirituality. Lectures with titles such as *Dajjal and The New World Order*, *Education of a Muslim Child* and *Secularism: The Greatest Danger of our Times* established his profile as an extremely knowledgeable, entertaining public speaker and made him a favourite among consumers of Islamic audio and video cassettes. He appealed to young British Muslims because of his status as a convert who had spent most of his early adult life travelling through the Muslim world to seek Islamic knowledge.[25] Though he did not explicitly advocate Sufism, his public talks reiterated the importance of spirituality and linked learning with action, a message which struck a chord with many in the activist scene who had grown disillusioned with the narrow rhetoric of existing Salafi and Islamist speakers. Tellingly people from across the spectrum of rival tendencies started to become drawn to his lectures, and it was then that he began to be invited to speak by most of the leading British Islamic activist organisations.

As interest in 'Traditional Islam' increased, Ibrahim Osi-Efa and website designer Masud Khan discussed the possibility of organising a regular study programme that would provide an introduction to the traditional Islamic sciences and help introduce other TI scholars to the UK scene. This decision led to the creation of three signature TI education programmes: the 'Light Study' courses, 'Deen Intensives' and 'Rihla' programmes. Each was intended to be a progressively deeper introduction to the core subject areas. Light Study programmes usually lasted one day and provided an introduction into a particular topic or text by an instructor. The three-day Deen Intensives were held over a weekend and were designed to reconnect participants with the Islamic intellectual heritage and provide an introductory knowledge of the major disciplines. Committed participants could then enrol on the summer month-long Rihla knowledge retreats, which were an opportunity for a longer immersion in Islamic studies, worship and sample of spiritually transformative experiences.

Ibrahim Osi-Efa by this point had also become active on the other side of the Atlantic, by developing networks with like-minded American Muslim activists such as Imam Zaid Shakir. Zaid Shakir, along with Hamza Yusuf, became a key component of the emerging transatlantic TI network and they worked together to produce one of the key documents of TI, the booklet *Agenda to Change our Condition*, which became a manifesto for individual and community change. Collaborating together, they expanded the work of the Zaytuna Institute and in 2009 relaunched it as the Zaytuna Liberal Arts College. Zaid Shakir, who converted to Islam in 1977 whilst serving as a member of the American Air Force, is regarded as one of the most influential Muslims in America and one of the few figures to have been invited to the UK to speak at Sufi, Salafi and Islamist events. A former Lecturer in International Relations and Arabic at Southern Connecticut State University, he has translated a number of classical texts, such as *The Heirs of the Prophets* and *Treatise for the Seekers of Guidance*, and authored *Scattered Pictures: Reflections of an American Muslim*. Shakir was encouraged by Osi-Efa to pursue higher Islamic studies in Syria, where he spent a total of seven years and is the first American graduate of Abu Noor University. Continuing his own personal quest for knowledge, Osi-Efa went on to study for three years in Syria, Mauritania and a further six years in Yemen, whilst in between helping to develop the growing demand for Deen Intensive and Light Study programmes in the UK.

The first Rihla programme in Britain was held in September 1996 in Nottingham, followed by others hosted in Morocco, Spain and Saudi Arabia. With the Rihla, the year 1999 proved to be another landmark for the TI network in the UK as it was hosted at the Islamic Foundation, Leicester. Its importance is due to the strategic planning meeting attended by many of the senior figures of the TI scene at the time. Ibrahim Osi-Efa described it as a 'pow-wow', a Native American word meaning spiritual gathering. This is an apt term, given the intention to bring together different perspectives and ideas in this emerging international neo-traditional Sufi network. Crucially in attendance was Umar Faruq Abd-Allah, another prominent American convert and widely respected scholar, who became Muslim in 1970. After spending several years teaching Islamic Studies in the US, Spain and Saudi Arabia, Abd-Allah founded the Nawawi Foundation in Chicago, where he is Scholar in Residence. At the Leicester meeting Abd-Allah gave a seminal paper outlining a vision for the TI network in the West, which was intended to galvanise a broad consensus of priorities, projects and a reinforcing of relationships. Among other issues discussed were the differences of opinion on what constituted Traditional Islam. According to Osi-Efa, Nuh Keller was quite adamant that adherents of TI should affiliate with an established *tariqa*, while Hamza Yusuf insisted that it was not necessary and should remain an optional personal choice.

An important outcome of the meeting was the commitment to a 'pact of non-aggression' among the different TI personalities, agreeing to revive the tradition of tolerance for diversity that has been the strength of the Islamic legacy and to refrain from attacking, slandering or backbiting fellow Muslims, even if their opinions differed.[26] In the end, all of the participants concurred that TI perspectives should reflect a distinctive set of conceptual themes and characteristics. This implied agreement came with a minimum set of normative theological beliefs, practices and pedagogical methods.

These ideas could be condensed down to these leitmotifs: the importance of classical theology, adherence to one of the four schools of Sunni law, transmission-based scholarship, traditional teaching pedagogies, practise of Sufism and social engagement. The emphasis on social engagement is a defining feature of this trend that distinguishes it from the followers of established Sufi *tariqas*. Individuals associated with the TI scene are more likely to be actively interested in current affairs and involved in activities that are aimed at inviting others to Islam. It is an increasingly popular current among young British Muslims, demonstrated by a growing infrastructure of educational centres, publishing houses, magazines, journals, websites, businesses, charities, campaigning groups, self-help groups and specialists in the arts. Within this unity of purpose is a wide diversity of backgrounds, nationalities, ethnicities, levels of scholarly authority and methods of engagement with other Muslim and non-Muslim groups.

Reconnecting with Classical Theology

The classical Sunni Muslim normative theological consensus that TI promoted was established over the centuries and is contained in a coherent body of creedal and legal positions. This concord is based upon the acceptance of the Asharite and Maturidi theologies and primacy of the four main Sunni schools of jurisprudence. The understanding relies on the accumulated wisdom of the great classical scholars such as al-Nawawi (1234–78), al-Ghazali, Ibn Qadi Abu Bakr (*b.* al-Arabi, 1076–1148), Hajar al-Asqalani (1372–1448), Imam al-Dhahabi (1274–1348) and Ibn al-Qayyim al-Jawzi (1292–1350) among others. This theme is particularly strong in the writings of American convert Nuh Keller. Keller, who became Muslim in 1977 whilst living in Egypt, has gained a significant number of followers in both the UK and US since the mid-1990s. A philosophy graduate of the University of Chicago and the University of California, his journey to Islam began in 1975 after he started to study classical Arabic in Chicago. He then began a prolonged study of the Islamic sciences with prominent scholars in Jordan and Syria, joined the Shadhili *tariqa* in 1982 and achieved scholarly seniority and title of Shaykh in 1996. He is best known for his translation of the classical Shafi'i manual of jurisprudence *Umdat al-Salik* (*The Reliance of the Traveller*), the first legal work in English to be endorsed by the historically important Al-Azhar University in Cairo. According to Marcia Hermansen, his approach to Sufism 'has been characterised as "techno-*fiqh*" or "ultra orthodoxy" by other American Sufis, whilst his followers perceive his style as being the most authentic and legitimate'.[27] Web designer Masud Khan introduced Keller to the UK speakers' circuit in January 1995. His lecture series delivered in London, Birmingham and Nottingham faced a hostile reception from members of JIMAS, who followed him around and heckled him on his tour. His speeches gained wider circulation through their publication later that year in *Q-News* magazine. The articles entitled 'The concept of Bid'a in the Islamic Shari'a', *Why Muslims follow Madhhabs*, *Literalism and The attributes of Allah* and *The place of Tasawwuf in Traditional Islamic Sciences*, became instrumental in foregrounding TI perspectives to British Muslims. Keller's deep but accessible scholarship explored the lightning-rod issues among British Muslim activists such as theological orthodoxy, normative Prophetic practice and the status of Sufism in Islam. His choice of topics was a deliberate attempt to address contentious issues that were being used by Salafis to define the boundaries of what constituted orthodoxy, and could be interpreted as the opening salvo of the Sufi fightback against Salafi and Islamist discourses. He attempted to vindicate Sufism by trying to demonstrate the organic link between orthodoxy and Sufism. He employed textual proofs, analogous reasoning and examples of historically famous Muslim scholars to validate his argument:

> From Umayyad times to Abbasid, to Mameluke, to the end of the six-hundred-year Ottoman period – Sufism has been taught and understood as an Islamic discipline, like Qur'anic exegesis (*tafsir*), hadith, Qur'an recital (*tajwid*), tenets of faith (*ilm al-tawhid*) or any

other, each of which preserved some particular aspect of the *din* or religion of Islam [...] Similarly *ilm al-tasawwuf*, 'the science of Sufism' came into being to preserve and transmit a particular aspect of the *shari'a*, that of *ikhlas* or sincerity [...] Indeed, to throw away every traditional work of the Islamic sciences authored by those educated by Sufis would be to discard 75 percent or more of the books of Islam.[28]

The recurring emphasis on the connection between the producers of orthodox theology and Sufism is not only intended to educate, but also to challenge Salafis and Islamists attempts to erase this historical narrative. The leading figures of the TI network did not support either the immanentism of Sufi figures such as Ibn Arabi (1165–1240) or popular practices associated with esoteric, ecstatic Sufism. Hamza Yusuf, keen to distinguish between genuine practitioners and charlatans, stated:

It is well known of the people claiming to be Sufis, putting on the garments of Sufis, and tricking simple followers and worshippers; getting them to give them their money, to slavishly serve them, and these types of things [...] happened historically in the Muslim world. The (pious) imams have always been the strictest at trying to prevent this deception, because there is nothing worse than deceiving somebody in religion.[29]

This clarification and distinction, and others like it, helped dispel the reluctance some young activists had towards Sufism and offered a persuasive alternative for those who wanted to escape the dominant Salafi/Islamist activist readings of Islam as well as the localised, ethnic Sufism of their South Asian heritage. This is not to say that all members of the TI scene joined a *tariqa*, as some took the view that '*tassawuf* is possible without *tariqa*'. Adherents of TI argue that the daily practise of Islam is best done through the mediation of one of the four madhabs. These legal schools represent the eponymous accumulated rulings of the four most widely followed jurists in early Islam. They function as reference points for believers trying to secure religious guidance in ascertaining what is religiously permissible and impermissible. Simply put, madhabs are accessed for matters that lie beyond the layperson's competence. Abdal-Hakim Murad, reasoned that:

We might compare the Qur'anic verses and the *hadiths* to the stars. With the naked eye, we are unable to see many of them clearly; so we need a telescope. If we are foolish, or proud, we may try to build one ourselves. If we are sensible and modest, however, we will be happy to use one built for us by Imam al-Shafi'i or Ibn Hanbal, and refined, polished and improved by generations of great astronomers. A madhhab is, after all, nothing more than a piece of precision equipment enabling us to see Islam with the maximum clarity possible. If we use our own devices, our amateurish attempts will inevitably distort our vision.[30]

The rationale argued here is that only people trained in the religious sciences are qualified to interpret the primary texts of the Qur'an and Hadith. Ordinary people are not equipped to consult them directly and are obliged to follow the jurisprudential reasoning of a legal school of thought. This explanation of the unwiseness of approaching the textual sources without the aid of specialists was meant to counter the prevalence of Salafi polemics against the 'blind following of a madhab'. This sentiment should be understood as a direct response to the popular slogan 'go back to the Qur'an and Sunnah' used by Salafis who claimed that madhab adherents follow the four legal schools blindly.

Abdal-Hakim Murad's role in helping to popularise TI perspectives in the UK is also very significant. One of Britain's most important scholars, he is well known for his academic work and highly regarded translation of two volumes of al-Ghazali's celebrated *Ihya Ulum al-Din*. Murad began his studies in Arabic at Cambridge University and graduated from Al-Azhar University before further private study with individual scholars in Saudi Arabia and Yemen. He first came to prominence in the mid-1990s through his regular articles in *Q-News* and became known for his erudition and frequently polemical tone towards Salafis and Islamists. Some of his most widely read essays include *Islamic Spirituality: The Forgotten Revolution, Understanding the Four Madhhabs* and *Recapturing Islam from the Terrorists*. He pulled no punches in arguing against what he saw as the corrosive affect of Saudi-funded Salafism and held the doctrinal excesses of Wahhabi thought, responsible for al-Qaeda terrorism, to account. He also singled out ideologues from the Muslim Brotherhood and the Jamaat-e-Islami for hyper politicising Islam and emptying it of its transcendent message. His counter narratives argued for a return to medieval theological Islamic consensus, adherence to a madhab and active commitment to Sufism. His prolific writings in the areas of Sufism, theology, law, interfaith relations, contemporary issues and engagement with mainstream media and government made him an important voice that commanded respect among educated Muslims across the UK and abroad. This is despite the 'overly academic style of writing, which even people favourable to his work consider as unconventional and cumbersome, especially those for whom he writes'.[31] The combined effect of the output of these three figures altered the terms of reference in activist circles and created interest in issues that until then had not been discussed by YM, HT or the Salafis. In effect, they re-established Sufism as a legitimate and necessary part of mainstream Islam and inspired young people to deepen their knowledge of religious tradition.

Adab, Isnad and Ijazah Paradigms

In his book *The Broken Chain*, Aftab Malik blames the demise of the caliphate, the rise of Islamist movements, the growth of modernism and the impact of the printing press for changing the relationship Muslims had with their religious knowledge. He was concerned that these factors perversely democratised the ability to access Islamic learning, resulting in people attempting to autodidactically educate themselves in specialised fields of knowledge.[32] The effect was to undermine *adab*, the correct etiquette, manners and respect one should have for teachers when learning Islam:

> Adab does not simply imply 'manners' but more so to *discipline* –
> the discipline of body, mind and the soul. Adab in the true sense
> of the word includes the discipline that assures the *recognition* and
> *acknowledgement* of one's proper place in relation to one's self,
> society and community; the *recognition* and *acknowledgement* of
> one's proper place in relation to one's physical, intellectual and
> spiritual capacities and potentials; the *recognition* and *acknowledgement*
> of the fact that knowledge and beings are ordered in degrees, levels
> and ranks.[33]

In his view, this levelling process caused the devaluing of religious knowledge and emergence of mediocre standards of scholarship which bore the imprint of Salafi and Islamist hermeneutics. This can be seen in the modern activist's tendency to claim the right to *ijtihad* – wanting to reinterpret directly from primary text and ignore the accumulated tradition available in the classical heritage. For seekers of traditional Islamic learning, having a trusted *isnad* (chain of transmission) and relevant *ijazah* (authorisation) is crucial to be able to demonstrate ones scholarly pedigree. The *isnad* paradigm provides 'a personally guaranteed connection with a model past, and especially with model persons, offers the only sound basis in an Islamic context for forming and re-forming oneself and one's society in any age'.[34] Masud Khan explained the importance of *adab*, *isnad* and *ijaza* pedagogy as:

> the transmission of knowledge from a living shaykh who has *ijazas*, or certificates of learning, for the material he is teaching. Students, not only gain the knowledge, but also benefit from the explanation of the subtleties of the text, which a casual reader may miss. Also, they gain the *barakah* or blessing from receiving the transmission of the text and take their place in a long chain back to the source, the Prophet (May Allah bless him and give him peace). Finally, and most importantly, the most beneficial thing they learn is the *adab,* or the etiquette of receiving knowledge. The importance of *adab* cannot be understated or underestimated, since one realises that the more he learns the more he realises he does not know and this is a very humbling experience.[35]

Studying Islam in this way with individual teachers also allows for the possibility of 'the spiritual power (*barakah*) of charismatic religious figure [...] perpetuated in a line of spiritual descent that links each new generation of adepts and lay followers of an order to the spiritual authority of the Prophet and ultimately to God – through the Companions and the best of their successors'.[36] The scholarly credentials are thus acquired through apprenticeship with individual teachers in the different Islamic sciences guiding them through 'learning, under-standing memorisation, recitation, exegesis and important works of Muslim piety and learning'.[37] The *ijazah* system is perpetuated by a method of knowledge transmission linking the past to the present through a network of personal rather than institutional certification.

The emergence of the TI network in the 1990s and its particular priorities reflects the resilience of the Sufi tradition in the modern era. The well-known historical Sufi orders and their South Asian varieties that migrated to the UK almost became irrelevant to a generation that viewed them as quaint remnants of their parents' immigrant culture. This changed dramatically after the emergence of the TI forms of Sufism because, unlike representatives of traditional *tariqas*, many TI figures commanded impressive scholarly credentials from both Muslim and Western academic institutions, had the cultural literacy to engage young Western Muslims and emphasised a spirituality thought to be missing in the other three Islamic currents. They changed the terms of reference within existing activist circles and inspired many to study the classical Islamic science overseas. Interestingly, figures like Hamza Yusuf initially entered the consciousness of wider British Muslim communities through the help of existing reformist Islamist infrastructures. Until they created their own, TI activists and speakers used organisational networks such as the IFE, YM, Islamic Society of Britain and even the Salafi-oriented Masjid Tawheed in East London. The neo-Sufism of the TI network demonstrates both continuity with history and change in relation to the impact of modernity but distinguished its religiosity from other Sufi currents and rival activist Islamic trends. The discourses of these four trends and the impact of dramatic socio-political change are explored in the next chapter.

CHAPTER 5

DAWAH DISCOURSES
UNDERSTANDING THE APPEAL
OF THE TRENDS

So we attract the youth, we purify them and we try to train them
by giving them tarbiyah, so that they will go back into and help
the society they live in [...] With HT it is to propagate the idea
that the Khilafah is the end and that the Khilafah will solve all our
problems [...] With JIMAS it is to change and purify the aqidah.[1]

Ahtesham Ali

The religious currents discussed in previous chapters all claimed to be
giving *dawah* – calling people to Islam. They were established either as
result of the transmission of religious ideas with the first generation of
Muslim settlers or have emerged out of the reproduction of globalised
transnational tendencies. The Islamist reformism of the Young Muslims
UK was developed as a result of UKIM wanting to produce a Muslim
youth leadership. Radical Islamists Hizb ut-Tahrir originally only
targeted overseas students in universities, but later attracted British-
born Muslims and made the UK its international communications hub.
Various Salafi trends were activated through the work of individuals
whose religious ideas aligned with a particular Islamic theological
orientation in Saudi Arabia. The Sufi Traditional Islam network emerged
as a response to these other currents and was strengthened through close
relationships with like-minded Muslims in the US and wider Muslim
world. This chapter links together these four narratives by looking at the

convergent and divergent discourses that they have produced, using analytical framing tools from Social Movement Theory. It offers a set of thematic frames which capture key issues prioritised by the trend to recruit and mobilise people to their cause. Understanding how these different frames are constructed help to explain why Islamic trends appealed to young British Muslims searching for religious indentities.

Social Movement Theories (SMT) were developed by social scientists working on the cultural and political impact of social movements. The pioneering work of Charles Tilly, Doug McAdam, Sidney Tarrow and Mayer Zald spanned various social and political movements in North and South America and Europe.[2] Social movement theories differ from existing interpretive frameworks that rely upon grievance-based models to explain collective action and offer analytical lenses that focus on group dynamics as well as individual members. Advocates of the SMT approach argue that most studies of Islamic activism 'are rooted in functionalist social psychology accounts of mass behaviour, which view collective action as derived from exogenous structural strains, system disequilibrium and concomitant pathologies, (alienation, anomie, atomization, normative ambiguity)'.[3] They also suggest that existing frameworks do not explain why and how people organise themselves into faith-based social movements, nor do they sufficiently take into account the rational strategic decisions made by movement leaders. The application of SMTs to the study of Islamic movements became more prevalent during the late 1990s, through the work of Islamic movements specialists who bridged the gap between faith-based activism and social science theories of collective action. Critically, they challenged the notion that process and organisation of Islamic activism is not *sui generis*, or somehow unique and unlike other social movements. Instead, they de-emphasise the specificity of Islam as a system of meaning, identity and the basis of collective action and point to the commonalties these movements share in the processes. Put simply, SMT focuses on the interaction between ideology, leaders and group members by analysing social movements through the way they frame issues, and is a useful way of looking at how Islamic activists rationalise their mission and mobilise their organisations. The groundbreaking volume *Islamic Activism: A Social Movement Theory Approach*, edited by Quintan Wiktorowicz, provided a diverse set of case studies in how SMT approaches illuminate cases of Islamic activism in very different contexts.[4] Wiktorowicz also wrote his own important study, *Radical Islam Rising: Muslim Extremism in the West*, in which he examined the extremist Al-Muhajiroun (AM) group in Britain. His application of the ideas of 'religious seeking', 'cognitive openings' and 'resource mobilization' in the decision-making process demonstrate how social networks and media are utilised to promote a movement's message. Resource mobilisation, for example, demonstrates how Islamic activists function as rational actors, rather than individuals who are guided purely by dogmatic adherence to religious ideology. From this perspective, these activists' decision-making processes can be said to be driven by tactical and strategic assessments of costs and risks and not only ideas about theology and piety.

Religious Seekers and Cognitive Openings

People interested in increasing their commitment to Islam, or those in state of religious seeking, are motivated by a number of different reasons. For many people, life cycle events such as getting married, becoming a parent or a death within the family can act as triggers for greater religious observance. For some, a turning point is reached through the influence of a sibling or a close friend who decides to take their faith seriously. This religious seeking can also be provoked by attending a public lecture or deciding to go on the pilgrimage to Makkah. For others, the traumatic effect of experiencing racism, Islamophobia, societal exclusion or blocked social mobility can prompt questions about what it means to be a Muslim in a non-Muslim society. This can lead to a process of enquiry and self-education gained through a combination of private study or attendance at public events. Heightened awareness of Muslims suffering from the impact of global events, as well as feeling the need to defend ones culture, is well-known factors in the process of young people reconsidering the role of faith in their lives. Cultural defence helps to sharpen religious identity and is not unique to Muslims, as similar processes can be seen among young British Sikhs and Hindus.[5] Cumulatively these different processes can lead to a 'cognitive opening' by the questioning of previously-held beliefs, consideration of alternative views and openness to the message of an Islamic trend. As indicated in earlier chapters, people feel liberated by the approach offered by the Islamic trends as they transcend the ethnic, culturally conservative attitudes prevalent in most mosques as well as providing an alternative subculture and social support structure.

Various studies suggest media coverage of Muslims and radicalisation also plays a role in increasing social disengagement and increasing receptivity to the messages of religious groups.[6] An example of the role of alienation in increasing religiosity and political consciousness is provided in a comparative study of young Muslim men in East London and Madrid by Justin Gest. His book, *Apart: Alienated and Engaged Muslims in the West*, demonstrates how social alienation from democratic processes can lead to what he calls 'apartism' – an active or a passive form of social exclusion.[7] Quintan Wiktorowicz's work on AM also found that discrimination and not being fully accepted as British citizens was also helpful in enabling recruitment. As Omar Bakri admitted to him, 'if there is no racism in the West, there is no conflict of identity [. . .] If there is no discrimination or racism I think it would be very difficult for us.'[8] Compounding this effect was anger over British and US foreign policy, which hardened into feelings of defeat and hopelessness. The pattern of international crisis events beginning in the 1990s – specifically, the first Gulf War, the US invasion of Somalia, ethnic cleansing of Muslims in Bosnia, persecution of Muslims in Chechnya and Kosovo, which continued into the 2000s with the second Palestinian Intifada and American invasions of Afghanistan and Iraq – all reinforced the perception of many Muslims that there is indeed a 'War on Islam'. A former member of HT lists the factors which he believed enabled cognitive openings for the organisation to recruit:

> A heightened perception of Muslims and Muslim countries being unjustly attacked (Gulf War I and II, Afghan War, Palestine, Chechnya). Double standards exhibited by the UN and USA with respect to Israel. Political Islam, being touted as a panacea for the Muslims problems. A lack of alternative scholarly voices advocating more traditional responses to state oppression and increased media awareness due to proliferation of Islamic literature on the Internet.[9]

All of the grievances coagulate to produce what Wiktorowicz calls 'moral shock', which occurs as response to distressing imagery of Muslim suffering or as revulsion towards decadent aspects of Western culture.

A popular technique of the moral shock tactics used by activists to elicit an emotional reaction is the graphic display of mutilated dead bodies of Palestinians under occupation, Afghan civilians killed by American and British troops or the humiliation of Iraqi prisoners in Abu Ghraib prison. This is usually followed by messages about the urgent need for action and why it is a religious duty for Muslims to become involved in collective work. The activist group presentation of Islam is often quite different to their parents' understanding of religion, which can then appear 'archaic, backward and ill-informed', a version that is 'focused on issues of ritual and tradition devoid of political import'.[10] This strategy allows groups to offer explanations and interpretations to young people who may not yet be able to evaluate the claims independently. Wiktorowicz observed during his research on AM that some experienced:

> cognitive openings through discussions with familiars and strangers [...] eventual joiners who responded to the opening through religious seeking found mainstream religious institutions and figures wanting [...] local imams and mosques failed to provide guidance on specific concerns of British Muslims, as a result they were more amenable to experimentation outside the mainstream.[11]

This in turn helps to solidify a particular form of Islamic identity and otherisation of non-Muslims. The effect produces a set of identities and values that challenge dominant cultural codes, or what Social Movement theorist Alberto Melucci, in his book *Challenging Codes: Collective Action in the Information Age*, called 'networks of shared meaning'.[12] In other words, they attempt to 'create a community of "true believers" tied together through a shared interpretation of Islam [...] characterised by high levels of tension with common religious understandings'.[13]

Framing Islamic Discourses

At a foundational level, all classical and modern Islamic discourses have a master narrative that agrees upon the root precepts of the uniqueness of God, the purpose of creation, the centrality of the Qur'an and Prophet Muhammad. The sacred texts of the Qur'an and Hadith provide the basis for these discourses, which were augmented and layered by the exegetical, legal and spiritual traditions accumulated over time and space to form a 'discursive tradition'. As anthropologist Talal Asad has argued, 'Islamic discursive traditions are characterised by their own rationality or styles of reasoning – couched in their texts, history, and institutions'.[14] These traditions are influenced as much by intellectual, cultural, sectarian and political conditions as they are by the burden of history. The multiple framing of ancient and contemporary events enable rival Islamic trends to manipulate traditions to present their own particular interpretation as the most authentic and correct reading of religion. Together these operate as a religious imaginary that filter sacred Muslim traditions and their application in different times and places. These discourses span several subject areas and vary in levels of sophistication and scholarly debate, though for the purposes of this book I am only interested in contempory populist discourses and how they focused into distinct frames.[15] The framing process has the effect of influencing what specific issues Muslim activists should be thinking and talking about and, more importantly, what target audiences should be doing. These framings are most potent and likely to be accepted when they resonate with a person's life circumstances and work best when they correlate with an individual's personal values, experiences, and viewpoints. In other words, the movement's discourses and framing strategy align with the individual's interpretative framework. The various Islamic trends operate in a highly competitive marketplace for religious seekers and have to 'stand out' when addressing issues and concerns shared by wider Muslim communities. For instance, when considering AM's framing of the causes of the Iraq war, Wiktorowicz wrote:

> The analysis of both mainstream organisations and *Al-Muhajiroun* on the Iraq war attributed responsibility for the crisis on the US. However, crucial differences remain. In particular, *Al-Muhajiroun* interpret US action as part of a 'Crusade against Muslims' and called for violent action in response. By contrast, many mainstream organisations interpreted it in terms of a general American drive for global hegemony and called for diplomacy and negotiation. However, this 'overlap in the diagnostic frames' means that the movement has the potential to attract audience participants outside their immediate community.[16]

Frames are most effective when they contain three core components: these are its diagnostic, prognostic and motivational features. In brief, the diagnostic frame defines the problem and who is to be held responsible for it, the prognostic frame offers the solution and the motivational frame provides incentives to inspire action. Once convinced of a particular diagnostic framing, an individual may become receptive to prognostic and motivational framing incentives for group membership. Framing as a process serves to convince target audiences by using well-rehearsed arguments that appeal to scripture, authoritative interpretation and prioritisation of action to elicit support and participation. In the case of Islamic revivalist discourses, the frames created by the individual groups aim to insert the particular movement or trend as the authoritative mediator between the sacred text and religious practices that are deemed to be the most correct and authentic.[17] Themes are strategically selected by a group to reflect its particular priority; it then attempts to convince its viewpoint in competition to rival 'framings' of the same issue. For example, when summarising the framing strategies used by al-Qaeda in Saudi Arabia, Wiktorowicz noted that they were:

> embroiled in a bitter 'frame dispute' with the Saudi ulama (religious scholars), where each asserts a particular interpretation and the right to sacred authority [...] Al-Qaeda emphasises the knowledge, character and logic of its scholars while attacking its detractors using the same criteria. Al-Qaeda supporters are framed as honourable, independent, and scientific in their approach to interpreting Islam. Opponents, in contrast, are framed as 'sheikhs of authority' or 'palace lackeys' inextricably linked to corrupt Muslim governments. The framing strategy is designed to insert al-Qaeda as sole mediator between the sacred texts and religious practice.[18]

Each trend has produced a large quantity of material that includes written or spoken artefacts in the form of books, pamphlets, audio, video, transcripts of speeches or the written texts, audio/visual, CD/ DVD media, internet and public lectures. After surveying them it is possible to identify a set of recurring themes that transcend the agendas of individual trends. I have grouped them into the following frames: '*To be a Good Muslim*', '*Islam is the Solution*', '*We are one* Ummah', '*Struggle* between *Islam and the Rest'* and *'The Search for a British Islam'*, which will be discussed in the following section.

'To Be a Good Muslim'

Among the most frequently cited reasons for participation in Islamic activism are to 'gain knowledge of Islam', to learn how 'to please God' and to 'encourage others to do the same'. A desire for personal salvation is perhaps the fundamental goal for most believers, so it is unsurprising that all of the different trends will construct frames around the importance of faith, values, ritual worship and pious behaviour. Islamic understandings of the development of personal piety are most often about increasing knowledge, strengthening religiosity through the performance of daily acts of worship and living a morally ethical life. This can be understood firstly as an act of religious faith and secondly as an empowerment strategy that enables people to challenge values and practices that are deemed as un-Islamic. This dimension is evident in the different types of material produced by the groups and usually links the importance of gaining knowledge as the first step to becoming a more observant Muslim. Underlying this emphasis are two main assumptions: first that acquiring knowledge is a faith imperative and, second, that Muslims today are in need of increasing their religious literacy. Gaining greater understanding of Islam is crucially linked to the idea of recognising the ultimate purpose for existence – the awareness of and submission to the will of the Creator – and that increasing religious knowledge is an act of faith that will generate spiritual reward and earn Divine favour.

A desire to achieve entrance to Heaven and be saved from Hell are also fundamental motivational incentives for encouraging and regulating correct behaviour and is self-explanatory. Islamic teachings provide vivid imagery describing what these two places look like and contrasting the fates of those who enter into them. These destinations are constantly evoked and contrasted with each other to remind people of the ultimate consequences of earthly conduct. The various Islamic trends begin to differ on how much they emphasise these core themes of Islamic salvationary doctrine. Groups such as YM, the Salafi trends and the TI network will in varying degrees connect correct belief and behaviour with judgement in an Afterlife. One of YM's core aims was to help young Muslims to reinvigorate their faith; Salafi's consider the correct understanding of the uniqueness of the Creator as the key to salvation; while in TI discourses spiritual purification and closeness to God are the means by which other-worldly success is achieved. All these themes are aspects of Islamic normative teaching and what distinguishes each trend from the other is the way it foregrounds a particular dimension. The 'to be a Good Muslim' frame can be interpreted as a perennial ethical challenge for all Muslims. It may also be seen as an emancipatory response to negative societal framing and can trigger a religiously inspired impulse to change the world. As mentioned earlier, Islam has always had a proselytising character and therefore wanting to share one's enthusiasm for Islam is a logical progression for those who have benefitted from applying its teachings. Hence engaging in activist work is seen as fulfilment of these Qur'anic injunctions.

'Islam is the Solution'

Some of the most persistent frames among revivalist groups are permutations of phrases such as 'Islam is the solution', 'Islam is the true religion' or 'Islam is the Truth', which reinforce a self-legitimising religious rationale and internal logic. As suggested earlier, reformist Islamist thought is very much a self-sufficient, closed system that vindicates itself by arguing Islam is a self-evident truth. This logic can result in feelings of religious supremacy and create forms of prejudice that both fear and desire many aspects of Western civilisation and highlight its less attractive cultural traits. Within this framing, 'British society is seen as woefully and perhaps fatally undermined by sexual promiscuity, alcohol abuse, psychological disorders, crime, drugs, and the collapse of the family and juvenile disobedience to parental discipline.'[19] This type of frame is used as a popular rhetorical tool by various Islamic trends across the spectrum and forms an oppositional positioning to the 'superiority of Islam' that can be still seen in the writings and propaganda of many Islamic organisations today. Islamic teachings are contrasted and extolled through moral values that discourage premarital sex, intoxicants, and promote family life and parental respect. This approach assumes a comforting set of discourses that often make unequal comparisons and carefully omit the fact that most contemporary Muslim societies are struggling with similar social problems. The presentation of this moral decline is interspersed with other difficult internal social challenges facing Muslim communities to counterpose the claim that only Islam – correctly understood and practised – is the solution to these problems. A bridging argument suggests that an absence of Islam will result in moral corruption, social destabilisation and a loss of God's favour.

This frame seamlessly connects to a narrative about the scientific rationality of Islam and serves to reassure people of the intellectual validity of their faith. Attempting to 'prove the truth of Islam' is a popular preoccupation of Islamist and Salafi groups who offer nostalgic re-readings of Muslim history and engage in 'Islam and science' based apologetics. This has spawned an entire genre, popularised by the book *The Bible, the Qur'an and Science* by French surgeon Maurice Bucaille, and continues in the work of Turkish writer Adnan Oktar (aka Harun Yahya). As a discourse it is a crude form of comparative religion which contrasts historical and scientific information in the Qur'an with the Bible and continues to be used by Muslim missionary groups around the world. The 'Islam is the solution' frame is also promoted by activist organisations keen to convert non-Muslims to Islam such as the Islamic Propagation Centre International (IPCI) in Birmingham. The IPCI distributes the writings and videos of South African polemicist Ahmed Deedat (1918–2005), who had a huge following around the Muslim world in the 1980s. Deedat's writings were circulated free of charge around the world and included combative titles such as: *Resurrection or Resuscitation?*, *Crucifixion or Cruci-Fiction?* and *Combat Kit against Bible Thumpers*. His approach has been taken up and enhanced by the Indian Salafi preacher Dr Zakir Naik on his popular satellite channel Peace TV. This strident polemical approach has gained widespread influence, was present in the material of most of the main trends, and was at one point promoted by YM. UKIM continues to promote leaflets with this kind of message, as do certain Salafi-oriented groups such as the World Assembly of Muslim Youth (WAMY). This mindset still pervades many Muslim activist groups keen to demonstrate the compatibility of Islam, science and the rationality of their beliefs. HT in the early 1990s was fond of claiming to prove the existence of God according to the latest findings of science in its various pamphlets. The works of 'Harun Yahya' are also important in this regard as his many books attempt to challenge the theory of evolution and have gained an international attention and readership among British Muslims.

This type of apologetic literature also contains widely circulated conversion stories (especially of celebrities), which are highlighted in booklets, books and on internet sites. There are many websites that stock such testimonies and they all tend to observe a formula that depicts those choosing Islam either after disillusionment with their religious upbringing, at the end of a pursuit of existential meaning, or following positive contact with Muslims. This type of missionary activism helps to validate the faith of young people in a climate of hostile critiques against Islam and Muslims and enables young people and new converts to feel intellectually convinced of the claims of their faith. The role of Islamic activists is then to persuade humanity to 'revert' to the *deen al-fitrah* (primordial religion). Running parallel to these frames of Islam being the solution, and the need to be a good Muslim, is the idea that Islam is the final universal religion. The universality of Islam and the notion of a community of faith are two of the defining features of the religion, and most Muslims at least on an emotional level will say that they feel a kinship with other believers from different parts of the world.

'We are One *Ummah*'

Indentifying with the political struggles across the Muslim world not only strengthens a sense of an 'Imagined Community', but serves to create virtual and real world ties of faith with fellow believers living under difficult circumstances.[20] Vicarious humiliation over Western military intervention in Muslim-majority countries such as Afghanistan, Iraq or the failure to solve longstanding political disputes in Palestine and Kashmir all help to reinforce a sense of shared responsibility towards people not within the realms of their everyday experience. This intensifies a sense of moral and political investment into the ideal of a universal Muslim *ummah*, which for some British Muslims became a powerful, emotional process of religious identification – motivating them to act on their behalf by giving charitable aid, awarenesss raising and in certain cases physical participation in conflict zones. This was particularly the case during the first Afghan war in the 1980s, Bosnia in the 1990s and more recently in Syria where hundreds of British Muslims were originally motivated to travel to protect innocents caught up in the civil war.

Unsurprisingly, pan-Islamic unity is a familiar theme in HT's discourse. HT rhetoric rejects any form of integration in non-Muslim societies and only recognises identification with their vision of a united Muslim *ummah*. Though HT's Zionist-like aspiration for the return of a caliphate may seem utopian, the idea of a single super state which could defend Muslims from aggression does resonate with some people and is one of the reasons Islamic State (IS) has been able to draw people to terrritory under its control. As Kirstine Sinclair perceptively suggested, HT ideology 'turns members into voluntary refugees who long for a lost homeland'.[21] These ideas can be more receptive when there is a perception that Islam and Muslims are under siege.[22] Other culture wars have acted as social flashpoints and continue to feed the belief that the West is at war with Islam. Events in recent years such as the Danish Cartoon crisis, banning the construction of minarets in Switzerland or the provocative YouTube film *The Innocence of Muslims* all serve to convince many Muslims that there is an ongoing struggle between Islam and its enemies and that only political unity at a transnational level can protect them.

'Struggle between Islam and the Rest'

This frame is premised upon the view that there is a cosmic battle between the forces of good and evil which began after the creation of the first human and his nemesis – Satan.[23] It is believed to have continued throughout human history with successive Prophets representing the forces of good struggling with those that challenged their message. This overlaps with the narrative about reviving a utopian 'Golden Age of Islam', lost through Muslim weakness and the violence of colonisation. It also functions to play upon modern experiences of 'marginalisation, exclusion, discrimination and disadvantage in education, housing and employment'.[24] Of the four trends HT has been the most vocal in supporting the idea of an inevitable clash of civilisations and even produced a booklet explaining why conflict with the 'forces of disbelief' is unavoidable. As a former international leader of HT explained:

> The fierce struggle between the Islamic thoughts and the *Kufr* thoughts and between the Muslims and the *Kuffar*, has been intense ever since the dawn of Islam [...] It will continue in this way – a bloody struggle alongside the intellectual struggle – until the Hour comes and Allah inherits the Earth and those on it.[25]

This frame is essentially a form of religious anti-imperialism and one of many similar 'oppositional group based narratives [which] have played a fundamental role in the construction of constituencies of shared grievance, rationales for action and legitimating exercises'.[26] Only ex-members are willing to acknowledge the pervasiveness of this polarising logic, as one conceded 'members constantly malign the Kafir [...] while not understanding that Islam came for the whole of mankind'.[27] This theological casting of enemies conspiring to suppress Muslims evinces the assertion that only Islam has the potential to threaten the world's great powers. However, this frame becomes less persuasive when Muslims are the ones oppressing fellow believers – as happens in various states in the Middle East and elsewhere. The framing of Islam versus the West becomes difficult to explain when 'Islamic nations' such as Iran transact economic deals with 'godless' communists in Russia, in spite of the Russian wars over Chechnya, or when Saudi Arabia supports autocratic regimes in the Gulf to persecute its own citizens. This reductionism not only obscures the complexities at play in international affairs, but also reinforces a sense of globalised victimhood.

'The Search for a British Islam'

While a number of Muslims still adopt an attraction/repulsion relationship with Britain, most have made the transition from feeling 'besieged to belonging' and are attempting to synthesise their religious and national identities into a distinct British Muslim cultural project. The term 'British Islam' was in limited use in the late 1980s but gained traction in the 1990s in the aftermath of the Rushdie Affair. Creating this hyphenated identity was intended to anchor the Muslim praxis with the cultural context of Britain and would require Islamic teachings to be indigenised, embodied and communicated within the cultural environment that they were growing up in. Activists advocating this perspective believed that giving *dawah* to non-Muslims effectively would mean that the *daiyee* (caller) needed to be grounded in the cultural norms and idioms of British culture and Islamic teachings yet were flexible enough to accommodate cultural practices that did not conflict with the essential principles of the faith. These ideas were taken up and articulated most enthusiastically in the pages of YM's *Trends* magazine and with a slightly different twist in *Q-News*. Both in their different ways argued that Muslims had chosen Britain as their home and Islam could find a home in Britain; in essence arguing that it is possible to be both Muslim and British. The idea of a British Islam refers to an ongoing attempt to separate core Islamic values from problematic ethnic cultural practices. This was a central theme in YM's work, articulated through the pages of *Trends*, public lectures and study circles. For instance, Mahmud al-Rashid, the YM President from 1992–4, explained that 'by creating a British Islamic culture, we will be carrying on what our great forefathers achieved, who developed Islamic cultures wherever they went. It is our job to be innovative, creative, adventurous, bold and chivalrous.'[28]

More sophisticated discourses, which attempted to demonstrate that Islam was not foreign to Britain or Europe at all and that Muslims had interacted and integrated in the region hundreds of years ago, started to develop in the late 1990s. Underpinning this argument was the fact that many prominent British people such as 'Shaykh of the British Isles' Abdullah Quilliam, Lady Evelyn Cobbold, Lord Stanley of Alderley and the famous translator of the Qur'an, Marmaduke Pickthall, had converted to Islam in the late nineteenth and early twentieth centuries and all contributed to the creation of an early form of British Muslim culture.[29] This project was possibly given its most powerful articulation in the writings of Abdal-Hakim Murad and Tariq Ramadan, who in their different ways crafted a theological basis for an Islam that was not only in the West but of the West. This perspective posits Islam and the West as having a shared history and an inevitable future, containing a set of interlocking narratives that have coexisted and learned from one another and whose interests lie in continuing to do so. In addition, this frame suggests that Muslims who live in Britain and other Western nations should not only demand their rights as religious minorities, but should take a full part in their societies and discharge their duties and responsibilities by contributing to the betterment of society as productive British citizens.

This narrative also frames Islam as having the creative potential to adapt to different cultural contexts and cites the historical establishment of various Muslim communities in minority contexts as examples of the ability of the religion to coexist comfortably within a plural setting. Promoting this has literally become a project for Muslims sympathetic to reformist and TI networks, with some organisations allocating resources to promote the idea of a British Muslim identity. On the other hand, most people associated with Salafism and HT continue to resist such reinterpretations and assert that Islam is culturally transcendent and therefore culture-free. According to this understanding, there is only one Islam and every cultural accretion threatens its theological/ideological purity and hence must be rejected. With this logic there can be no British Islam/Muslims, only Islam/Muslim in Britain, as HT spokesman Farid Kassim once reasoned: 'There is no such thing as British Muslims. There are only Muslims.'[30] HT's position on this subject within its various publications remains the same today. They subscribe to the idea that any allegiance to national citizenship identity threatens their quest for the Khilafah superstate and is a capitulation to the 'kafir society' in which they live. For them, the idea of Britishness cannot be delinked from its cultural or political manifestations and argue that to do so would condone types of behaviour forbidden in Islamic teachings, such as the right to consume alcohol or drugs, premarital sex and laws that are incompatible with the religion. HT, like most Salafis, is unable to admit the formation of an encultured identity, because they understand it as something that undermines Islamic theology and law. Neither do they have time for contemporary reformist Islamic thinkers who advocate a *wasatiyyah* position, which is based on a middle-ground ideal that argues Islam is a religion of balance. Members of HT interpret *wasatiyyah* as a compromise, or a capitulation to Western capitalism that is a covert attempt to secularise the religion:

> The middle position or compromise solution is an idea that is alien to Islam. The Western nations and those Muslims loyal to them have attached this idea to Islam to sell it to the Muslims in the name of moderation and tolerance, intending to deviate the sincere Muslims from the clearly defined rules and limits of Islam.[31]

Using this reasoning, they reject the idea of showing any kind of loyalty to Britain. HT is not alone in advocating a model of citizenship that does not recognise the possibility that Islamic teachings can accommodate cultural adaptation. Many Salafis are also uncomfortable describing themselves as British Muslims and will argue against the notion of a British Muslim culture by relying on fatwas developed by Middle

Eastern Salafi scholars who argue that Islam is culture free and that hyphenated identities are a *bid'a*.

The construction of these frames is contingent upon context and Islamic activist discourses cannot be understood simply by the slogans that they brandish. The construction of each trend needs to be understood in relation to the ideas of their foundational figures and how these ideas were localised and negotiated in changing circumstances. Each conceptulisation, narrative, critique and response has to be contextualised within the time it was produced and in relation to competing narratives that made similar or counter claims. The framing of issues by different trends sometimes agree – especially on issues around moral decline, the need for reform and outreach to young Muslims and non-Muslims. This is due to their shared theological heritage and from a general consensus that Muslim communities in Britain have largely lapsed in the practice of Islam. In this view, they are vulnerable to losing their faith identities in the midst of secular Western lifestyles and only a full recommitment to Islamic teachings in both private and public will bring about the renewal of a lost Muslim civilisational greatness at micro and macro levels.

These narrative frames in essence combine identity maintenance, moral hazard and religious revival arguments at the centre of their discourses. They also display deep differences in the details of the causes of Muslim civilisational decline, the extent of the problem, priorities and how these challenges should be addressed. Whilst the trends may agree with most of the main discourse frames, they clearly interpret them differently and have unique ways of presenting their particular vision. These differences of opinion on the relationship between faith, citizenship and loyalty illustrate the deep differences of opinion that continue to fracture British Muslim communities. These divergences lead to Muslims belittling other Muslims and to branding fellow believers as deviants, sinners or even non-Muslims. These frames and accompanying discourses cannot exist without the mediation of culture, theology and politics. The various currents all invest in a set of self-legitimising arguments that claim to diagnose the causes of problems facing British Muslim communities, but are mediated through the registers of sectarian or ideological orientation. A closer examination of their discourses reveal that these Islamic tendencies share far more in common then they would admit; this is unsurprising given the shared textual sources, histories, religious references and experiences of living in Britain as minority faith communities. For instance, scholastic traditionalists from South Asia like the Deobandis and Barelwis, though bitter enemies, actually share a common adherence to the Hanafi school of law, revere many of the same historical figures, such as Shah Wali Allah, and even subscribe to the same Sufi masters. These tendencies also have internal factions that contain hard liners and pragmatists in a state of dynamic tension. While they would all agree on the need to be pious Muslims, that Islam is the best way of life and the importance of cohesive global *ummah*, they would differ on what the priorities of Muslims living in Britain should be, how best to bring about internal reform, the degree of integration possible within a majority non-Muslim society and the possibility of a British Islam. These various iterations function as comprehensive, emotionally satisfying interpretations of Islam that resonate with their values, life experiences and preferences.

People join the different Islamic trends in relation to their own personal, intellectual, emotional and psychological positions at various points of their lives. They choose to join or associate with groups that align with their own world view and benefit from social networks that they feel most comfortable with. Many British Muslim activists remain loyal to the first Islamic trend that they encountered, even if they are no longer active in them, and will often retain an emotional or intellectual attachment to them. All of the differing trends have been successful in attracting young people to their cause at different points in their individual histories, for the various reasons explained here. A factor perhaps meriting further study is the role and degree to which individual psychological dispositions and personal histories play in the choice to join a particular trend. Prominent Muslim psychologist Professor Malik Badri suggests that Islamic trends all carry elements which appeal to either the intellectual, emotional, behavioural or spiritual dimensions of an individual life experience. He argues different individual trends offer only one or two of these characteristics and hence tend to attract people who are already inclined to a certain outlook.[32] As one female ex-member of HT reflected:

> I think that it is possible, for example, most people who would join HT may be extrovert, confident and appear to possess a positive self-image – that has been my experience. On the other

hand, people who work with YM or ISB appear to be calmer characters, who wish to integrate into the society and are more laid back.[33]

For some, the messages framed by YM opened their awareness to international issues and political Islam, other people were attracted to HT's theo-political framing of issues and its confrontational approach. YM struggled to compete with HT on university campuses and suffered from a weakness in trying to defend their message, which left HT and JIMAS to battle each other. As a result, HT often gained the advantage in this rivalry; as one observer wryly noted:

[HT] were offering something that JIMAS wasn't, they had literature, politics and a theology that was testosterone driven. Their talk of revolution and sense of violence tapped into a type of psychology that proved exciting to youth, but couldn't keep people as the adrenaline rush couldn't be sustained. Those that stayed on invested so much that they couldn't afford to lose. While YM/ISB were a bunch of middle-class people that did study circles among themselves in the leafy suburbs.[34]

Despite all their differences, they shared the idea of inviting people to Islam. What was more contentious was whether this was an individual or collective religious obligation. Most argued it was a religious obligation and attempted to provide textual evidences to show how all Muslims must be involved in organised activism and preferably only with their particular group. This premise placed pressure on newcomers to both join and stay within these movements and leaving was said to be sinful. This mindset was particularly overt in HT and YM and former members confirmed the use of emotional blackmail for expressing doubts or thoughts of departing from the group. The next chapter discusses the impact of socio-political change upon the religious discourse of these trends and their modes of operation.

CHAPTER 6

FRAGMENTATION AND ADAPTATION: THE IMPACT OF SOCIAL CHANGE

We bring together the youth, men and women from all social and
ethnic backgrounds, and different schools of thought, for the
benefit of all. As such, our membership largely reflects the
diversity of the British Muslim landscape. We welcome all
Muslims and non-Muslims.[1]

Young Muslims UK

Throughout this book I have reiterated how the 1990s were the critical
period in both the formation and transformation of religious trends
among second-generation British Muslim communities. Multiple
anxieties about maintaining religious identity, solidarities with
transnational politics, competing claims over religious authenticity,
scholarly authority and group priorities have all converged to define
these trends and what it means to be a Muslim in Britain. The impact
of generational change, the repercussions of international and domestic
crisis events, internal organisational disagreements and the introduction of new technologies have forced change within communities and
has led to the evolution of the complex varieties of Islamic activism
observable today. In order to give a sense of periodisation, I suggest
that they have passed through six stages which can described as *Arrival*,
Inception, *Establishment*, *Fragmentation*, *Renewal* and *Contemporary*:

Arrival: Correlates with the migration and establishment of the settler generation between the 1960s and 1970s. In this period, a host of reformist Islamist organisations, such as the UK Islamic Mission, Federation of Students Islamic Societies, Muslim Student Societies, Muslim Educational Trust, Islamic Foundation and Dawatul Islam, laid their roots and tried to cater for new immigrants. It was the period that saw the emergence of FOSIS as a national student organisation, whose membership contained people who went on to become prominent British Muslims such as Ziauddin Sardar, Azzam Tamimi and Fuad Nahdi. It was also the period in which UKIM developed the Muslim Youth Movement and the creation of the Bengali Islamist, Young Muslim Organisation.

Inception: Refers to the 1980s, where three of the main trends launched their organisations: Young Muslims UK, JIMAS in 1984 and the British branch of HT in 1986. This was made possible by the coming of age of young Muslims born in the 1970s. This key transitional second-generation were beginning to search for their place in society and those inclined to religious reform joined the groups and experimented with the first Britsh forms of Islamic activism that proliferated in the next decade.

Establishment: Describes the early 1990s when YM, HT and JIMAS all acquired a national following and became visible outside of activist circles. All of them had representation in most cities and towns with Muslim communities and were able to attract young people and adults into their activities until their membership peaked around 1995. During this time HT, YM and JIMAS were very active on most university campuses; HT and YM also formed branches and created public profiles. Similarly, JIMAS had a strong presence within communities in London, Birmingham and Ipswich and competed with YM and HT in universities. However, this decade was also the inception stage for the TI network.

Fragmentation: Covers the period from 1995–2001, when YM, JIMAS and HT all suffered internal organisational problems due to conflicts within the leadership. Senior members of all three groups resigned or left to create successor organisations, as in the case of JIMAS and HT. This left the organisations in a state of confusion, uncertainty and crisis. For YM the departure of two of its national presidents left the organisation in limbo and caused many people to question its ideas and direction, while some defected to other trends such as the TI network.

Renewal: Overlaps with the end of the 1990s and the beginning of the 2000s in which YM and HT spent time trying to salvage their organisations and re-launch their work. HT began to reassess its position in the UK, but the process was complicated by the competing claims of a second HT organisation. YM struggled to reassert itself, as former members were either moving to MAB, the TI network or withdrawing from activism. JIMAS had to compete with various competing Salafi trends as well as the spread of ultra-radical Jihadis that were hovering around Abu Hamza and Abdullah el-Faisal. The other themes that distinguish this period are the self-critical reformulations of tradition, the appearance of post-Islamism, neo-Sufism, new types of Salafism, growth of cosmopolitan British Muslim cultural expressions and eclectic Islamic activism.

Contemporary: This stage began in the early 2000s and was deeply affected by the terrorist attacks of 9/11 in 2001, 7/7 in 2005 and subsequent changes in the political climate in the UK and Europe. This marked a point in which the British activist scene saw a significant displacement of the three ideological trends (YM, HT and JIMAS) and witnessed the increasing popularity and the establishment stage of the TI network. It also signalled the appearance of new forms of activism that grew from either the work of former members of the ideological groups, people who had decided to become activists during this period and a third generation of activists that had grown up and become involved in Islamic work in the post-9/11 era. It is also a period of very public contestation for the representation of Islam in Britain between the various Islamic organisations and self-styled 'moderate Muslims' who argued that their voices had been ignored or marginalised by the dominant Islamic trends and umbrella organisations such as the MCB. This intra-Muslim competition for government approval and funding saw the emergence of 'reformed radicals' and new liberal Muslim voices seeking attention in the public sphere. This most recent stage is also characterised by a new social milieu that presents Islamic activism as fashionable, exciting and much less of a minority interest than it was in the preceding three decades. There is a tangible sense of a British Muslim cultural scene manifested in forms of pious art, music, fashion, humour and the widespread availability of Islamic products, services and new media technologies.

Each of these periods corresponded with the demographic growth, maturation and indigenisation of Islam in Britain. The movements most influential in the mid-1990s transformed dramatically towards the end of that decade by a complex combination of changing intra-community dynamics and shifting external socio-political realities. The membership of each of the main groups – YM, JIMAS and HT – experienced protracted internal disputes around the same time, resulting in successive leadership resignations in YM and HT and breakaway groups from JIMAS. Two presidents of YM resigned after becoming disillusioned and some were won over to the emerging TI network, the former leader of HT went on to form the more extreme Al-Muhajiroun organisation, while in JIMAS a number of influential members broke away to form other organisations and precipitated divisions that still remain. This period was marked by diversification and movement of people between the trends – a pattern indicative of the activist eclecticism beginning to arise towards the end of the 1990s and 2000s.

Discussing the dynamics of social change in Muslim societies, Olivier Roy has suggested that they have transformed over the last 20 years as a result of three paradigm shifts – the religious, social and political.[2] He argues that this has resulted in three developments: a *new global generation*, a *shift in political culture* and a *new religiosity*. There has been a huge demographic increase in the youth population across the Muslim-majority states, particularly in the Middle East, North and sub-Saharan Africa.[3] Within this new global generation various trends are shaping these societies in very significant ways, such as: more women entering higher education and employment, young people marrying later, couples having fewer children and nuclear families replacing extended households. This has been accompanied by greater access to mobile phones, satellite TV and the internet, which has changed young peoples' attitudes towards their religion, culture and societies.[4] This new generation is causing a shift in the political culture by young people being less attracted to totalising ideologies, whether they be nationalist or Islamist. They are more challenging of authority and interested in democratic systems of governance, a fact dramatically illustrated in the demonstrations in the Arab uprisings of early 2011. Many in this generation also display a new religiosity that grew out of the re-Islamisation phenomena over the last 30 years – visible in increased mosque attendance, more women wearing the *hijab* and a greater demand in Islamic goods and services – but at the same time they are seeking greater individualisation and diversification of the religious field. One of the clearest examples has been that traditional religious authorities have lost a great deal of their legitimacy to the self-taught religious entrepreneurs found on satellite TV and the internet. Informed people, aware of the various options available, exercise their personal choice and enact an avant-garde approach to religious practices.

The religious currents profiled in this book have also felt the repercussions of these global developments. Internal centripetal and external centrifugal forces have imposed changes upon these trends, pressuring them to make a number of adaptive changes to their objectives, organisational structures, personnel and modes of operation. I suggest that there are five internal and external factors that have had the greatest effect in transforming British Muslim communities and by extension the environment in which activist trends operate. The internal are: *demographic, the new elite* and *youth acculturation* and the external are: *the impact of 9/11 and 7/7* and *new communication technologies*.

Demographic Factors

The most obvious change in British Muslim communities is in their composition. They have grown in both number and internal diversity, officially reaching 2.7 million according to the 2011 census, an increase of more than one million over the preceding decade. Muslim communities have grown relatively faster than other minority faith groups in places such as Birmingham, Bradford, Manchester and parts of London.[5] This represents one of the most important changes as it points to a growing youth population with its accompanying challenges and opportunities that range from issues of identity, gender relationships and educational opportunties to concerns about discrimination, Islamophobia and criminality.[6] Though predominately of South Asian heritage, in the last 15 years Muslim communities in Britain have diversified through an influx of economic migrants, refugees and political asylum seekers from various nations originating in South Asia, the Middle East and Africa. New Muslim arrivals have visibly reconfigured the visual and spatial arrangement of established Muslim communities in large cities like Manchester, Birmingham and London, bringing with them different ideas about religious practice and culture. This gradual transformation has sometimes created tensions between the newer and the older settled Muslim communities, as well as non-Muslims concerned about the latest cycle of immigration. The creation of new mosques and Islamic centres figure prominently in the new urban landscape with institutions such as the East London Mosque becoming significant landmarks and sites of religious mobilisation. Converts to Islam have also enriched Muslim communities in Britain by perhaps up to 100,000 and growing each year, with women and people of African-Carribean heritage seeming to be changing their faith in the greatest numbers.[7] Some are well known, such as ex-MTV presenter Kristiane Backer and Lauren Booth, the sister-in law of ex-Prime Minister Tony Blair, and the journalist-converts Yvonne Ridley and Myriam Francois are both known for their activism inside and outside Muslim communities.

The New Elite

Describing changing patterns of political representation, social anthropologist Sean McLoughin has suggested the emergence of what he calls a 'New Muslim Leadership' that has 'human, social and cultural capital gained through education, business and professional experience'.[8] This has been the inevitable outcome of the university-educated second- and third-generation professional elites that are making their mark in Muslim communities. This new elite is increasingly national and not local, with increasing numbers of councillors, Members of Parliament and holders of senior position in national organisations such as the MCB. This represents a strand of Muslim political activism where the objectives are in a sense secular and about securing rights. I would add a complementary category, the 'New Islamic Elite', which is another middle-class generation of individuals who are less ideologically committed than formal members of the four trends and who have developed new modes of Islamic activism. The New Islamic Elite is composed of former second-generation activists that have grown older and have come to terms with the complex realities of adult life, as well as younger third-generation activists. This maturing of the second generation had the effect of making them question their previous ideological interpretations of Islam, other Muslims groups and their relations with wider non-Muslim society. The New Islamic Elite are making spaces for themselves in civic and public life and are engaging Muslim scholars and thinkers to help them fashion an indigenised Islamic culture that has social relevance. Furthermore, the new third generation of British Islamic activists do not necessarily share the convictions and approach of their predecessors. The entrance and participation of these activists into secular, civil society organisations has changed the ethos of their Islamic organisations and tempered their previous youthful idealism. This has been most notable in the work of YM/ISB and JIMAS and they appear more prepared to build bridges across sectarian/ideological divisions and engage seriously with Islamic scholarship to create new types of religious authority.

Youth Acculturation

A generation has grown up in the late 1990s and 2000s that has become disconnected both from their communities as well as wider society by living through a political climate still tense from anti-terrorist legislation, aggressive policing tactics and increased Islamophobia. These young people live in increasingly deprived areas and poorer housing, under-perform educationally compared to their peers and suffer higher rates of unemployment.[9] This has taken its toll in various ways; perhaps the most disturbing is the disproportionately high number of young Muslim men within the criminal justice system, which currently stands at around 13 per cent of the total prison population.[10] Major lifestyle changes can be seen in the ways in which young Muslims spend their free time and the aspirations that they hold. Most have imbibed much if not all of the behaviours of their non-Muslim peers in the realms of cultural tastes, clothing, music, sport, career ambitions and relationships with the opposite sex and are no less likely to participate in anti-social behaviour, crime and risk-associated activities. They also tend to have a greater political consciousness because of discrimination they may have suffered due to their Muslimness and are more likely to identify with Muslim causes abroad. All of these changes form a very different cultural milieu for third-generation activists who have joined the Islamic scene in the early and mid-2000s, taking for granted the challenges faced by the people who established the trends in the 1980s and 1990s and with different expectations for the future.

The Impact of 9/11 and 7/7

The New York and London terrorist attacks had major repercussions upon social attitudes towards British Muslims and prompted controversial government legislation and social policies, such as the anti-terrorism strategy known as 'Prevent'.[11] These events focused unprecedented public attention upon Muslim communities, by forcing them to deal with those who questioned their loyalty, and made them participate in public debates around the value of multiculturalism. Voices from across the media and political spectrum began to very publicly question the presence of Muslims and their integration into British society. The increasingly hostile climate put Islamic activists under the spotlight through right-wing think-tank policy publications and television exposés of 'extreme' Salafi and Islamist speakers and groups. Government attempts to define a 'Moderate Islam' in addition to the legal implications of new counter-terrorism legislation created a very public struggle for representation among British Muslim organisations.[12]

The post-9/11 and 7/7 era also corresponds to the shift in public rhetoric among the dominant Islamic trends which rushed to proclaim their 'Moderate Muslim' credentials. For some it was a result of genuine introspection, a desire for acceptance and engagement with wider society, while for others it was merely tactical. Islamist-rooted organisations toned down their rhetoric and adapted their positions to become less ideological. In Britain, nearly all of the Islamist organisations affiliated with the MCB supported its aim of seeking the 'common good' rather than the communal good. This in practice meant working around religious differences with other Muslim groups and seeing non-Muslim organisations as partners and not objects of *dawah*.[13] This has resulted in what some scholars have called a 'multicultural convergence', which seeks 'the same point of agreement (with others) but from its own point of origin and by its own route'.[14]

This centre ground is characterised by agreement upon the need for increasing mutual understanding through dialogue, partnership, trust and the promotion of pluralism and opposition to separatism. As Sean McLoughlin noted, the leadership within organisations such as the MCB are populated by 'professionals who have middle class investments to create an Islam rooted in the UK that is in the process of creating a normative, some would say elite, Islamic cosmopolitanism that seem(s) to

reinscribe certain oppositions and power relations in Muslim communities.' This rapprochement around liberal values was also motivated by
a necessity to 'accommodate to prevailing political conditions and
structures in pursuit of power'.[15]

However, while there appears to be a convergence at leadership
level among the dominant trends, at the grassroots deeply entrenched
theological and political divisions remain within British Muslim
communities. The historic stand-off between Barelwi and Deobandis
still exists, the majority of Salafis have no time for Sufis, and vice-versa,
and differences continue to exist below the surface even between Islamist
organisations such as the Dawatul Islam, IFE and the MAB. These
developments occurred in addition to other battles for representation
that were being played out between the MCB and people associated with
Q-News. This realignment of the activist landscape was complicated
further by the appearance of Muslims for Secular Democracy, the Sufi
Muslim Council (SMC), the British Muslim Forum (BMF) and the self-
styled 'ex-Islamists', Ed Husain and Maajid Nawaz of the Quilliam
Foundation.

This period of transition was significantly influenced by the Labour
government, who were looking for more compliant community
partners to deal with the issue of radicalisation. The MCB, which was
regarded as the main umberella body for British Muslims, had already
fallen out with the government due to its refusal to support the US-
UK led intervention in Iraq, and after the London Bombings came
under intense pressure to curb radicalisation within communities.
Relationships soured further as it was accused of being dominated at
leadership level by Islamists sympathetic to the Jamaat-e-Islam and
the Muslim Brotherhood. Instead, the Labour leadership looked to
the SMC, BMF and QF as interlocutors. This was seen by some as a
return to a colonial model of dividing and managing minorities
by exploiting oppositional relationships for those seeking state
partronage. The Radical Middle Way project was an example of the
precarious situation that Islamic activists tried to negotiate. It began
as a community-led initiative that received government funding to
promote mainstream Islamic teachings and challenge religious extremism
by hosting lectures and cultural events. Originally a partnership
between YMO, FOSIS and Q-News, it succeeded in engaging large
numbers of young people but was criticised for preaching to the

converted and had its independence questioned by those who said it was tainted by receiving state funding. Furthermore, the predominance of TI scholars at programmes eventually caused YMO and FOSIS to abandon its cooperation.

New Communication Technologies

British Islamic activists have always tried to use every available means to communicate their messages. With the arrival of new information communication technologies, space, geography and time were redefined, enabling activists to exploit opportunities previously unavailable as they made the transition from analogue to digital. In the 1980s and 1990s, didactic approaches to activism took the form of educational lectures, seminars, conferences and activity-based camps, and information was disseminated via leaflets, booklets, magazines, books, audio and video cassettes. In the post-9/11 era the trends devised new strategies, such as e-activism, social networking groups, structured educational courses, faith-sensitive services, multimedia tools, CDs, DVDs, MP3s and podcasts. Latterly the internet has become the most popular means of accessing religious information, and prerecorded or live programmes can now be broadcast from community radio stations or widely viewed on satellite stations and watched or listened to on their corresponding websites. The impact of sophisticated technological globalisation has shrunk distances and made physical borders irrelevant in the transfer of ideas and practices. A religious text published in Singapore can be automatically purchased in Scotland and a message posted on Facebook by a user in Morocco is instantly available for readers in Malaysia, enabling unprecedented opportunities for religious networking and a more globalised, disembedded identity.[16] These instant global flows of information and images have raised a sense of international Islamic solidarity previously unattainable and helped people to identify with a 'virtual ummah'. It has helped create new ways of thinking about being a Muslim in the modern world as well as creative, diasporic and indigenous forms of 'Living Islam'. Those exploring their faith became much more informed consumers that shop around in the global Islamic marketplace of ideas and selectively adopted figures of religious authority. As Peter Mandaville observed, 'the age-old interaction of the individual going to their local imam, of the individual going to their

Sheikh [...] and having nuanced almost very specifically constructed answers for a given situation, for a given circumstance, for a given complexity' has passed.[17]

Fierce public scrutiny of Muslim groups and the increasing political literacy of activists also caused most groups to minimise or drop previous triumphalist and exclusivist themes popular in the 1980s and 1990s. At the same time, other younger Muslims and converts who were either dissatisfied with the ideological groups or were independent of them began to experiment with developing other forms of expressing their religious identity, especially in the area of culture. This period witnessed a flowering of indigenised forms of Islam, illustrated by the proliferation of 'Islamic pop music', Muslim rap artists, fashion, Muslim humour and even the 'Islamic Novel'. These social changes cumulatively affected the social ecology that Islamic trends functioned in. During the course of these changes a number of people within the trends questioned their self-understanding of Islamic activism and how their work had remained largely irrelevant to the needs of most young Muslims. These developments highlighted emergent forms of religiosity that attempted to reconcile and integrate minority faith communities into secular post-modern societies and are discussed further in the next chapter.

No Longer Younger Muslims

As already indicated, people within the leadership of YM were developing deep differences over issues of ideology and direction. The crisis in 1995–6 took around five years to resolve and in the process YM lost its position as a leader in the activist scene. A relatively recent website mission statement provides a starting point for understanding how the group evolved its self-identity. A striking feature is how the language and reference points dramatically changed. In the 'about us' section of its home page in 2012, it described its history and purpose in the following way:

> YM UK was set up in 1984 to provide a vehicle for committed young British Muslims to combine their knowledge, skills and efforts for the benefit of one another and British society as a whole. We bring together the youth, men and women from all social and

ethnic backgrounds, and different schools of thought, for the benefit of all. As such, our membership largely reflects the diversity of the British Muslim landscape. We welcome all Muslims and non-Muslims, helping them understand Islam and live by its teachings and principles. We strongly believe that working for Islam is not just about campaigning for Muslim rights, but also about sharing Islam's view on God, life and society. We do so as an organised and dedicated group, engaging in sincere and constructive dialogue.[18]

This contrasts heavily with its 1993 manifesto booklet *Striving for Revival*, which stated its mission as:

The Young Muslims UK, (like its parent movement, The Islamic Society of Britain) is a limb of the global Islamic Movement, sharing its understanding with all the major world-wide movements. Our situation here in Britain reflects the domination of ignorance and the absence of Islam [...] Unfortunately for the people of this country, batil (falsehood) reigns. And one of its manifestations is the prevalence of *shirk* (associating partners with Allah) – the greatest injustice of all. It is our responsibility that Islam should be introduced to the people of this country not as 'the religion of the Saracens' nor as 'the next threat to the West' but rather as the cure to its many diseases.[19]

This hard line prescription is taken from another era in YM's history. Written in the early 1990s, the vocabulary and mood reflects both the influence of Islamist rhetoric and a need to compete conceptually with HT and JIMAS. Its most recent website claimed that 'YM UK is a leading force in encouraging positive contributions to British society through the development of a British Islam.' Compared to the rhetoric of the early years, it illustrates the tension that was always present in the goals of YM. The idea of belonging to an 'international Islamic Movement' is difficult to reconcile with its desire to create a 'British Islamic Culture'. The inconsistent visions between past and present aims either reflect the organisation's maturation or a surrender to the realities of twenty-first century Britain. The organisation, in contradistinction to its peers in YMO, HT and MAB, went through a corrective adjustment into non-ideological entity keen to promote its pro-integrationist credentials. According to former YM president Ahtesham Ali, the organisation changed in the late 1990s and early 2000s as a result of the 'rise in individualism and self-interest and the availability of a wider choice of alternatives and concerns over the rise of radicalisation made people reluctant to commit to a movement in the same way people did in the 1990s.'[20] These sentiments were echoed by former ISB executive member Robina Ahmed, who argues that 'a generational culture change occurred when new members took certain things for granted and did not have to fight for the issues the earlier ones did, and they are more Westernised'.[21]

I would argue that among Islamist groups YM has journeyed the greatest distance from its reformist roots and original mission to convert Britain to Islam. People associated with YM/ISB have adapted consciously or unconsciously to post-Islamist positions. The term post-Islamism was originally coined by sociologist Asef Bayat and developed in his book *Making Islam Democratic: Social Movements and the Post-Islamist Turn* to describe the pragmatic orientations of the Iranian leadership and other alternative Islamic socio-political projects emerging in Egypt in the mid-1990s.[22] These new movements have attempted to fuse religiosity with modern ideas of freedom, plurality and liberty and are unsurprising given similar patterns occurring within former avowedly Islamist organisations coming to terms with and making the most of their minority status in Europe. As other observers have noted, dogmatic Islamism became abandoned for pragmatic considerations, influenced equally by the experience of coming to terms with secular, liberal British culture as well as the maturation enabled by exposure to serious Islamic scholarship and various contempory Muslim and non-Muslim intellectul trends. This has been the most pronounced among individuals who were obliged to engage with journalists, academics and policy makers. The following reflections of three former members of YM after the Arab Uprisings of 2011 are illustrative. Sarah Joseph, one of YM's brightest stars in the 1990s and a former editor of *Trends*, in an *emel* magazine editorial about the repercussions of the protests, declared that:

> I am no longer a Utopian. I once believed that we could create an
> ideal community or society, where justice reigned and people

committed themselves to its maintenance because it was worth the sacrifice. However, life has shown me that this is unlikely, and idealized communities are probably not possible on this earth. Not even the Prophet's community was filled with faultless individuals, all living in perfect harmony and peace.[23]

Dilwar Hussain, a research and policy consultant who was previously an executive member of YM, president of ISB and well known in English-speaking Islamist circles also wrote in that issue of *emel*:

> While some are hailing this [the Arab Spring] as a success of 'Islamism,' I would like to suggest – perhaps counter-intuitively – that it is actually an indication of the demise of Islamism; at least old-style, traditional Islamism of the type that sought to create an 'Islamic state,' an Islamic version of a Hobbesian Leviathan to govern society.[24]

Later he writes that:

> For decades now, some activists have looked to the Islamist movements for inspiration. But with recent developments post-Arab Spring, the evolution of the AKP in Turkey, and the natural process of settlement, some are arguing that the stratification developing within Islamist Movements is just as important as the split between Islamists and non-Islamist Muslim activists. If the old slogans of 'Islam is the solution' are being replaced with notions of 'freedom and justice' [...] what does that mean for Islamist-influenced Movements and their agendas in the West?[25]

Similarly Inayat Bunglawala, also most active in YM during the 1990s, a loyal spokesman for the Muslim Council of Britain and someone who has embraced more liberal Muslim perspectives over the last decade, wrote in his blog in January 2012:

> When I was younger I was taught by many senior Muslim leaders in the UK and elsewhere that secularism was akin to atheism and that only a truly Islamic state which enforced the Shariah would

provide the real answer to humanity's problems. Looking back,
I just shake my head and can't believe I actually swallowed
that argument for so long. It is just so embarrassing.[26]

These examples from some of the more well-known former members
of YM demonstrate the 'growing up and out', process described
earlier. With age they grew out of their youthful enthusiasm for
religious identity politics but retained a personal commitment to their
faith and now contribute to the debates about Islam in Britain in more
sophisticated ways.

Still Waiting for the Khilafah

From 1996–2001, HT in Britain struggled to reorganise after Omar
Bakri's departure and a markedly low public profile concealed the
strategic reappraisal that was quietly taking place. In the days after
9/11, the HT central leadership issued a communiqué to the British
national executive to adopt a strategy to 'rhetorically streamline
localised international incidents, specifically the Middle East peace
process, the Balkans conflict and continued US presence in the Gulf,
into a narrative of the West's "oppression" of Muslims and a "War on
Islam"'.[27] HT attempted to rebrand itself as a moderate Islamist
movement and made efforts to tone down its anti-Western rhetoric and
distance itself from allegations associating the organisation with
violent extremism. The movement was forced to adapt further due to a
change in their position within Muslim communities, which diminished
as most activists learned how to counter their argumentation strategies.
HT was further marginalised by the increased profile and mobilising
capacity of the MAB.

While HT had in the past been able to organise demonstrations to
protest various Western interventionist policies in the Muslim world, in
the early 2000s they were displaced by the alliance-building strategies of
MAB and its work with large numbers of Muslim and non-Muslim
organisations. Notably, its association with the Stop the War Coalition and
various civil society organisations helped to mobilise millions of people
during the anti-war marches of 2003. HT's reputation for provocation also
worked against them when the National Union of Students (NUS) passed a
'No Platform' motion in 2004 against their activities on university

campuses. During this period HT struggled to get its message across within communities, which by then had realised HT was merely a talking shop. The irrelevance of their agenda was highlighted by their argument that all mainstream political processes, including calling on the United Nations to oppose military action in Iraq, was *haram* (religiously unlawful) and by their unfortunate campaign slogan; 'DON'T STOP THE WAR – except through Islamic politics.'

A Conveyor belt to Terrorism?

During the early 2000s, HT raised an alarm within the US administration for its activities in the ex-Soviet republics in Central Asia, in particular for its alleged attempts to destabilise the government of Uzbekistan. This prompted some analysts to claim that it was a 'conveyor belt for terrorism', a catchphrase picked up by commentators seeking to exaggerate the role of the movement in Islamic radicalism in Britain. A number of neoconservative think-tanks, analysts and politicians overstated HT's potential threat by reproducing alarmist judgments that relied on speculation and guilt by association. The movement was accused of being an intellectual precursor for more violent subversive groups because of its fierce anti-Western rhetoric and support for Muslim liberation groups in occupied territories such as Palestine, Kashmir and Iraq. This assessment appears at face value to locate it in the violent company of al-Qaeda, however in reality they differ from each other considerably. HT's historical record demonstrates its non-violence, as well as its inability to gain popular support among the Muslim masses in any way comparable to similar movements. The unease about the group in certain Western circles is motivated more by a general fear of the rise in popularity of Islamist opposition groups in certain regions of the world and how they could endanger geo-strategic relationships with Muslim countries with large energy reserves.

Following the 7/7 bombings in London, HT was once again thrust into the media spotlight for alleged links with violent extremism, though given its aggressive rhetoric and radical profile the scrutiny was expected. The accusation that HT has links to terrorism surfaces periodically, especially after individuals arrested for terrorist offences are alleged to have attended HT events. The evidence for these charges is tenous at best. The issue of British Muslims and terrorism has multiple causes that include social dislocation, racism, anti-Muslim discrimination and ideology, but often has its roots in anger at Western foreign policy. Various think-tank assessments, academic research institutions, security specialists and even the British government's own intelligence agencies have agreed upon the link between US- and UK-led military interventions in Muslim countries and the increase in terrorist attacks.[28] Many British Muslims feel targeted after increased police and search tactics, high profile dawn raids, detentions and a feeling that the anti-war movement had failed. In fact, up until 7/7 it was the motley crew of London-based preachers, Abu Hamza, Abdullah el-Faisal and Abu Qatada, who totally eclipsed HT radical credentials and facilitated the circulation of jihadist ideas among young British Muslims.

Mustafa Kamel Mustafa, or Abu Hamza as he was popularly known, was an Egyptian who claimed to have fought in Afghanistan during the Russian occupation in the 1980s and during the civil war in Bosnia in the 1990s. Settling in the UK, he eventually became Imam of Finsbury Park Mosque before being removed in 2003 by the police and British Charity Commission. Prior to this, he gained a profile for fronting his Supporters of Shariah (SOS) organisation, which at one point was part of a jihadi transnational network linked to the Algerian GIA movement. He is also believed to have mentored 9/11 suspect Zacarias Moussaoui and the attempted shoe-bomber Richard Reid. He was arrested in 2004 under the Terrorism Act for various charges of encouraging murder, incitement to racial hatred and active recruitment for militant groups in places such as Yemen. After serving a sentence in the UK, the US government extradited him at the end of 2012. While HT advocated a non-violent approach to establishing a caliphate, Abu Hamza was more concerned with radicalising Muslim conciousness and fighting the 'forces of kufr' than establishing the institution of *khilafah*. This prioritisation brought him closer to the tactics of Omar Bakri's Al-Muhajiroun movement rather than HT's goal. Even though they had their differences, the two men shared platforms at rallies and press conferences to support each other's work. This tactical partnership was of mutual benefit and helped Bakri to bolster his transnational activist credentials, while at the same time gave Abu Hamza opportunities to promote his agenda.

Similarly, Jamaican convert Abdullah el-Faisal was a prolific radical speaker who acquired a reputation for outrageous rhetoric. After being removed from Brixton Mosque in the early 1990s, he gained a following across the UK for trying to persuade young people that Muslims should use the 'bullet, not the ballot'. This eventually led to his imprisonment in 2003 – for soliciting murder, inciting racial and religious hatred – and later deportation to Jamaica in 2007. HT distanced itself from these individuals and groups, categorically denying any connection between their work and the activities of Al-Muhajiroun and other Jihadists. However, what is not clear, is how many disillusioned individual HT members went on to join Al-Muhajiroun or its successor groups. Even when this happened – and it would have been in spite of HT ideology and not because of it – HT was perceived by most people as 'all talk and no action'. One ex-member, when discussing if HT had contributed to the process of radicalisation, commented:

> only to a certain degree, but only in the arena of the war of ideas. I don't think they contributed to people becoming radicalised enough to carry out 'terrorist' attacks. Even though HT has a revolutionary streak, I don't believe the idea of violent take over (even though it was deemed a part of the method to restore the Caliphate) was ever touted in enough detail to make people think about direct use of violence to achieve political aims.[29]

HT is not a proto-terrorist movement, nor a radicalised force brainwashing thousands of Muslim youth, as some in media and policy circles have suggested. Sensing the serious possibility of HT being proscribed post-7/7, Abdul-Wahid, media spokesman at the time, tried to explain why Hizb ut-Tahrir removed incriminating material from the party's website:

> It would be ridiculous to assume that rhetoric relevant to a population that sees itself under occupation is symptomatic of the viewpoint of Muslims generally, and Hizb-ut-Tahrir specifically, on all issues relating (say) to Jews and Americans. Yet that is all too often what we see in these so-called challenges to our political ideas. In fact, the decision to remove some of our overseas literature from our British website was a considered response to the legitimate proposition that people who read it out of its context might see it as offensive.[30]

This dissimulation represented a more sophisticated defence of the party's ideas for non-Muslim public consumption that would have been unheard of during Bakri's era. This pragmatism by a new media-savvy leadership proved more effective in advancing their public relations efforts and masked the fact that pamphlets and websites for other countries still retained standard HT propaganda. In response to 7/7, it created new front organisations such as the 'Stop Islamophobia Campaign' to lobby support against any future ban. In a media pack aimed to counter popular criticisms against HT in the eyes of politicians, local authorities and civic institutions it stated:

> In the UK our work with the Muslim community is focused on directing Muslims to make a positive contribution to society whilst preserving their Islamic identity [...] In recent times we have held panel discussions with non-Muslim politicians, thinkers and personalities. These events have helped to overcome the intellectual entrenchment that characterises most of today's debate. Furthermore, we believe the Muslim community, with her Islamic values and culture, can contribute in solving many of the social problems affecting Western society – such as racism, alcohol abuse, substance misuse, family breakdown, sexual abuse and the decline in morality.[31]

Ironically, HT rhetoric ignores the fact that 'racism, alcohol abuse, substance misuse, family breakdown, sexual abuse and the decline in morality' also occurs within Muslim societies and also affects British Muslims. Other examples of HT's growing pragmatism was evidenced in the run-up to the May 2006 local elections, where instead of condemning Muslim participation in the election as *haram* – which was previously the standard policy position – HT asked Muslims to 'consider Muslim issues when voting'. It also began sharing a platform with non-Muslim agencies and politicians to convey its message. Following the London bombings, HT contacted MPs in a bid to shore up its non-violent credentials and build support against the threat of proscription. It managed to persuade well-known Labour MP Clare Short to organise a meeting in the House of Commons in 2006 and even wrote a 'thank you' letter to Conservative Party leader David Cameron for his criticism of the Israeli bombardment of Lebanon.[32] Since 7/7, HT has made significant changes in strategy by sharing the stage with other Islamic organisations to both distance itself from associations with violent radicalism and reach out to other Muslim constituencies. In February 2008 it participated in a public debate organised by the MB-associated Cordoba Foundation on whether political participation had failed British Muslims. Another development post-7/7 was the promotion of Dr Nasreen Nawaz as Women's Media Representative on mainstream TV and in radio interviews. These positions seem at odds with the uncompromising ideas and methods of its founder, but is not surprising given that HT, like other political movements, is interested in self-preservation.

The overriding appeal of HT in the 1990s was its total ideological packaging and inability of other Islamic trends to offer more compelling alternatives. Part of the attraction to HT were the attention-grabbing tactics developed by Omar Bakri. Other Islamic activists hated HT for turning up at their events, hijacking question and answer sessions and distributing their literature. To HT, the Young Muslims and JIMAS were viewed as being weak or compromising the militant message of Islam. Like other rigid social and religious groups, members were taught to think of themselves as part of a collective movement and not as individuals who think independently.

This partly explains its ideological consistency and disciplined public image. Though the core HT ideology and specific methodology has essentially remained unchanged in over 60 years, it has developed new strategies in Britain over the last 15 years. It represents an intellectual half-way house of sorts between moderate reformist Islamism and violent jihadism. Young people who completed their education and settled down into adult life usually left. A factor that influenced HT's approach in Britain was the ageing of those first generation of activists who were most prominent during the mid-1990s. The process of finishing their studies, gaining employment, getting married, buying a house and raising familes all brought new practical challenges for loyal members that were not addressed by HT's ideological architects.

The New Salafis

The repercussions of 9/11 and 7/7 were also major factors in the mutation of British Salafism, as media attention began to focus on the possible link between Salafism and terrorism. A connection between the two was also implied in a collection of articles published in *Q-News* after the 9/11 attacks by three leading figures of the TI network, particularly Abdal-Hakim Murad's provocative piece entitled *Recapturing Islam from the Terrorists*.[33] In November 2001 Usama Hasan, who was keen to prevent Salafis from being implicated in the attack, wrote a widely circulated response to Murad, *Recapturing Islam from the Pacifists*, in which he attempted to critique the suggestion that Wahhabi/Salafi teachings motivated the hijackers.[34] It was an emotionally charged piece that was even sceptical of Muslim involvement in 9/11 and made a number of attacks against Sufism. He has since regretted writing the article and apologised to Murad. This is significant, as it indicated a gradual mood change among leading Salafis during that period. The attacks in London on 7 July 2005 became Britain's 9/11, and proved to be another crucial milestone in the evolution of British Salafism. It is also worth noting that those associated with Salafi publications had for years opposed rebellion against Muslim governments and had reproduced a fatwa by Grand Mufti of Saudi Arabia, Sheikh Bin Baz, condemning the theology and tactics of Bin Laden and his followers. Most British Salafis are publicly apolitical and more interested in trying to recreate an idealised collective piety that 'posits a golden age in the past and a historical utopia that can be reproduced in contemporary Islam'.[35] However, other strands of Salafism started to become more self-critical.

The increased media and political scrutiny, as well as the force of new anti-terrorist legislation, brought home the potential danger of extremist exclusivist Salafi discourses and provided an impetus for intra-Muslim cooperation and consensus building. Many Islamic groups organised lectures to explain the difference between jihad and terrorism. At a City Circle event in mid-2005, Abu Muntasir broke down in tears and made a public apology for potentially contributing to violent Salafism. He, along with other JIMAS members, began sharing platforms with figures like Hamza Yusuf in an effort to undo the logic of polarisation accumulated after years of hard line Salafi rhetoric. According to Usama Hassan, in the past the 'separatist ideas of JIMAS stemmed from their dependence on Ibn Taymiyyah which produced an "us" and "them" mentality'.[36] Whatever the cause, Abu Muntasir made extra efforts to reach out to other Muslims across the sectarian divide.

Today JIMAS has transformed from being the incubator of British Salafism to a friendly, voluntary organisation with charitable status. On its current website, the 'about JIMAS' section states:

> JIMAS is a Muslim educational charity which works to create greater understanding about Islam amongst Muslims and People for other faith and no faith backgrounds. JIMAS works to do this through Education, Engagement and Service.

> Our vision is to establish a pride of place for Muslims in the UK where our strengths are reared and recognised in all that is good; to unlock our potential and help create a society where every citizen functions with dignity; where communities work together, have mutual understanding and thrive, through fostering respect and understanding.[37]

This is a far cry from the language and priorities of JIMAS in the 1980s and 1990s. Today the former *Amir*, Abu Muntasir, is now Chief Executive of JIMAS and has built many bridges with non-Muslim organisations, and is keen to demonstrate his Britishness and commitment to civic duty. His current *dawah* lectures are now peppered with references to Western philosophy, British history and the importance of interfaith work. JIMAS now seems to be reluctant to use the word 'Salafi' at all, as Usama Hassan believes the purists have hijacked the term. Other observers remain to be convinced that there has been a true conceptual departure from the organisation's intellectual reference points, as evidenced by the presence of hard line Salafi tracts that were until recently available on its website.[38]

In contrast, the purists at the Salafi Institute have remained loyal to Salafi symbols and vocabulary in their work. Their institute is housed in a multipurpose complex in Birmingham, which also houses a primary school, counselling services, a translation centre, publishing house, a bookstore and a mosque. In recent years it claims to have printed and distributed more than a million free leaflets detailing its anti-terrorism stance in the years between 9/11 and 7/7. These leaflets are often colourful, printed on high-quality paper and have eye-catching titles, such as *The Corruption of Terrorism & Suicide Bombings: Exposing the Perpetrators of evil*; *Think for Yourself (Do you Really Believe Evolution is true???)*; and *Who are the Salafis*. Its websites dominate search engine entries for the word 'Salafi', which will link to 20 mirror sites such as salafimanhaj.com, salaf.com, salafipublications.com and islam4kids.com.

However, this particular form of Salafism has not gone unchallenged by other Salafis. Abdul Haqq Baker, from the Brixton Mosque, feels that the Salafi Institute is too aggressive and has contributed to giving British Salafis a bad name. At the same time, Baker disassociates himself from JIMAS and questions the direction taken by its leader, who he suggests was influenced by the ideology and methodology of the Muslim Brotherhood, saying that 'the statements of Abu Muntasir became increasingly negative against students of knowledge and their scholars – the very people he had introduced us to'.[39] Other image problems arise out of allegations that some Salafi men carry out multiple marriages and serial divorces in areas such as Birmingham and London.[40]

A recent development towards the end of the 2000s is what some obervers have called 'Salafism Lite'. Conscious of the negative connotations that the term 'Salafi' had accrued, particularly after 9/11, some Western Salafis attempted a strategic de-emphasis of Salafi motifs in their language and literature and instead will use phrases like 'orthodox Islam' or 'normative Islam', to encode their Salafi loyalties. The British activities of the American AlMaghrib Institute and the work of British Salafi Imam, Haitham al-Haddad, provide interesting examples of this subtle strategy.

The US-based AlMaghrib Institute, led by Muhammad Alshareef and Yasir Qadhi, has been successful in offering professional online and face-to-face Islamic educational packages that offer an Islamised self-help approach to religious revival.[41] AlMaghrib services provide a self-accredited degree, weekend courses, conferences and online media services. Using modern pedagogical approaches that include portfolio building, case study analysis and virtual interaction quizzes and community events, they were able to build a corporate structure that used market research methods, targeting Muslim young people in specific localities in the US and UK. Haitham al-Haddad, born and raised in Saudi Arabia before taking up residence and pursuing higher education in Britain, has developed a significant following. He is associated with the Arab Salafi Al-Muntada al-Islami organisation in London, works closely with the iERA, has links with AlMaghrib Institute and has a team that runs the Islam21c.com website.

The Islam21c.com site is careful not to make references to Salafism on its web pages and instead presents itself as trying to 'articulate Islam in a modern context and address the unique situation and challenges faced by Muslims in the West'.[42] This implicit Salafism transcends individual organisations and has been boosted by the popularity of satellite TV stations such as the Islam Channel and Peace TV. This development, along with the continued ubiquitous presence of pro-Salafi literature, has helped to promote the Salafisation of popular religious discourses.

Muscular Sufisms

Salafism's main competitor in matters of scholarly authority is the TI network, which has steadily gained popularity since the mid-1990s and seems to have offset the influence of the other three trends. TI perspectives integrate Sufism with a worldly engagement not found in established Sufi orders and according to Fuad Nahdi has 'provided charismatic leadership and "edutainment" that British Muslim youth were looking for'.[43] According to Aftab Malik, the TI trend has developed in three phases: the first is the period beginning in 1995, when it established its identity in contradistinction to the other trends;[44] the second occurred in the post-9/11 period, with leading proponents such as Hamza Yusuf becoming publicly more self-reflective and attempting to contextualise the Islamic tradition in relation to the challenges facing modern Western Muslims.

Malik suggests that the second phase also witnessed a broad split within the TI network between what he calls 'conservative' and 'progressive traditionalists'. The conservatives preferred to focus on core themes around spirituality, following madhabs and distinguishing themselves from the other Islamic currents. In contrast, the progressives were interested in broadening their concerns to contextualise tradition in light of the contemporary challenges facing Muslims. The differences at this point were a matter of emphasis rather than a serious disagreement among the leading figures. Conservative figures such as Nuh Keller continue to concentrate consistently on the Sufi-related topics they are well known for. On the other hand, progressives such as Hamza Yusuf attempted to reconcile the need to maintain traditionalist themes with the demands of Muslims living in the West by engaging the media, politicians and non-Muslim audiences. This divergence of approach drew new people to TI perspectives and generated hostility from other traditionalists who felt that this distracted from the importance of emblematic Sufi concerns. Influential British Muslim commentator Yahya Birt, writing about Sufi–Salafi dynamics in the post-9/11 era, observed three responses within the TI network – the first was promoting of unity in the face of the 'war on terror', toning down public critique of Salafis and Islamists and 'even moving towards some kind of public entente on occasion', maintaining that 'theological intolerance lends itself more readily to violence than does more tolerant theology'. The second response witnessed some people in the TI network seize the 'political opportunity in aligning themselves with the war on terror and attacking Salafis and Islamists as their political star was falling', whilst the third was initiated by a segment who 'were keen to stay out of public engagement altogether for various reasons'.[45]

According to Aftab Malik, the third phase in TI's development occurred around the mid-2000s and saw the appearance of factionalism among those who had wrapped themselves in the TI banner. Some younger Barelwis, who had previously been drawn to the messages of Hamza Yusuf, Nuh Keller and Abdal-Hakim Murad, began questioning their scholarly authority and started to publicly attack them for some of their religious positions. For instance, some mocked Yusuf by calling him a 'Saturday Sufi'. Inter-*murid* rivalry is not new, but took on abusive forms in recent years with some young British Barelwis being dubbed the 'Super Sunnis' for challenging the credentials of leading TI figures. It was also aggravated by the perception that figures such as Hamza Yusuf was not sufficiently critical of the West, or that he had been co-opted by the UK and US governments.[46] These fractures increased over internal differences about perspectives, strategies and engagement with the public sphere.

The TI scene has gone on to become populated with dozens of young Shaykhs and *ustadhs* (teachers), many of whom are converts, and has developed to a point where it has acquired a distinct aesthetic branding and grammar. This has led to the development of institutes and centres that hold regular study circles, courses, and seminars teaching 'sacred knowledge' in many British towns and cities with significant Muslim populations. Notable among these educational initiatives are the Ibn Abbas Institute and Greensville Trust, both in Liverpool, the Abu Zahra Trust in Keighley, the Shifa Trust in Oxford, the Sacred Knowledge Trust in Dewsbury and the Habiba Institute in London. Magazines promoting TI perspectives include the now defunct *Q-News* and *Islamica*, *Seasons* and *Illume* journals. The most prolific publishers include: Amal Press, the Islamic Texts Society, StarLatch Press and White Thread Press and Alhambra Productions. Prominent internet sites include Deenport.com and Masud.co.uk, the Sunni Path (now Qibla.com), the Seekers Path, Zhikr.org, ShadhiliTeachings.org (now UntoTheOne.com) and Lamppost Productions. Interestingly, these sites tend not to emphasise their sympathy towards Sufism but instead claim that they represent traditional Islamic teachings within the parameters of classical orthodoxy.

The leading websites, such as Deenport.com, are strikingly modern, English-language based websites, which combine concerns about the importance of classical Islamic knowledge, spirituality and current affairs, and also have an active eclectic forum that discusses everything from fatwas to football. Masud Khan's personal website was one of the first information points for TI internationally. It contains articles by Abdal-Hakim Murad, Nuh Keller, a section on British Muslim Heritage, audio lectures and links to other TI-oriented sites. Qibla, formally the Sunni Path website, uses cutting-edge technology to 'take sacred knowledge to households all over the world by realizing the principles of traditional learning in an online environment. Qibla's pioneering online learning system uses the latest [. . .] tools to make location and distance to teachers no longer an obstacle.'[47] Another popular site, the Seeker's Digest, was set up by young Canadian-Pakistani scholar, Faraz Rabbani, and has now developed into a full educational Seeker's Hub, comprising courses, online study circles, blogs and podcasts. The Seeker's Hub contains both opportunities to ask questions on Islamic law and browse articles that address contemporary Muslim concerns which 'function as pedagogical material for young supporters of tasawwuf and recruitment devices for the uncommitted'.[48]

The net effect of the adaptations and changes within these four trends is that they have simultaneously attracted and repelled young people and have consciously or unconsciously perpetuated existing differences based upon theology or ideology. People began to 'shop around' at other groups to see if they could find a better religious experience. This resulted in people making choices about future participation within a trend. The highly competitive Islamic scene of the 1990s, and the fragmentation that occurred during the middle of it, caused a number of people at both leadership and follower level to broaden their horizons and reconsider their loyalties. Some people never joined a particular trend after they started to become observant and many sampled the different trends after first encountering them whilst at college, university or within their communities but did not commit to membership. Those that had negative experiences left the trend or ceased practising the faith. Within these organisations were those that occasionally participated in the activities of other trends and others that defected because they found another more compelling. Many people made long-term commitments and stayed loyal to one particular trend into their adult lives. For others, disillusionment with a trend motivated them to develop their own localised activist projects and in some cases prompted new initiatives that gained a national profile. This flow of traffic between different trends became more visible after the internal problems within YM, HT, JIMAS and the emergence of the TI network.

Today the most popular forms of activism are eclectic, as people choose to participate strategically in what they get involved with and will alternate and consume Islamic activities according to their interests and needs. Despite the fact that most British Muslims are not members of these four trends, their understanding and practise of Islam is likely to have been influenced by them. The changes that have taken place in these communities altered the social ecology in which the Islamic trends operate and demographic, political and religious changes taking place with Muslim societies globally have reverberations in the UK. After recovering from leadership crises and organisational splits, three of the four trends that underwent the most dramatic change in the mid-1990s have renewed their outlook and modes of operation. The threat of violent radicalisation and potential links with Islamic groups floated like a cloud over the work of many of them in the post-9/11 and 7/7 eras. Though radical Islamic activism is minuscule, it has provoked many leading British Muslims such as Abdal-Hakim Murad to ponder:

> What attracts young Muslims to this type of ephemeral but ferocious activism? One does not have to subscribe to determinist social theories to realise the importance of the almost universal condition of insecurity, which Muslim societies are now experiencing. The Islamic world is passing through a most

devastating period of transition. A history of economic and scientific change, which in Europe took five hundred years, is, in the Muslim world, being squeezed into a couple of generations [...] Such a transition period, with its centrifugal forces, which allow nothing to remain constant, makes human beings very insecure. They look around for something to hold onto, that will give them an identity. In our case, that something is usually Islam. And because they are being propelled into it with this psychic sense of insecurity, rather than by more normal processes of conversion and faith, they lack some of the natural religious virtues, which are acquired by contact with continuous tradition, and can never be learnt from a book.[49]

In response, after feeling governmental pressures to deal with the problem of religious extremism British Muslim communities gradually became more introspective. The membership of many of the groups dropped as people began to question the expectations of rigid loyalty. Activist-oriented trends, as well as civil society agencies, were forced to adapt to the new political climate. These processes have shaped the rhetoric of all the religious orientations and have indirectly helped create new forms of Islamic activism, which are discussed in the next chapter.

CHAPTER 7

CONTEMPORARY BRITISH ISLAMIC ACTIVISM

Put your tawheeds up, ones in the air and praise Allah.[1]

Poetic Pilgrimage

I have tried to demonstrate how four global Islamic trends have helped second- and third-generation British Muslims learn about and express their faith. I have discussed how organised groups of young people grappled with issues of religious identity, culture, reform and how they were instrumental in shaping re-Islamisation trends in Muslim communities between the mid-1980s into the early 2000s. The spirited work of YM, JIMAS, HT and the TI network in the 1990s was the precursor for the multiple forms of Islamic activism visible today. They tried to resist cultural assimilation, attempted to respond to the failures of traditional mosques and tried to provide alternative Islamic youth education in every town or city with a significant Muslim population. This activism also tapped into a sense of a globalised Muslim consciousness, which enabled these groups to mobilise Islamic symbols and political causes for their work in Britain. They have evolved their goals and methods over time due to a variety of internal and external societal factors which produced both convergences and divergences in their rhetoric and strategies.

The impact of social change and the repercussions of international and domestic political crises triggered internal debates, divisions and changes in leadership direction. The reflective mood was particularly pronounced in the aftermath of the terrorist attacks of 9/11 and 7/7 and led to surprising new developments. The trends still continue to function, some with diminished capacity and presence while others have grown organically in different ways. Many former members and participants of these trends are now leading influential Islamic organisations and initiatives today. During the 1990s the various Islamic trends worked in a very competitive climate, each purporting to represent 'true Islam'. Ultimately, they differed upon scriptural interpretation and the best way to deal with the realities of living in a non-Muslim society. This diversity and intense competition between them is not unique to Muslims and is present in every lived religious tradition. The contestations between them are not so much a 'Battle for British Islam', but an attempt to define and position themselves within a contentious minority context. This politics of representation can be seen in other faith groups too, but does not receive the same attention. The next section provides an overview and assessment of each of the four trends in the 'contemporary stage'.

The Young Muslims UK

Of the different orientations, YM was first to have an impact upon a wide group of second-generation Muslims. YM pioneered the teaching of Islam in the English language, as well as 'halal alternatives' in sports, music, recreation, leadership training and peer-networking opportunities. They helped to build pride in religious identities, popularised large national youth conferences, produced a national Muslim youth magazine, introduced Islamic speakers' tours – which provided platforms for many popular Islamic speakers – and was instrumental in shaping emerging discourses around Muslim Britishness. A number of YM's leading members from the 1990s generation went on to acquire prominent places in British Muslim communities and a handful are influential outside it. Original YM President Farooq Murad went on to lead one of the biggest Muslim charities in the UK and the MCB, Inayat Bunglawala was a deputy secretary of the MCB and Ahtesham Ali is Muslim Advisor to the Prison Service. Others joined political parties and became local government councillors, and some tried to become MPs. In 2014 founding member Afzal Khan was elected to the European Parliament.

Despite these achievements YM was conflicted ideologically and lacked a realistic long-term vision, which caused many members to lose faith in it. To outsiders it appeared elitist, appealing mainly to young people from stable, 'easy to work with', middle-class backgrounds. People who did not always have the required competence were selected, rather than elected, to its executive committes. Ambivalence towards Islamist reference points generated tensions with its claim of trying to create an indigenous 'British Islam'. Attempting to do too many things caused disorientation and disorganisation, and a number of its branches became distracted in turf wars with HT and JIMAS. There were also allegations of inappropriate relationships developing between some unmarried male and female members, leading to an accusation of YM being a 'dating agency'.

Its biggest failure was its inability to address the growing number of social problems facing young British Muslims. Former members and outsiders accused YM of lacking intellectual depth and religious scholarship, which was seen to be a major weakness in the organisation. During its heyday, none of the leaders of the YM movement had any Islamic scholarly training, a situation which was acknowledged in the mid-1990s, when a handful of individual executive members, such as Dilwar Hussain, went to study Arabic and Islamic studies for a year at the L'Institut Européen des Sciences Humaines in France. Others like Mostahfiz Gani (brother of former YM president Mahbub Gani), and ex-presidents Munir Ahmed and Ahtesham Ali, embarked upon Islamic studies with scholars such as Shaykh Abdullah ibn Judai in Leeds. Neither were any of the organisational leadership professionally trained in youth work or specialists in community development, which is quite remarkable given their rhetorical slogans around 'training the youth' and 'changing society'.[2] Equally surprising is that very few had more than a surface awareness of the history and methods of the reformist movements with which they associated themselves. This partly demonstrates the failure of reformist Islamism to fully embed itself in the British landscape and its inability to respond intellectually to the socio-political challenges facing Muslims in Britain.

Since its creation in 1984, the organisation has changed beyond recognition. Following 7/7, YM was forced to move away from its ideological inspirations and it is now closely managed by its adult destination organisation the ISB, and after pressure to indigenise their

Islamic discourse the YM dropped the heady rhetoric of being the representatives of the international Islamic movement in Britain. The most recent third generation of activists, from the 2000s onward, represent a different type of young British Muslim. They are religiously conscious but more cosmopolitan and have different priorities and life experiences to their predecessors. Former YM member, Dilwar Hussain explained: 'The ambience has changed, people are more relaxed as Islamic groups have shifted to a consensus and there is great similarity in the outlooks of YM/ISB, City Circle and the Radical Middle Way project.'[3] Today YM works much more closely with the ISB, but still uses its traditional means of recruitment through large camps, residential training programmes and study circles. After the London bombings it repackaged its image and invested in electronic media, revamped its website and also created a Facebook group. To boost its public image it has also helped raise money for local and national Muslim and non-Muslim charities such as Cancer Research UK.

The organisation has now become a marginal player in a very competitive contemporary Islamic activist scene and has failed to achieve the original mission of Islamising Britain. Critics of YM/ISB claim that they have no clear agenda, only appealing to a narrow middle-class constituency and have a liberal 'happy-clappy' image compared to current Islamic trends. According to former member Robina Shah: 'YM/ISB is too apologetic, and too concerned with developing a media-friendly appearance, by showing that they are doing things like raising money for charity – all of which in my opinion is very middle-class.'[4] Other, more damaging, concerns expressed about YM/ISB are that its current intellectual trajectory appears to have liberal, modernist tendencies among some prominent members. For instance, one British Muslim blogger recently asked 'Is ISB Living Islam or Reforming Islam?'

ISB was at one point in time, a highly respected organisation with classical Islam as its beating heart. Over the years, ISB has taken some disconcerting decisions. Platforming [...] dangerous individuals is not a presentation of living Islam but an attempt at killing Islam.[5]

This comment represents a hyperbolic, but recurring, sentiment by other contemporary Islamic activists who question YM/ISB's Islamic credibility. Another example is the fallout after a paper written by Usama Hasan seemed to suggest that there was no religious basis for Muslim women covering their hair in public. Though this opinion is considered a minority view within Islamic scholarship, a number of YM/ISB female members stopped wearing *hijab* and this caused controversy both inside and outside YM/ISB circles.[6] YM/ISB supporters will argue that they pioneered forms of Islamic activism that have been taken up by other Muslim activists, such as the Islam Awareness Week, inaugurated in 1994, and its well-attended bi-annual 'Living Islam' camp, which attracts thousands. Despite this, YM has suffered a major decline in its profile due to an inability to offer relevant activities and retain membership. Today they are thought of as a youth club to 'baby-sit' the children of the 1980s and 1990s generation of members and are considered largely irrelevant within current activist circles.

Nationalisation of HT in Britain

Since the 7/7 London bombings of 2005, HT faced the threat of government proscription and was keen to prove its non-violent credentials and rebut allegations linking the party's ideas with terrorism. Since then, discussion about banning HT is demanded every so often by politicians but is mostly stifled by the fact that they have always operated within the law, and that any ban would have little or no effect as it would simply lead to the creation of other front organisations. The Association of Chief Police Officers, the Intelligence services and elements within the Home Office have opposed a ban on the grounds of insufficient evidence, and others believe that HT is actually useful in drawing young Muslims away from violent forms of radicalisation. HT has based its international headquarters in London, which became a hub for coordinating its international communications, administrative and publishing operations. It continues to push its ideology within local communities and retains tried and tested recruitment tactics in educational and community settings. For instance, between 2004 and 2008 in Tower Hamlets, East London it focused on creating front organisations to do youth work, as one HT insider explained:

> The main purpose of all the organisations in Tower Hamlets including Newgen was to be a front for HT, to promote HT and its

ideas and to have influence over youths in Tower Hamlets [...] We would invite a local role model from the community like the councillor and amongst them we would include a member of HT just to make it look like HT members are role models.[7]

One of the other most challenging developments for HT in Britain has been the sustained high-profile attacks by its ex-members, Shiraz Maher, Ed Husain and Maajid Nawaz, who vigorously tried to discredit them. Maher was the first to do this, but it was the publication of Husain's *The Islamist* and the subsequent creation of the Quilliam Foundation with Nawaz that brought further unwanted attention to HT from 2007–10. Perhaps the greatest problem for HT in Britain is the fact that most of its members eventually leave. This suggests a major retention problem and an inability to remain relevant to young Muslims in a highly competitive Islamic activist scene. Though there appears to be HT activity in certain localities, support for its ideas has dwindled since the mid-1990s, and diminished further after the anti-war protests of 2003. There also appear to be different factions at leadership level, between hardliners and pragmatists, who debate the discrepancies between party ideology and realities on the ground in British Muslim communities. This is a more subtle challenge, according to HT insider and academic Noman Hanif:

> The current generation feel a sharp sense of being orphaned, in that they are largely South Asian and are living in a minority Muslim context, which is outside of the founders original thinking, and they have little understanding or connection with HT as an international movement. [so they] have an identity problem, not really belonging anywhere.[8]

The organisation's biggest struggle remains one of relevancy, as HT has long lost its ability to shape the agenda. British Muslims are far less receptive to HT's efforts compared to 20 years ago, as its radical message has grown tiresome and most people interested in Islamic activism find them unpersuasive. It also struggles to compete with the increasingly crowded alternatives in the Islamic landscape and the fact that many universities have made it difficult for them to recruit on campuses. Recognising its image problem, the UK branch has publicly moderated its confrontational rhetoric and attempts new outreach strategies by addressing community issues such as drugs, forced marriages and Islamic alternatives to the global financial system. It attempts to deal with the lack of interest in its message by piggybacking onto the most emotive issues of the day, organising or participating in public events which discuss concerns around how anti-terrorism legislation, policing and government policy impacts on Muslim communities. It tries to reach out to new constituencies by exploiting issues such as opposition to the invasion of Iraq, demonstrated against former Pakistani President Pervez Musharraf during his visits to the UK and has tried to shape British Muslim opinion on debates around multiculturalism and integration. The leadership continues to search for issues which will draw interest to their work, a notable example was its attempt to capitalise on the early stages of the Arab Uprisings. Initially, HT tried to claim that the Tunsian protests were driven by a desire for 'Islamic Rule' and were quick to post a YouTube clip purportedly showing a demonstration on 15 January 2011, 'where the masses can clearly be heard calling for Islam and Khilafah'. When it turned out that the footage was of a small group of Salafis on the streets, HT moved back to familiar themes.

New Trends in British Salafism

Salafism in the early days of JIMAS was a radical new perspective for many young Muslims. Like HT, it offered a rejection of what they believed was a corrupted version of Islam and the attraction of Salafism for young British Muslims can be attributed to a set of interrelated factors which were transnational in character, well funded and timely. First among them was the globalisation of Saudi Salafi discourse through the public and private financing of certain British Muslim institutions, the distribution of Salafi literature, saturation of Salafi perspectives on the internet and free scholarships to study in the University of Medina in Saudi Arabia. Second, there was a fertile reception of salafi-oriented themes among British-born Muslims who were in search of religious identities that would restore their religious pride. Thirdly, for those inclined to Salafism it appeared to offer an apparently evidence-based, uncompromising, 'uncontaminated' Islam which provided ethical certainty in a confusing, rapidly changing world, privileging their claims to authenticity as the only Muslims adhering to the concept of *tawhid*, 'the authentic Sunnah' and 'manhaj of the Salaf'. Salafism aggressively rejected theo-cultural diversity within South Asian forms of Islam, branded them as impure and led to an ultra-orthodox elitism over 'lesser Muslims' and separation from a disbelieving British society. The Salafi *dawah*, like HT activism, became notorious for its uncompromising attitude to other Muslims, whom they frequently criticised for following weak Hadiths. This led to clashes with others about their approach to theology and ritual practice. The religious truth claims made by Salafis were used by some young people as a justification to rebel against parental culture; others went further and charged their parents with the accusations of unbelief.[9]

Leading British Salafi figures such as Abu Muntasir, Usama Hasan, Surkheel 'Abu Aliyah' and Abdurraheem Green do not publicly define themselves as Salafi anymore, even though they may privately refer to Salafi scholarship for religious guidance. This viewpoint is echoed by other Salafis, who do not consider these individuals as true Salafis either and have accused the first three of becoming liberals and Sufi sympathisers. I would suggest that Salafi perspectives in Britain today can be categorised into six sub-tendencies: puritan, apolitical 'Super Salafis', Politicised Salafis, Jihadi Salafis, the Liberal Progressive Salafis of JIMAS and the 'Methodological Salafism' of the iERA/AlMaghrib nexus, whose religious praxis is not aligned with any particular group but is more of an approach to Islamic textual sources and scholarly reference points. The latter approach is illustrated by the outlook of well-known activist Moazzam Begg:

> I still believe that this was correct in terms of following Islam scripturally, but not in terms of the interpretation being exclusionary. I continue to regard myself as Salafi in the proper sense of the term, as a seeker after a pure, unadulterated Islam. However, I don't associate or ally myself with the people today who call themselves the Salafi Movement, in that isolationist sense.[10]

New hybridised identities are emerging which indicate the evolving nature of contemporary British Salafi trends. This stands in contrast to the simplistic representations of Salafism and reflects the dynamic and organic nature of religious identity formation. Those who consider themselves Salafis today are more sophisticated than their predecessors and tend to be open to non-Muslim sources of knowledge, but ultimately remain loyal to their Salafi theological convictions.

British Traditional Islam Scene

One the main reasons for the appeal of TI perspectives has been its reference to tradition and continuity. For its adherents, TI provides a rootedness missing from the deculturising rhetoric of Salafis and an alternative to the politics of Islamists. As TI insider Jahan Mahmood explained, 'it encouraged a level-headed approach [that was] much more grounded and encouraged a sense of calmness that didn't dehumanise people like those who were talking about kafirs, or other Muslims'.[11] The scholarly erudition of people like Abdal-Hakim Murad and others was compelling as they are seen as possessing an untainted authenticity and connection with ancient tradition. This prompted a number of young British Muslims to seek the guidance of a teacher, pledge allegiance to a Sufi shaykh, or to travel to Muslim countries for extended studies to emulate the charismatic example of Hamza Yusuf's romantic narrative of personal transformation and learning. However the personal appeal of some of its leading figures later became a source of criticism, as some TI adherents were said to be preoccupied with following the personality of the scholar.

This can be seen in the pop-star like status held by Hamza Yusuf. Though he does not approve or encourage it, many young people became attracted to him, obsessively attending his every lecture, buying all his books, dressing like him and even imitating his speech patterns. An almost 'groupie'-like following occured around him and those who attended his educational institution, leading to them being disparagingly called 'Zaytunees'. This type of behaviour is a feature of Sufi charismatic religious leaderships that command a large band of followers, and in some cases descend into a cult-like relationship between the shaykh and *murids*.[12] The loss of independent personal judgement and partisanship invited ridicule from Salafis and Islamists, who felt vindicated in their negative assessments of Sufism and accusations of personality worship.

Some observers watching the rise of TI argued that it has undermined the intentionality and moral qualities required by those embarking on seeking religious knowledge, resulting in people promoting themselves rather than Islam. Some Western TI adherents who went on to gain qualifications in the Islamic sciences in Syria, Yemen or Mauritania, returned wanting to be recognised as shaykhs and to become inundated with offers to teach. As traditionalist American Imam Abdul Hamid Ali observed:

> Today, there are many people with ijaza, with expertise and without the same sort of integrity [...] an extreme has developed where people think that ijaza is equivalent to achieving mastery of a subject or that it makes a person a scholar when in fact an ijaza in 9 out of 10 cases merely means a person completed the reading of a book with a learned person, not that the person has mastered the science. The rebirth of the ijaza discussion has also led to a negative anti-Western [...] politics as well which is also an extreme that needs to be avoided. Both are 'means', not 'ends.' True scholarship results from living, continuing to learn, continuing to study, continuing to teach, making mistakes and correcting them.[13]

Another concern voiced by people both inside and outside TI circles is about the balance between individual and social transformation. Critics point to the continuation of a quietest strand of historical Sufism that is considered to excessively focus on spiritual matters. They argue that while it provides personal solace, it ignores the societal relevance of Sufism and its socially transformative possibilities. Much of the activity in TI circles is about seeking 'sacred knowledge', 'maintaining tradition' and celebrating the sacred status of the Prophet. Though a small number of high profile TI initiatives are at the forefront of social projects, most TI-affiliated organisations are more interested in religious pedagogy than addressing problems within Muslim communities. Fuad Nahdi, for instance, laments the tendency of TI adherents to be 'held hostage to the past'.[14] Noting the limited appeal TI perspectives have to young 'non-practising' Muslims, Abaas Choudury suggests:

> Traditional Islam still only touched a very small amount of people compared to the other, more established, trends, like the Salafis, HT, Al-Muhajiroun, Young Muslims and others. I think part of

the reason has been, although I sense a shift, the accessibility of traditional Islam. Young Muslims are amongst the lowest performers in education and inner-city Muslims have very few analytical, academic and educational skills. Traditional Islam was presented in an intellectual manner and often it did not make sense to the mainstream youth because it required them to try and understand it in a way that was alien to their intellects.[15]

This could also be attributed to the lack of centralised leadership, which is difficult to create given its diffuse overlapping networks. TI activists such as Aftab Malik argue that there is a desire to identify a figure that could be formally declared as the figurehead in the West. Hamza Yusuf appears to be the first choice, with Abdal-Hakim Murad considered as the representative for Britain. Individuals within the networks claim that the TI networks do not have any political ambitions or tendencies and that people are free to make up their own minds about issues of society and politics. This is both a strength and a weakness, as some were frustrated that certain senior figures within the network, such as the former Grand Mufti of Egypt Shaykh Ali Goma and the late Shaykh Sayyid Ramadan al-Buti, did not provide moral leadership during the Arab Uprisings and capitulated to their governments in Egypt and Syria. In contrast, American TI figures Hamza Yusuf and Zaid Shakir, and Syrian Shaykh Muhammad al-Yaqoubi', did support the Arab Uprisings.

It is also clear that while the TI network has helped to popularise higher religious learning among young Muslims in the West, only a handful of individuals such as Abdal-Hakim Murad and Umar Faruq Abd-Allah have engaged some of the intellectual challenges of the Western tradition. Moreover, living as minorities in the West has produced a multitude of questions that cannot be addressed solely by recourse to sacred religious knowledge and surely needs to be complimented by the acquisition and mastery of 'secular' knowledge. There is also an uncritical romanticisation of 'tradition' in TI discourse which avoids discussion of the problematics of applying the Shariah today and has little to say about the sensitive issues being debated by contemporary Islamic intellectuals and academics. For example, the chapter on the practise of slavery was omitted from Nuh Keller's translation of the legal manual *The Reliance of the Traveller*. Leading scholars within the TI network appear reluctanct to address difficult problems, such as the patriarchal construction of religious authority; nor is there any appetite to explore apparent inequalities in the interpretation of Islamic family laws or whether capital punishment should be applied today.

Some observers sympathetic to the TI trend suggest that, despite an impressive range of institutions appearing in the UK and US, TI activism has not been able to match the activism of the various Salafi and Islamist currents in their localities and cannot draw people to their ideas in the same way. The outcome of this competition is difficult to measure, as TI perspectives seem more visible in some areas and less in others. Interestingly, the rise in popularity of the TI Network has provoked some Salafis to reposition themselves based on the popularity of TI discourse. Well-known Brixton Salafi Imam and academic Abdul Haqq Baker, recently pondered the following:

> References to traditionalism and Sufism being synonymous are relatively recent and in this authors's opinion, threatens to isolate significant segments of the Muslim community that also consider themselves in the same light historically, especially from the perspective of adherence to the four main schools of jurisprudence/Islamic law [...] should not Salafism, by virtue of its subscription to the first three generations of Islam (which incorporates the four main schools of jurisprudence) also be considered traditionalist?[16]

Usama Hasan, though appreciating the contributions of the TI approach, has expressed reservations about the emphasis and approach its proponents have taken, accusing it of going overboard with ijaza and becoming dogmatic by excessively promoting madhabs and replacing scriptural literalism with what he terms 'madhabi literalism'.[17] This sentiment reflects an ongoing divide that has yet to be fully bridged by those that define themselves as Sufis and Salafis. At the same time most Sufis find it difficult to transcend the divide not only with Salafis but also with Islamist-inspired organisations whom they resented for decades of representational hegemony within communities.

One of the biggest criticisms of reformist Islamist movements is that they try to do too many different things in their attempts to prove the comprehensiveness of their message. This has been a general critique of twentieth century reformist movements, in that trying to be ideological movements, political parties, religious educators, reform organisations and welfare groups all at the same time hampered their ability to excel at one specific goal. The Islamist influenced organisations in the UK, like their mass-movement counterparts in the Muslim societies, have suffered similar overreach and are criticised for trying to do too much and not being particularly good at any one thing. YM have been attacked in the past for reproducing the elitism of the Jamaat-e-Islami, remaining aloof and irrelevant to the concerns of young, working-class Muslims. HT in Britain is also accused of being out of touch with the day-to-day concerns of Muslim communities and their vision of a supranational caliphate remains an unfullfilled dream. Similarly the overemphasis on matters of doctrinal difference with other Muslims and social isolationism means Salafism has a limited appeal to the majority of British Muslim communities. The TI network, although containing elements that are tuned into the social realities in British Muslim communities, have yet to address 'worldly issues' with most of its adherents, preferring instead to focus on improving their personal religiosity. Therefore, no single trend has yet offered a detailed vision for betterment of the Muslim communities in the present or future. As professor of religious studies, Sophie Gilliat-Ray, perceptively observed; 'the most successful trends and traditions within Muslim communities in Britain will be those that have the human, economic and technological capital to provide "authentic" Islamic teachings in ways that chime with the spirit of personal choice that characterises the religious worldview of many young British Muslims'.[18]

The trends are likely to continue to evolve organically as their adherents go through the processes of self-reflection, experimentation and adaptation to the culture in which they live. The cyclic pattern of British Islamic activism would suggest that every so often charismatic new speakers and scholarly figures will appear and attract a following in the British scene by either rising up through local communities or residing in the UK, as happened with Omar Bakri, Abdullah Faisal, Abu Hamza, Tariq Ramadan and to a lesser extent with Haitham al-Haddad. It is important to note that in this contemporary period, younger people from more conservative religious trends such as the Deobandis and Barelwis have become much more assertive and are trying to carve their own territories in the new Islamic landscape. Other sectarian, ethnic and ideological trends with some localised influence have also emerged in recent years, such as the Al-Khoei Foundation among British Shi'a, the Turkish Gulen movement inspired Dialogue Society and organisations that attempt to offer a kind of secular–religious synthesis.

The Evolution of British Islamic Activism

British Muslims have been experimenting with different ways of expressing their religious identities and methods of inviting non-Muslims to understand them. Reformists, Salafis and radicals tended to be preoccupied with pedagogical approaches to imparting a religious understanding of Islam which were limited to rules that regiment daily life. This started to be challenged in the mid-1990s by those associated with *Q-News* magazine and their attempts to generate indigenous forms of British Islam. It was perhaps the first popular media outlet that explored what living as Muslims in Britain meant and contained lively features on Muslim communities with all their diversities, issues and contradictions. *Q-News* covered stories on Muslim artists, poets, philosophers and engaged in issues affecting wider society. The magazine also became a training ground for different kinds of Muslim socio-political activism, as well as an apprenticeship for future Muslim journalists. Its provocative, creative style impacted on individuals both within the various trends and outside them.

This critical outlook corresponded with a general frustration among Muslim activists who felt that the revivalist organisations had failed to articulate a vision for Muslims to feel at home in Britain. Those who became impatient with the narrow rigidities of religious conservatism but were still committed to their faith began searching outside the dominant trends for inspiration. The need to feel integrated was a double challenge for many who regularly faced different forms of discrimination and were unconvinced of the exclusivist, isolationist interpretations of Islam that most activist groups where promoting. For people inside and outside Islamist trends, the work of Reformist thinker Tariq Ramadan has been influential, particularly his two books *To Be a European Muslim* and *Western Muslims and The Future of Islam*, which provided contemporary scholarly arguments for an inclusive vision of Islam in Europe. Ramadan is now a recognised figure within British Muslim communities and has helped to develop Islamically-informed ethics of active citizenship as well as creating imaginative ways of reconciling Muslim faith within modern Britain.

This influence can be seen in the transformation of many activist discourses, which moved away from a rules-based approach – with its familiar themes of 'how to give *dawah*' and 'halal and haram' distinctions – to exploring different ways of living authentically as both Muslim and British. This outlook led to attempts to develop a creative cultural synthesis and the production of material culture and arts. British Muslim journalists, film makers, photographers and playwrights have started to help shape and critically examine what it means to be a British Muslim, as well as other issues affecting the community at large. In this regard Navid Akhtar, a former BBC producer and founder of the Muslim lifestyle digital media platform Alchemiya, has made many thoughtful programmes such as 'Who wants to be a Mullah?' and 'Ramadan Reflections' which have been broadcast on British mainstream terrestrial television.

Many other documentaries and films have helped to positively shape the perception of the Muslim experience in the UK, ranging from programmes broadcast on terrestrial channels such as 'Shariah TV', 'Make me Muslim' and 'Koran and Country' as well as critical investigative documentaries such as 'Undercover Mosque,' which provoked controversy and debate within both Muslim and non-Muslim communities. While the ever-increasing number of satellite channels have contributed to normalising religious identities, at the same time these have also displaced Islamic organisations in their ability to outreach and set the agenda. For instance, British Muslim TV, the Islam Channel and Peace TV made people like South African speaker Zakir Naik into Muslim celebrities. He has become a household name among Muslims, with a large following in Britain through his lectures and debates with Christian missionaries, and such exposure demonstrates the possibilites of creating a following through mass media.

Another example of growing cultural confidence is the beginning of a British Muslim literary genre. In the 1970s and 1980s there were only a handful of Muslim novelists, such as Farrukh Dhondy, Salman Rushdie and Hanif Kureishi, but from the mid-2000s onwards a number of second-generation British Muslim memoirs and fiction started to make an impact on mainstream readership. Though not all of them write on overtly Muslim themes, some authors have won critical acclaim, such as Leila Aboulela for her novel *Minaret* and Robin Yassin-Kassab for his *The Road from Damascus*. These two novels in particular explore the tensions between maintaining religious identity and living in secular milieus. Autobiographic accounts by the convert Na'ima Robert, who wrote *From My Sisters Lips*, and Lucy Bushill's *Welcome to Islam*, provided British Muslim conversion stories intended to encourage an interest in Islam. Other memoirs, such as *Unimagined: A Muslim Boy Meets the West* by Imran Ahmad, Zaiba Malik's *We are a Muslim, Please* and *Only Half of Me: Being a Muslim in Britain* by Rageh Omaar have provided entertaining accounts of the rich diversity of being Muslim in Britain. These works of fiction and non-fiction all illustrate how Muslims have come of age as citizens and are actively thinking through what it means to be a Muslim in a globalised world. Prior to becoming published some authors have used the internet to develop their writing skills on blogs, which have also helped them to create a readership base, such as Shelina Zahra Janmohamed, who created the Spirit21 blog about life as a Muslim woman before writing her memoir, *Love in a Headscarf*. The internet has also become an easy way for Islamic activists that lack the resources to maintain organisations to set up campaigning websites and personal blogs.

The influence of interaction with American Muslims is sometimes overlooked, despite the fact that scholars and preachers from the US are regularly invited to speak by British organisations. American Muslim artists share similar cultural experiences with their British counterparts and have influenced them in many areas. The cumulative result was the birth of an Islamic activism that was at once celebratory and experimental, carrying a creative impulse that nurtured British forms of pious arts, poetry, humour, fashion, fiction, film making and Islamic music. YM were among the first British Muslim organisations to experiment with music with English lyrics and released a number of audiocassette albums in the early 1990s. Though production quality was weak, their *nasheed*s – simple songs celebrating Muslim identity and the challenges of living life as a Muslim – paved the way for more professional productions in the early 2000s.

The desire to produce Islamic popular music paralleled patterns in Europe and North America, where Muslim entrepreneurs have capitalised on the emerging appetite of young Muslim consumers for Islamic alternatives to non-Muslim products and services, in what has been dubbed the new 'Muslim Cool'.[19] This has taken the form of 'Islamic Rap', which has among its proponents well-known mainstream artists such as Yasiin Bey (aka Mos Def), Q-tip and Napoleon. The Islamist-inspired Awakening Worldwide production company launched the career of British Muslim pop star Sami Yusuf, who has sold more than 8 million albums. There is also a proliferation of other British Muslim singers populating the Islamic music scene, such as Hamza Robertson, Kamal Uddin, Nazeel al-Azami and a generation of Muslim rappers and hip-hop artists such as Mecca 2 Medina, Mohammed Yahya and the female duo, Poetic Pilgrimage.

Parallel to the proliferation of music artists has been the appearance of 'Islamic comedy', inspired in part by the American Muslim creative scene. American Muslim performers like Azhar Usman, 'Baba Ali' and Preacher Moss have encouraged British Muslims to experiment with humour as a way of tackling prejudice and exploring issues of faith and culture. Jeff Mirza, Shaista Aziz, Prince Abdi and the YouTube sensations 'Diary of a Bad Man' and 'Guzzy Bear', self-consciously explore various aspects of Muslim life in Britain, poking fun at both Muslims and the wider society's perception of their faith and culture.

British Muslim interest in purchasing religiously lawful products has caused the huge growth in what could be called 'halal-certified consumerism', a growing phenomenom that includes both Muslim and non-Muslim companies offering faith-compliant goods and services. Food and drinks, such as Ummah Chocolate and Mecca-Cola attempt to reassure the religious convictions of its customers by donating a portion of their profits to Islamic causes. Another obvious indicator is the increasing appetite for Islamic sartorial forms for women and men that fulfil their desire to be 'visibly Muslim', who look good and dress modestly.[20]

In this new British Islamic landscape, the four Islamic trends coexist alongside new cultural trends, public engagement forums, social entreprises, electronic activists and service-based organisations. This has been one of the most interesting developments, as individuals inside and outside the activists' trends realised the need to move beyond religious education into civil society and social entrepreneurship. Complementing older pioneering agencies such as the An-Nisa Society are the service-based organisations such as the Muslim Youth Helpline, the Nafas drug education and rehabilitation project, groundbreaking charities such as

Al-Mizan Trust, the National Zakat Foundation and a plethora of social enterprises and religiously-themed social events organisations such as the Emerald Network, faith-sensitive training consultancies like Faith Associates and Muslim marriage websites. In addition to which there are informal networks of academics, intellectual and professional associations, social networks and a growing number of institutes for Islamic education that are trying to increase the intellectual capital of British Muslim communities.

In the current era most Islamic activists prefer to express their particular Islamic values on advocacy platforms and in network hubs rather than formal, hierarchical socio-political movements. Nearly all have a web presence synchronised with multiple social media feeds on Facebook, Twitter and WhatsApp, which enable them to make cross-ideological alliances and de-centre some of the established organisations and institutions. They are more strategic in their approach and make interventions in mainstream media, as well as discussing traditional topics such as highlighting and defending discrimination against Muslims. These new trends, in contradistinction to the four trends examined in this book, do not have a single defining message or particular religious features. They are different in that they occupy a post-ideological position, which is eclectic, hybridised and heavily uses digital communication technologies.

CONCLUSION

At a time when activist groups are struggling to keep their own
talented people on board, underperforming in leading their own
communities and often getting weaker by internal squabbles,
replicating the same old thing in the same old way is not going
to work.[1]

Muhammad Abdul Bari

Are Muslims in Britain becoming more religiously observant? Yes
and no. A significant number have clearly decided to take their faith
seriously but not as many as it might appear. Would Muslim activism
be so visible without the work of the Islamic trends? Perhaps not, given
similar developments that have taken place across the world where
revivalist movements have been instrumental in (re)Islamising
significant sections of their societies.[2] Increased religiosity among
British Muslims is not necessarily a problem and none of these trends
has achieved a mass following, people participating in these four
orientations represent a very small percentage of the total number of
Muslims in Britain. Beyond their ability to shape popular religious
discourses, the actual influence of these groups in communities is very
limited and this is due the the fact that most young British Muslims,
despite surface impressions, are not strongly committed to observing
their faith. Though most Muslims will acknowledge a personal
emotional attachment to Islam, the majority will admit they do not
'practise' Islam on a daily basis and are even less likely to be involved in
organised Islamic activism.

There are various reasons why this is the case. Even though British Muslims have an extensive infrastructure of mosques, institutions, educational services and no shortage of opportunities to learn about Islam within community venues or online, there are equally strong forces which are drawing young people away from their religion. Many different factors explain this anomaly, such as shifts in popular culture, secularisation, a generally decreased interest in religion among young people and a religious education in most mosques that was failing to engage Muslim children. Many Imams and religious teachers are recent immigrants who cannot deliver religious instruction in English and struggle to connect with the life experiences and needs of young people. The four Islamic trends have also yet to fully engage with 'unmosqued Muslims' – that is, young people who feel alienated from religious institutions and are not interested in their faith.

A pessimistic view of reformist Islamist movements would suggest that their future in the UK is unlikely to be sustainable in the long term and will be made irrelevant by new emerging networks. This contention is supported by the fact that the most talented people in reformist organisations tend to leave after becoming frustrated with organisational rigidities and the expectation to conform. The reality which few leaders will admit to in public is that Islamist organisations in the UK are in crisis and cannot offer anything of substance other than their educational and welfare activities in Muslim communities. Though many offer helpful services in certain localities, the main trends have yet to meaningfully address the difficult social problems within British Muslim communities, let alone show they are capable of positively contributing to wider society.

An optimistic assessment would suggest that while these formal organisations may decline or dissapear, the globalised nature of Sufi, Salafi and Islamist paradigms are not going to vanish anytime soon. Most of the existing trends have demonstrated their durability in remaining visible after three decades, pointing to the deeply-rooted appeal of their ideas and an ongoing activism that seems to resonate within elements of British Muslim communities. Sufism is entrenched as part of the historical Islamic tradition in most Muslim cultures and Salafi perspectives are increasingly popular due to the proliferation of a well-financed media presence in satellite and digital forms. Islamist outlooks represent a widespread desire for Muslim autonomy and a freedom to choose systems of governance inspired by Islam. Tensions and contestations between Sufis, Salafis and Islamists are also taking place in Muslim majority societies outside Western nations.[3] Within various countries these trends have gone through similar stages of growth, fragmentation and competition for the attention of their citizens. In many Muslim majority societies in South Asia and Africa, Sufis are actively reasserting themselves in order to challenge Salafis and Islamists, while in the Middle East generally, and Eygpt and Tunisia specifically, Islamist movements have splintered into various factions as disgruntled former members have left and formed new organisations, as in the case of the Muslim Brotherhood. During the turmoil of the Arab Uprisings, many people were surprised by the successful entrance of apolitical Salafis into electoral politics, despite previously considering concepts such as democracy to be religiously prohibited.[4] In a globalised world these developments will continue to have repercussions at a local level.

Based upon the cycles of growth and decline evinced by the British Islamic activist movements examined here, it is perhaps possible to anticipate future patterns likely to occur in the short and medium term. In coming years it is likely that the two broad *participation orientations* outlined in Chapter 1 as 'Conservative Isolationist' and 'Intergrationist' tendencies will continue to assert themselves as the true representatives of Islam. At the same time, the struggle for representation and authority between the four dominant trends will carry on alongside the emergence of more activist Deobandi and Barelwi voices. In addition, new hybrid, re-culturalising Islamic trends will continue to experiment with what it means to be a religiously committed Muslim in Britain. We might also find diverse secular and progressive Muslim perspectives that offer more liberal critiques of established religious positions rising to challenge conservative activist trends more convincingly. This may result in a more 'individualistic and politically quietist disposition – in which religiosity and pro-capitalist consumption practices intertwine'.[5] The next decade could equally see a further emeshing of different orientations until they are unrecognisable from their origins, as well as new unexpected permutations and alliances which emerge in a different social environment, resulting in an even more complex spectrum of Islamic activist terrain. Furthermore, it is unlikely that extreme voices will disappear as long as the geopolitical conditions that gave rise to them continue to exist.

The Challenges of Remaining Relevant

Understanding the complex diversity of British Islamic activism described in this book is vital for anyone interested in faith minorities and the ways young people can politicise and develop religious subcultures. It is also highly relevant given the exceptionally politicised public debates these communities are forced to deal with. British Muslim communities have in many ways succeeded in establishing themselves and significantly contributed economically, culturally and politically to British society. They are largely well integrated with an emerging middle class, are represented in most professions and have representation in academia, local and central government. Muslim communities also have a vibrant internal media, with a growing number of online magazines, journals, newspapers, radio stations and satellite channels that have made it an international hub of religious activism. However, most Muslims living in inner-city areas are structurally disadvantaged in numerous ways and are trying to cope with a growing number of social problems, particularly among their young people. One of the main questions facing all the trends is where they fit within the social, political and cultural life of Muslims in Britain today and what they can offer.

Most of them emerged in a very different period of British history. The 1980s presented its own set of challenges, which changed in the 1990s and again in the early 2000s. In the last 15 years, attitudes have hardened against British Muslims and tensions have heightened after various failed and successful terrorist plots, continous negative media coverage, mainstreaming of Islamophobic sentiment, increasing anti-Muslim hate crimes and the pressure to comply with the latest government diktats. Such pressures have left many people in these communities with an acute sense of feeling demonised. Educational achievement, though improving among girls, still lags behind other minority groups as do employment rates, issues that are complicated by the increasing numbers of young Muslim men entering the criminal justice system and the challenges facing new Muslim immigrants from the Middle East, South Asia and Africa. When pressed to respond to this context, many leaders from the main tendencies will talk about British society in terms of a moral critique and struggle to understand the scale of complexities facing them. Addressing these issues requires profound thought and not just well-rehearsed lip service and occasional publicity stunts that talk about the need to tackle drug use, homelessness and crime. Herein lies a role for wider society, media, policy makers and government agencies to work more effectively with Muslim communities in addressing socio-economic inequalities and challenging discrimination.

Islamic trends interested in attracting the attention of British Muslims would benefit by being more reflective and self-critical. A common shortcoming cited by former activists is the lack of transparency within many Islamic organisations. Few are willing to be open about their funding sources and how they spend their money. Fewer still have mechanisms that allow for internal accountability or external criticism of their leadership and decision-making processes. These are standard practices which can be learnt from the new generation of activist organisations that are registered as charities, voluntary organisations and social enterprises. It would also be in their interest to learn from successful national and international Muslim and non-Muslim civic organisations. For those wanting to work with young people this would mean volunteer training, maintaining recognised professional standards in health and safety, child protection policies and paid roles within organisations. This is in addition to training in areas such as organisational leadership, management, capacity building, problem solving, innovation, future scenario planning and conflict resolution.

If the challenges within Muslim communities are to be addressed, respectful dialogue and cooperation between religiously-oriented and non-religious elements within communities would also need to take place. Essential to this process is the need to fully realise the potential of 50 per cent of their population, by representing the voice and presence of females at the leadership level of these groups and mosque-based institutions. Muslim women tend to be the most active at a local level but, aside from a handful of exceptions, do not seem to rise to leadership positions within Muslim organisations.[6] Another obvious problem of many activist organisations is a lack of intellectualism. Whilst most value Islamic scholarship, very few people in the various trends engage in critical thinking about their religious heritage, history, science or contemporary ethical debates.

These trends could benefit by taking research, analysis and policy development more seriously and devoting part of their work to understanding society and the complex dynamics of the world in which they live. A problem-solving mindset would be needed to penetrate their thinking and replace a preoccupation with ideology and sectarianism and a tendency to want to represent the views of all Muslims. In practice this means inspiring and supporting increasing numbers of young people to combine sacred and secular scholarship so that emerging religious scholars and Muslim academics can develop the knowledge, skills and experience to address these challenges. Practically it requires transcending deeply entrenched theological, ideological and political differences to develop long-term functional cooperation and shared vision for the future. This is no easy task and is one of the most difficult challenges facing British Muslims. To begin to address this would require an agreed common ground, putting aside differences, rediscovering the Islamic ethics of managing disagreements and developing a shared vocabulary which facilitates intra-community conversations between young people, religious scholars, intellectuals and activists from every element of British Islam.

In relation to wider society, the Islamic trends would better serve their communities by jettisoning exclusionary, supremacist apologetics that compare Islam with other faiths and world views. A more fruitful approach would be to offer an increasingly sophisticated engagement with the diverse intellectual and philosophical currents that define modernity by drawing upon the historical richness of Islamic civilisation and learning from other faith traditions and world views. Rather than engage in rhetorical shadow boxing or moralising, the trends should positively contribute to pressing global and local debates about the relationship between faith and reason, secularism, public–private distinctions of religion, social pluralism, social exclusion, human rights, economic justice, peacemaking and the potential ecological disaster facing the planet. To do all of this of course requires synergy; an energy created by collaboration and a mature, inclusive outlook and seriousness about cooperating with people from different religious traditions and those with none. It remains to be seen whether young Islamic activists within Muslim communities can rise to these challenges – the future of Islam in Britain might be shaped by them.

NOTES

Introduction

1. Adapted from Peter Mandaville, 'Europe's Muslim youth: Dynamics of alienation and integration', in S.T. Hunter and H. Malik (eds), *Islam in Europe and the United States: A Comparative Perspective* (Washington: Center for Strategic and International Studies, 2002), p. 23.

2. It is very difficult to measure religiosity, as personal identification to faith does not necessarily correlate with personal piety and active observance. According to historian Clive D. Field, analysis of the data from 27 different national polls conducted among British Muslims since 2001 shows that religion does matter for young British Muslims. Overall, for four-fifths their faith was more important than their ethnicity. For further information, see Clive D. Field, 'Young British Muslims since 9/11: A composite attitudinal profile', *Religion, State and Society* 39/2–3 (2011), pp. 247–61. At the same time, whether or not Muslims in Britain are becoming more observant is more contentious. See, for example, Lucinda Platt, in 'Is there assimilation in minority groups' national, ethnic and religious identity?', *Ethnic and Racial Studies* 37/1 (2014), pp. 46–70. Platt draws upon empirical data to demonstrate that younger Muslims tend to attend mosques less and do not maintain a daily commitment to religious discipline and worship.

3. These concerns have been discussed extensively in a number of publications such as Tariq Modood, *Multicultural Politics: Racism, Ethnicity and Muslims in Britain* (Edinburgh: Edinburgh University Press, 2005), Tahir Abbas (ed.), *Muslim Britain: Communities Under Pressure* (London: Zed Books, 2005) and Sophie Gilliat-Ray, *Muslims in Britain: An Introduction* (Cambridge: Cambridge University Press, 2010).

4. Hizb ut-Tahrir is sometimes spelt as Hizb Al-Tahrir, but I have chosen the rendering used by the organisation on its English language website, which is also the one most commonly used in academic literature; see for example: http://www.

hizb.org.uk/. For further information on Sufis, see Ron Geaves, 'Transformation and trends among British Sufis' in R. Geaves and T. Gabriel (eds), *Sufism in Britain* (London: Bloomsbury Academic, 2013). For a more detailed background on Salafis from an international perspective see Roel Meijer, *Global Salafism: Islam's New Religious Movement* (London: Hurst Publishers, 2009).

5. See for example Kerry Moore, Paul Mason and Justin Lewis, *Images of Islam in the UK: The Representation of British Muslims in the National Print News Media 2000–2008* (Cardiff: Cardiff School of Journalism, Media and Cultural Studies, 2008), available from http://www.channel4.com/news/media/pdfs/Cardiff%20Final%20Report.pdf (accessed 18 May 2015) and Julian Petley and Robin Richardson (eds), *Pointing the Finger: Islam and Muslims in the British Media* (London: Oneworld Publications, 2011).

6. These fears are vocalised in a number of alarmist books, such as *Celsius 7/7* by Conservative government minister Michael Gove and *Londonistan: How Britain Created a Terror State Within* by Melanie Phillips, and by publications produced by right-wing think-tanks such as the Centre for Social Cohesion and Policy Exchange. The latter produced one interesting report, *When Progressives Treat with Reactionaries: The British State's flirtation with radical Islamism* by Martin Bright, which contains a number of internal Labour government documents detailing its assessment and policy responses to Islamic groups during the mid-2000s.

7. For background see Wajahat Ali, Eli Clifton, Matthew Duss, et al., *Fear, Inc.: The Roots of the Islamophobia Network in America* (Washington: Center For American Progress, 2011) and Nathan Lean, *Learn more The Islamophobia Industry: How the Right Manufactures Fear of Muslims* (London: Pluto Press, 2012).

8. For a sober theoretical analysis of contemporary Islamism see Richard C. Martin and Abbas Barzegar (eds), *Islamism: Contested Perspectives on Political Islam* (Stanford: Stanford University Press, 2009). For more background into the variants of Islamism see Mohammed Ayoob, *The Many Faces of Political Islam: Religion and Politics in the Muslim World* (Ann Arbor: University of Michigan Press, 2011).

9. Broadcast by the BBC on 12 January 2015.

10. This is evident in the observations and conclusion of BBC journalist, Innes Bowen's recent *Medina in Birmingham, Najaf in Brent: Inside British Islam* (London: Hurst Publishers, 2014).

11. There is an expanding area of research into British Muslim radicalisation and violent extremism ranging from think-tank assessments such as: Jytte Klausen, *Al Qaeda-Affiliated and 'Homegrown' Jihadism in the UK: 1999–2010* (London: The Institute for Strategic Dialogue, 2010), Robin Simcox, Hannah Stuart, Houriya Ahmed, et al., *Islamist Terrorism: The British Connections* (London: The Centre for Social Cohesion, 2010) to government-commissioned reports such as Tufyal Choudhury, *The Role of Muslim Identity Politics in Radicalisation (a study in progress)* (London: Department of Communities and Local Government, 2007)

and studies into violent radicalisation: Yahya Birt, et al., *Studies into Violent Radicalisation; Lot 2 The Beliefs, Ideologies and Narratives* (London: Change Institute, 2008). Academic surveys include: Tahir Abbas (ed.), *Islamic Political Radicalism: A European Perspective* (Edinburgh: Edinburgh University Press, 2007), Basia Spalek, Salwa El Awa and Laura Zahra McDonald, *Police–Muslim Engagement and Partnerships for the Purposes of Counter-Terrorism: An Examination* (Birmingham: University of Birmingham, 2009), to books such as Quintan Wiktorowicz, *Radical Islam Rising: Muslim Extremism in the West* (Lanham: Rowman & Littlefield, 2005) and Sean O'Neill and Daniel McGrory, *The Suicide Factory: Abu Hamza and the Finsbury Park Mosque* (London: Harper Collins, 2006).

12. For incisive scholarly reflections on these issues see Muhammad Umer Chapra, *Muslim Civilization: The Causes of Decline and the Need for Reform* (Markfield: The Islamic Foundation, 2007) and Ali A. Allawi, *The Crisis of Islamic Civilization* (London: Yale University Press, 2009).

13. Ron Geaves provides an important overview of the establishment of Deoband, Barelwi and Jamaat-e-Islami in Britain up to the mid-1990s in his *Sectarian Influences within Islam in Britain: With Special Reference to Community* (Leeds: Department of Theology and Religious Studies, Leeds University. PhD Thesis, 1994), which is complemented by Philip Lewis, *Islamic Britain: Religion, Politics and Identity among British Muslims* (London: I.B.Tauris, 1994), while Suha Taji-Farouki, *A Fundamental Quest:* Hizb al-Tahrir *and the Search for the Islamic Caliphate* (London: Grey Seal, 1996) covers the group's activities up to 1994. See also Innes Bowen's *Medina in Birmingham*. To date, the most penetrating research on any single Islamic trend in the UK is Wiktorowicz's, *Radical Islam Rising*.

14. Husain calls himself 'Ed' as an abbreviation of Mohammed, in a story recounted in his memoir *The Islamist*. Nawaz made similar capital out of his former association with HT and wrote his own book *Radical: My Journey from Islamist Extremism to a Democratic Awakening*. Both made careers as native informants touting their claim of expertise in countering religious extremism. For critical commentary on Husain's *The Islamist*, see Riazat Butt, 'How Mohammed became Ed', *The Guardian*, 9 May 2007. Available at http://www.guardian.co.uk/commentisfree/2007/may/09/thereismuchexcitementabout (accessed 18 May 2015) and Ziauddin Sardar, 'The Islamist by Ed Husain; Journey into Islam by Akbar Ahmed', *The Independent on Sunday*, 1 June 2007. Available at http://www.tribuneindia.com/2007/20070610/spectrum/book6.htm (accessed 18 May 2015). The most damning criticism of the book is the allegation that it was ghostwritten in Whitehall: see Nafeez Ahmed, 'The Circus: How British Intelligence Primed Both Sides of the 'Terror War', *Middle Eastern Eye*, 27 February 2015. Available at http://www.middleeasteye.net/columns/circus-how-british-intelligence-primed-both-sides-terror-war-55293733 (accessed 18 May 2015). For more on the opaque relationships between the British government and radical Islamists see Mark Curtis, *Secret Affairs: Britain's Collusion with Radical Islam* (London: Serpent's Tail, 2012).

15. This decline of formal religious authority can be traced back to the impact of colonialism and more recent factors such as migration, globalisation, digital telecommunications and the filling of this void by activist organisations, lay intellectuals and scholarly preachers. See for example; Martin van Bruinessen and Stefano Allievi (eds), *Producing Islamic Knowledge: Transmission and Dissemination in Western Europe* (Abingdon: Routledge, 2012).

16. My personal introduction to Islamic activism began in 1983 at the Muslim Youth Foundation in Manchester. I have worked with various organisations between the late 1980s until the early 2000s. The majority of the material for this book draws upon my PhD research conducted from 2005–11 and is based upon more than 50 interviews with current and former male and female activists, sympathisers and observers of the four trends. It utilises primary sources found in organisational books, magazines reports, leaflets, audio tapes of public speeches, internet sites, chatroom discussion, internal organisational manuals and is also informed by observations from attending their events.

17. It also necessary to note that there is a growing Shiite minority that includes Ismaili (followers of the Agha Khan), Bohras, and Khojas. For further background on internal diversity of British Muslim communities, see Sophie Gilliat-Ray, *Muslims in Britain.*

18. The Barelwis, or followers of Muslim scholar Ahmed Riza Khan (1856–1921) from Barelwi, India, emphasise popular Sufi devotional practices that are unique to Muslims from the Indian subcontinent. These religious practices and customs focus on celebrating the Birthday of the Prophet, individual piety, and remembrance of deceased pious Muslims. Deobandi refers to the scholastic reform movement founded in 1866 in the Indian City of Deoband, in response to British colonialism. Among its prominent leaders were Rashid Ahmad Gangohi (1829–1905) and Muhammad Qasim Nanotvi (1833–80). The *Ahl al-Hadith* tradition, which emerged in India the mid-1800s, is credited to the work of Syed Nazeer Hussain (1805–1902) and Siddiq Hasan Khan (1832–90) and bear a strong resemblance to Salafis in their approach to sacred texts and social attitudes.

19. See for example the work of Alom Shaha, *The Young Atheist's Handbook: Lessons for Living a Good Life Without God* (London: Biteback Publishing, 2012) and the Council of Ex-Muslims of Britain: http://ex-muslim.org.uk/ (accessed 18 May 2015).

20. For more background see Lewis, *Islamic Britain,* Jessica Jacobson, *Islam in Transition: Religion and Identity Among British Pakistani Youth* (London: Routledge, 1998) and Serena Hussain, *Muslims on the Map: A National Survey of Social Trends in Britain* (London: I.B.Tauris, 2008).

21. For a detailed anaylsis of these developments see Nasar Meer, *Citizenship, Identity and the Politics of Multiculturalism: The Rise of Muslim Consciousness* (London: Palgrave Macmilian, 2010).

22. Asad Yawar, 'Seven years of Q-News', *Q-News* 302–3, March 1999. Cited in Jonathan Birt, 'Islamophobia in the construction of British Muslim identity

politics', in P. Hopkins and R. Gale (eds), *Muslims in Britain: Race, Place and Identities* (Edinburgh: Edinburgh University Press, 2009).

23. For further background on Saudi religious influence internationally, see Jonathan Birt, 'Wahhabism in the United Kingdom: Manifestations and reactions', in Madawi al-Rasheed (ed.), *Transnational Connections and the Arab Gulf* (London: Routledge, 2004) and Khaled Abou El Fadl, *The Search for Beauty in Islam: A Conference of the Books* (Oxford: Rowman & Littlefield, 2005). For more background on Iranian efforts to influence British Muslim institutions see Gilles Kepel, *The War for Muslim Minds: Islam and the West* (Cambridge MA: Harvard University Press, 2004).

24. See for example his *The Islamic Threat: Myth or Reality?* (New York: Oxford University Press, 1992).

25. See John Obert Voll, *Islam: Continuity and Change in the Modern World* (Syracuse: Syracuse University Press, 1994).

26. See Tariq Ramadan, *Western Muslims and the Future of Islam* (Oxford: Oxford University Press, 2004), pp. 24–8. Saied Reza Ameli, in his book *Americanisation, Globalisation and British Muslim Identity* (London: ICAS Press, 2002), claims that Ramadan's typology is inadequate in dealing with British-born Muslims because it fails to consider the 'the invention and institutionalisation of "instantaneous communication" and does not include categories such as secular, westernised or hybrid' (p. 36). This assertion actually fails to recognise that Ramadan's schema focuses upon macro-religious trends, which are also manifested on a micro scale and are not intended to include the development of encultured social identities. Ameli's own typology is open to criticism in that it was based solely upon a small sample of British Muslims in the London borough of Brent. I would argue that all of the tendencies suggested by Ramadan can be identified in Britain; however, there are new hybrid syntheses developing and which are highlighted in the chapter on contemporary Islamic activism. Other British Muslim classifications worth mentioning are also developed by Jørgen S. Nielsen in 'Muslims in Europe: History revisited as a way forward?', *Islam and Muslim Relations* 8/2 (1997), pp. 135–43, and the Institute of Community Cohesion's report, *Understanding and appreciating Muslim diversity: Towards better Engagement and Participation* (London: ICoCo, 2008) has a number of interesting different theological, sectarian and legal classifications.

27. For more on Al-Muhajiroun see Wiktorowicz, *Radical Islam Rising* and on Abu Hamza, see O'Neill and McGrory, *The Suicide Factory*.

28. Launched by Husain, Nawaz and fellow ex-HT member Rashad Ali in 2007, the Quillium Foundation has cultivated a positive profile in the Western media and was a recipient of millions of pounds of British government funding until 2011. However, it has also succeeded in alienating nearly every section of Britain's Muslim community as a result of its policies and has little credibility with them. For a critical analysis see Jonathan Githens-Mazer and Robert Lambert, 'Quilliam on Prevent: the Wrong Diagnosis', *The Guardian*, 19 October 2009. Available at http://www.theguardian.com/commentisfree/

belief/2009/oct/19/prevent-quilliam-foundation-extremism (accessed 18 May 2015), Ahmad Shaikh, 'Quilliam Foundation: All Muslims are Dangerous Except Us,' *MuslimMatters.org*, 2 September 2010, available at http://muslimm atters.org/2010/09/02/quilliam-foundation-all-muslims-are-dangerous-except-us/ (accessed 18 May 2015) and Nafeez Ahmed, 'How Violent Extremists Hijacked London-Based "Counter-Extremism" Think Tank', *AlterNet*, 28 April 2015. Available at http://www.alternet.org/world/how-violent-extremists-hi jacked-london-based-counter-extremism-think-tank (accessed 18 May 2015).

29. The SMC was created before the QF and it also generated a large amount of criticism among British Muslim communities. For a scholarly analysis of the SMC see Simon Stjernholm, *Lovers of Muhammad: A Study of Naqshbandi-Haqqani Sufis in the Twenty-First Century* (Lund: Centre for Religion and Theology, Lund University. PhD Thesis, 2011). In his thesis, Stjernholm explores the stated claims of the SMC and upon closer inspection of the organisation reveals that its founders had close links with the Labour party and connections with neoconservative think-tanks in American and Israel. The SMC failed to gain any traction and its founder Haras Rafiq went on to become the Managing Director at Quilliam.

*. As this is an academic text, I have not added the customary designation PBUH, (Peace and Blessings be Upon Him) when referring to the Prophet Muhammad, which Muslims are expected to recite upon hearing his name.

Chapter 1   'Taking Islam to the People': The Young Muslims UK

1. This quote encapsulates YM's founding mission. From Khurram Murad, 'Message to Young Muslims'. Talk given to members of Young Muslims in 1996, reproduced in *Q-News International* 248–50, 27 December 1996–9 January 1997.

2. From the Sunan of Abū Dawūd, Book 37: *Kitab al-Malahim*, No. 4,278.

3. For more on the genealogies of reformist Islamist thought see Ibrahim M. Abu-Rabi, *Intellectual Origins of Islamic Resurgence in the Modern Arab World* (New York: State of New York Press, 1995), Esposito, *The Islamic Threat* and Graham Fuller, *The Future of Political Islam* (London: Palgrave Macmillan, 2004).

4. For more on his life and thought see John Calvert, *Sayyid Qutb and the Origins of Radical Islamism* (London: Hurst Publishers, 2010).

5. For further background see Azzam S. Tamimi, *Rachid Ghannouchi: A Democrat within Islamism* (Oxford: Oxford University Press, 2001).

6. Salwa Ismail, *Rethinking Islamist Politics: Culture, the State and Islamism* (London: I.B.Tauris, 2006), pp. 1–2.

7. The Ikhwan al-Muslimun are an Islamist religio-political reform movement founded by Hasan al-Banna in Egypt in 1928. For further background see Brynjar Lia, *The Society of the Muslim Brothers in Egypt: The Rise of an Islamic Mass Movement 1928–1942* (New York: Ithaca Press, 1996), Brigette Maréchal, *The Muslim*

Brothers in Europe: Roots and Discourse (Leiden: Brill, 2008), Alison Pargeter, *The Muslim Brotherhood: The Burden of Tradition* (London: Saqi Books, 2010) and Lorenzo Vidino, *The New Muslim Brotherhood in the West* (New York: Columbia University Press, 2010). For more on Jamaat-e-Islami and Mawdudi, see Seyyed Vali Reza Nasr, *Mawdudi & The Making of Islamic Revivalism* (Oxford: Oxford University Press, 1997) and his *The Vanguard of the Islamic Revolution: Jama'at-i Islami of Pakistan* (London: I.B.Tauris, 2002). Other recent monographs of the Jamaat-e-Islami include Humeira Iqtidar's *Secularizing Islamists? Jama'at-e-Islami and Jama'at-ud-Da'wa in Urban Pakistan* (Chicago: University of Chicago Press, 2011) and Irfan Ahmad, *Islamism and Democracy in India: The Transformation of Jamaat-e-Islami* (Princeton: Princeton University Press, 2009).

8. Marcia Hermansen cited in Omid Safi (ed.), *Progressive Muslims: On Gender, Justice and Pluralism* (Oxford: Oneworld Publications, 2002), p. 309.

9. For multiple perspectives on al-Qaradawi, see Bettina Graf and Jakob Skovgaard-Petersen (eds), *The Global Mufti: The Phenomenon of Yusuf al-Qaradawi* (London: Hurst Publishers, 2009).

10. The most well-known texts in this genre are Bat Ye'or, *Eurabia: The Euro-Arab Axis* (Madison: Fairleigh Dickinson University Press, 2005) and Bruce Bawer, *While Europe Slept: How Radical Islam Is Destroying the West from Within* (New York: Anchor Books, 2007).

11. Murad's works, particularly his translation of Mawdudi's *Let us Be Muslims* (Markfield: The Islamic Foundation, 1985) and *The Islamic Movement: Dynamics of Values, Power and Change* (Markfield: The Islamic Foundation, 2007), form part of the reading lists of YM and its Bengali peer group, YMO.

12. Cited in Larry Poston's *Islamic Da'wah in the West: Muslim Missionary Activity and the Dynamics of Conversion to Islam* (New York: Oxford University Press, 1992), p. 82.

13. Khurram Murad, *Muslim Youth in the West: Towards a New Education Strategy* (Markfield: The Islamic Foundation, 1986), p. 18.

14. Ibid., p. 16.

15. For a survey of his ideas and influence see Ataullah Siddiqui (ed.), *Ismail Raji al-Faruqi: Islam and Other Faiths* (Markfield: The Islamic Foundation, 2007).

16. His son, Farooq Murad, was until recently the Leader of the MCB and was also the first national President of YM.

17. Interview with the author, April 2009.

18. Sophie Gilliat, 'A Descriptive Account of Islamic Youth Organisations in the UK', *The American Journal of Islamic Social Sciences* 14/1 (1996), pp. 99–111.

19. Qureshi later went on to become Chairman of the Lancashire Council of Mosques and is today a senior member of UKIM.

20. Interview with the author, May 2009.

21. Today Zahid Pervez is an educationalist and senior figure in UKIM. He wrote a book applying his understanding of reformist ideas to the British context entitled *Building a New Society: An Islamic Approach to Social Change* (Markfield: Revival Publications, 1997).

22. He is currently Academic Director at the Traditional Islam-oriented Cambridge Muslim College and the author of *Wandering Lonely in a Crowd: Reflections on the Muslim Condition in the West* (Markfield: Kube Publishing, 2010), which is a collection of his blog articles and observations on Islamic activism and the changing social challenges for British Muslims.

23. Atif Imtiaz, *Striving for Revival* (Markfield: The Young Muslims UK, 1995).

24. Interview with the author, January 2008.

25. Interview with the author, January 2008.

26. He is a human rights lawyer, former Deputy Secretary General of the MCB and husband of Sarah Joseph, the CEO and editor of *emel* magazine.

27. Interview with the author, February 2008.

28. This was quite a turnaround for Imtiaz, as he had previously viewed the emerging TI network as a threat to Islamist organisations and went as far as organising a competing educational training camp with notable Islamist speakers and scholars at the Islamic Foundation, Leicester in August 1996.

29. Interview with the author, August 2006.

30. See article by Shiv Malik, 'Youth wing of UK Muslim group calls for jihad', *The Independent*, 31 July 2005. Available at www.independent.co.uk/news/uk/this-britain/youth-wing-of-uk-muslim-group-calls-for-jihad-302698.html (accessed 19 May 2015).

31. Cited in Shiv Malik, 'The attacks on London, part three: Conflict within Islam', *The Independent*, 31 July 2005. Available at www.independent.co.uk/news/uk/crime/the-attacks-on-london-part-three-conflict-within-islam-302702.html (accessed 19 May 2015).

32. Shiv Malik, 'Youth wing of UK Muslim group calls for jihad', *The Independent*, 31 July 2005.

33. According to former YM president, Ahtesham Ali, there were exceptions. For example, there was an attempt at cooperation between YM and JIMAS when they planned a joint exhibition on Islam at Regents Park Mosque in the early 1990s, but which ultimately failed. Interview with the author, November 2011.

Chapter 2   'Khilafah Coming Soon': The Rise and Fall of Hizb ut-Tahrir in Britain

1. Hizb ut-Tahrir, *Hizb ut-Tahrir* (London: Al-Khilafah Publications, 2000), p. 12. For further examples of HT's understanding of the Khilafah see Taqiuddin an-Nabahani's *The Islamic State* (London: Al-Khilafah Publications, 1998) and *The System of Islam* (London: Al-Khilafah Publications, 2002).

2. For a critical analysis of Islamist theorisations of the Khilafah see Abdelwahab El-Affendi, *Who needs an Islamic State?* (London: Seal Press, 1991), Wael B. Hallaq, *The Impossible State: Islam, Politics, and Modernity's Moral Predicament* (New York: Columbia University Press, 2013) and Madawi al-Rasheed, Carool Kersten and Marat Shterin (eds), *Demistifying the Caliphate: Historical Memory and Contemporary Contexts* (London: Hurst Publishers, 2013).

3. See Taji-Farouki's study, *A Fundamental Quest* and security-oriented studies targeting policy makers such as Zeyno Baran (ed.), *The Challenge of Hizb ut-Tahrir: Deciphering and Combating Radical Islamist Ideology* (Washington: Nixon Center, 2004), Michael Whine, 'Hizb ut-Tahrir in Open Societies' in Baran, ibid. and Houriya Ahmed and Hannah Stuart, *Hizb ut-Tahrir: Ideology and Strategy* (London: The Centre for Social Cohesion, 2009). Other useful sources include: Jean-François Mayer, 'Hizb ut-Tahrir – The Next Al-Qaida, Really?', *PSIO Occasional Paper* 4 (2004), Sarah Swick, *From London to Andijan: The Rising Global Influence of Hizb-ut-Tahrir on Muslim Youth* (Bethesda: Minaret of Freedom Institute, 2005). In the UK, Shaqwir Shaheen wrote an MA thesis entitled *The Evolution of Hizb ut-Tahrir in Britain* (London: Muslim College, 2008). A number of doctoral studies of HT have recently been completed such as Kirstine Sinclair, *The Caliphate as Homeland: Hizb ut-Tahrir in Denmark and Britain* (Odense: Centre for Contemporary Middle East Studies Institute for History and Civilization University of Southern Denmark, 2010), Nomaan Hanif's *The Securitisation of Hizb ut Tahrir: A Comparative Case Study* (London: Royal Holloway University. Unpublished PhD thesis, 2014), British HT activist, Reza Pankhurst's *The Inevitable Caliphate?: A History of the Struggle for Global Islamic Union, 1924 to the Present* (London: Hurst Publishers, 2013), Farhaan Wali's *Radicalism Unveiled* (Farnham: Ashgate Publishing, 2013), another former HT member and Reza Pankhurst's recent *Hizb ut-Tahrir: The Untold History of the Liberation Party* (London: Hurst Publishers, 2015).

4. Edward William Lane, *Arabic-English Lexicon, Book I* (Cambridge: Islamic Texts Society, 1984), pp. 797–8.

5. Al-Rasheed, Kersten and Shterin, 'Introduction', in al-Rasheed et al., *Demystifying the Caliphate*, p. 2.

6. Ibid., p. 3.

7. Abdelwahab El-Affendi. *Who Needs an Islamic State?* 2nd edn (London: Malaysia Think Tank, 2008), p. 32.

8. Al-Rasheed, Kersten and Shterin, *Demystifying the Caliphate*, p. 5.

9. Olivier Roy, *Globalised Islam: The Search for a New Ummah* (London: Hurst Publishers, 2004), p. 288.

10. See for example David Commins, 'Taqi al-Din al-Nabhani and the Islamic Liberation Party', *The Muslim World* lxxxi/3–4 (1991), pp. 194–211, and John Gray, *Al Qaeda and What it Means to be Modern* (London: Faber and Faber, 2007) for an analysis of how modern Islamist movements adopt Western political ideas and stylistic motifs.

11. Taji-Farouki, *A Fundamental Quest*, pp. 71–2.

12. Commins, 'Taqi al-din al-Nabhani' citing Nabhani, *Mafahim*, pp. 6–7.

13. Ibid.

14. Ibid.

15. Taji-Farouki, *A Fundamental Quest*, p. 57.

16. This bears a strong resemblance to Mawdudi's Vanguardism in JI. For further background see Nasr, *The Vanguard of the Islamic Revolution*.

17. Abdul Qadeem Zallum, *How the Khilafah was Destroyed* (London: Khilafah Publications, 2000), p. 1.
18. Hizb ut-Tahrir, 'Adopting Secularism in Government is Apostasy from Islam', *Hizb ut-Tahrir Leaflet*, 2 July 1996. Available at http://www.islammuslims.com/article/discussion_q_a/discussion_forums/adopting_secularism_in_government_is_apostasy_from_islam (accessed 19 May 2015).
19. Hizb ut-Tahrir, *The American Campaign to Suppress Islam* (London: Khilafah Publications, 2001), p. 16.
20. Zallum, *How the Khilafah was Destroyed*, p. 193.
21. Ahmed and Stuart, *Hizb ut-Tahrir*, p. 65.
22. Wali, *Radicalism Unveiled*, p. 39.
23. Ibid., p. 76.
24. 'Umm Mustafa', 'Why I left Hizb ut-Tahrir', New Statesman, cited in Ahmed and Stuart, *Hizb ut-Tahrir*, p. 82.
25. Cited in Birt, et al., *Studies into Violent Radicalisation*, p. 103.
26. Interview with male respondent 'A', August 2006.
27. Sinclair, *The Caliphate as Homeland*, p. 135.
28. Interview with the author, November 2011.
29. Mahan Abedin, 'Al-Muhajiroun in the UK: An Interview with Sheikh Omar Bakri Mohammed' *Spotlight on Terror* 2/5 (2005), p. 5. Also available at http://www.jamestown.org/single/?tx_ttnews%5Btt_news%5D=290&no_cache=1#.VUuH_vlViko (accessed 7 May 2015).
30. This claim is rejected by British Salafis and others who regarded this assertion as a spurious tactic.
31. Interview with female respondent 'B', August 2006.
32. Wali, *Radicalism Unveiled*, p. 162.
33. Interview with male respondent 'A', August 2006.
34. Although its large conferences attract thousands of attendees, this is not an accurate guage of its influence within the British activist scene or its actual membership, which is likely to be in the hundreds.
35. al-Rasheed et al., *Demistifying the Caliphate*, p. 3.
36. Taji-Farouki, *A Fundamental Quest*, p. 29.

Chapter 3 'Returning to the Qur'an and Sunnah': The Salafi *Dawah*

1. Quoted from *A Brief Introduction to the Salafi Da'wah* (Ipswich: Jamiyyah Ihya' Minhaj as Sunnah, 1993), p. 1. This quote epitomises Salafi approaches to Islam.
2. Sami Amghar, 'Salafism and Radicalization of Young European Muslims' in S. Amghar, A. Boubekeur, M. Emerson (eds), *European Islam: Challenges for Public Policy and Society* (Brussels: Center for European Policy, 2007), pp. 39–40.
3. This Hadith is recorded in *Sahih al-Bukhari* 3: 48: 820.

4. Hadith recorded in Abu Dawud, no. 4,597; Ibn Majah, no. 3,992, cited in Surkheel Sharif, *The Seventy-Three Sects: Are the Majority of Muslims Innovators?* (Jawziyyah Institute, 2012). A summary of the paper can also be found under Sharif, 'Muslims Splitting into Seventy-Three Sects', *The Humble 'I'*, 12 February 2013. Available at http://thehumblei.com/2013/02/12/muslims-splitting-into-seventy-three-sects/ (accessed 19 May 2015).

5. Henri Lauzière, 'The Construction of *Salafiyya*: Reconsidering Salafism from the Perspective of Conceptual History', *International Journal of Middle East Studies* 42/3 (2010), pp. 369–89. He states that: 'Written sources make it clear that medieval scholars used the notion of *madhhab al-salaf* primarily in theological contexts where it served as an authoritative and prestigious synonym for the Hanbali creed (*aqida*). In essence, it harked back to the idealized state of theological purity that existed in early Islamic history, when Muslims had not yet faced the challenge of speculative theology (*Kalam*) and had not yet embarked on a systematic search for answers regarding the nature of God and the Qur'an', p. 372.

6. Yunus Dumbe and Abdulkader Tayob, 'Salafis in Cape Town in Search of Purity, Certainty and Social Impact', *Die Welt des Islams* 51 (2011), pp. 188–209.

7. For more background on these two figures, see Albert Hourani's *Arabic Thought in the Liberal Age: 1798–1939* (Cambridge: Cambridge University Press, 1983).

8. See Roy, *Globalised Islam*, p. 233. For examples of representative Salafi critiques of reformist Salafism, see 'Historical Development of the Methodologies of al-Ikhwaan al-Muslimeen and Their Effect and Influence upon Contemporary Salafee Dawah', *Salafi Publications*, March 2003. Available at http://www.salafi publications.com/sps/downloads/pdf/MNJ180001.pdf (accessed 19 May 2015).

9. A critical perspective can be found in Hamid Algar, *Wahhabism: A Critical Essay* (New York: Islamic Publications International, 2002). Also see Khaled Abou El Fadl, *The Great Theft: Wrestling Islam from the Extremists* (New York: HarperCollins, 2007). A sympathetic scholarly view can be found in Natana J. Delong-Bas, *Wahhabi Islam: From Revival and Reform to Global Jihad* (Oxford: Oxford University Press, 2004).

10. An apologetic tract has been written addressing this very point in 'The Wahhabi Myth' by Haneef James Oliver, which provides a representative polemic against the usage of the term 'Wahhabi'. Available from http://www.islamdaily.org/Media/Documents/EN-thewahhabimyth.pdf (accessed 19 May 2015).

11. Roel Meijer, 'Introduction', in Meijer (ed.), *Global Salafism*, p. 10.

12. Khaled Abou El Fadl, 'Islam and the Theology of Power', *Middle East Report* 221 (2001). Also available at http://www.merip.org/mer/mer221/islam-theology-power (accessed 8 May 2015).

13. See El Fadl, *The Great Theft*. He has also described this fusion as 'Salafabism' and as interpretative methodology that retreats to the 'security of the text' and empowers followers to project their socio-political anxiety onto it; see his 'The Orphans of Modernity and the Clash of Civilizations', *Global Dialogue* 4/2 (2002), pp. 1–16.

14. Bernard Haykel, 'On the nature of Salafi thought and action. Appendix: al-Qaeda's Creed and Path' in Meijer (ed.), *Global Salafism*, p. 3.

15. Peter Mandaville, 'Globalization and the Politics of Religious Knowledge: Pluralizing Authority in the Muslim World', *Theory, Culture & Society* 23/4 (2006), p. 12.

16. For an interesting analysis of the role of psychological, cognitive and emotional dispositions in explaining the appeal of Salafism, see Jonas Svensson, 'Mind the Beard! Deference, Purity and Islamization of Everyday Life as Micro-factors in a Salafi Cultural Epidemiology', *Comparative Islamic Studies* 8/1–2 (2012).

17. The other two main schools of Sunni Islamic theology are Ashari and Maturdi, which share most of the basic positions of the Atharis but have significant differences on the relationship of belief and piety. Further background can be found in Tim Winter (ed.), *The Cambridge Companion to Classical Islamic Theology* (Cambridge: Cambridge University Press, 2008).

18. Roy cited by Haykel in Meijer (ed.), *Global Salafism*, p. 3.

19. The Green Lane mosque's management would describe themselves as following the *Ahl al-Hadith* tradition and is hospitable to Salafism, given their theological and methodological similarities. There are other Salafi institutions such as the Arab Al-Muntada Al-Islami in London.

20. The organisation is today primarily educational but until recently continued to promote a number of booklets whose titles reflects Salafi concerns, for example: *The Concise Legacy* by Shaikh ul-Islaam Ibn Taymiyyah, *Al-Walaa' wal-Baraa'* by Shaikh Saalih bin Fouzan al-Fouzan, *The Knowledge of Current Affairs* by Shaikh Muhammad Naasir-ud-Deen al-Albaani, *From the ways of Our Pious Predecessors*, Shaikh Ahmed Fareed, *A Statement and Clarification of Al-Salafiyya* by Shaikh 'Abd al-'Aziz ibn 'Abd Allah ibn Baz.

21. It is worth noting these individuals have been through different phases and forms of Salafism. Usama Hasan has evolved from being a politically active Salafi literalist to adopting controversial positions on a number of issues and now works for the anti-Islamist Quilliam Foundation. After converting, Abdurraheem Green was briefly associated with the Iranian Islamist-oriented Muslim Parliament, set up by the British Pakistani activist Kalim Siddique (1931–96), to being with JIMAS, to becoming co-founder of the missionary iERA organisation. Surkheel Sharif locates himself in the Hanbali legal tradition and is open to Sufism and reflects on contemporary debates on his blog page http://thehumblei.com/. Abdul Haqq Baker, former chair of Brixton Mosque and now an academic, is well known for his anti-radicalisation work and willingness to engage with mainstream political debates.

22. In the beginning the credibility of JIMAS was helped through the personal backing of the influential scholar Dr Suhaib Hasan, who was once leader of the British *Ahl al-Hadith* Network and founder member of the UK Islamic Shariah Council through Abu Muntasir's friendship with his son, Usama Hasan.

23. Haykel in Meijer (ed.), *Global Salafism*, p. 4.

24. Ibid., p. 4.

25. Quintan Wiktorowicz, 'Anatomy of the Salafi Movement', *Studies in Conflict & Terrorism* 29/3 (2006), pp. 207–39.

26. Interview with the author, September 2007.

27. Interview with the author, December 2012.

28. Wiktorowicz, 'Anatomy of the Salafi Movement.'

29. Abu Khadeejah, '1995: End of the JIMAS Era, One Year before the Inception of Salafi Publications', *abukhadeejah.com*, 5 December 2013. Available at http://www.abukhadeejah.com/1995-salafi-dawah-in-1995-one-year-before-the-inception-of-salafi-publications/ (accessed 19 May 2015).

30. Interview with the author, September 2007.

31. For more background, see Umar Lee, *The Rise and fall of the Salafi Dawah in North America* (Kindle Edition, 2014). Available at http://www.amazon.com/Rise-Fall-Salafi-Dawah-America-ebook/dp/B00I1AEYL2 (accessed 19 May 2015).

32. Salafitalk.net, 'Terms and conditions'. http://www.salafitalk.net/st/index.cfm (accessed 19 May 2015).

33. Term coined by Abdal Hakim Murad in his article 'Islamic Spirituality: The Forgotten Revolution', *Cambridge Mosque Project*, n.d., available at http://www.masud.co.uk/ISLAM/ahm/fgtnrevo.htm (accessed 19 May 2015).

34. Abu Khadeejah, 'Giving Da'wah to the innovators, its nature, conditions, and context', *SalafiTalk.net* 11 July 2002. Available at http://www.salafitalk.net/st/viewmessages.cfm?Forum=6&Topic = 562 (accessed 8 May 2015).

35. Bilal Philips, 'Reply to the Critics'. Reposted on *siratemustaqeem.com*, 28 August 2006. Available at http://www.siratemustaqeem.com/phpBB/viewtopic.php?f=28&t = 3956 (accessed 19 May 2015).

36. The sheer bitterness of these polemics of the 'Super Salafis' is evident in salafitalk. net: http://www.salafitalk.net/st/index.cfm and Salafi Manhaj.com: http://salafimanhaj.com/. Rival responses can be found on sites inspired by the *Sahwa* Shaykhs such as Islamic Awakening.com: http://www.islamicawakening.com.

37. For more background see Fawaz A. Gerges, *The Far Enemy: Why Jihad Went Global* (Cambridge: Cambridge University Press, 2009).

38. For a detailed account of these dynamics, see Wiktorowicz's *Radical Islam Rising* and O'Neill and McGrory's *The Suicide Factory.*

39. Ron Geaves, 'Tradition, Innovation and Authentication: Replicating the "Ahl as-Sunna wa Jamaat" in Britain', *Comparative Islamic Studies* 1/1 (2005), pp. 1–20.

40. This is evidenced by viewing the JIMAS annual conference guest speaker lists between the 1990s and the early 2000s.

41. Algar, *Wahhabism: A Critical Essay*, p. 52.

Chapter 4   Sufism Strikes Back: Emergence of the 'Traditional Islam' Network

1. Cited in Nazim Baksh, 'In the Spirit of Tradition', *Cambridge Mosque Project*, n.d., available at http://masud.co.uk/ISLAM/misc/tradition.htm (accessed 8 May 2015).

2. The following quote illustrates the diverse understandings of the term: 'One of the etymological roots of the word "sûfî" is stated by the imams of lugha (linguistics) to be "sûf-cotton" which is mentioned in Hadîths to be clothing worn by Prophets ('alayhimus-salâm) and groups from among the Sahâba (radiyallâhu 'anhum). The group who wore clothes made from sûf became known as "Sûfîs" so this is a source in the Sunna for the word'. An example of the differences of etymology is provided by 'Ali b. 'Uthman al-Jullabi al-Hujwiri (d. 1071). In early Muslim History: 'The true meaning of this name has been much discussed and many books have been composed on the subject. Some assert that the Sufi is so called because he wears a woollen garment (jáma'-i súf); others that he is so called because he is in the first rank (saff-i awwal); others say it is because the Sufis claim to belong to the Asháb-i Suffa.' Cited in Jamal Malik and John Hinnells (eds), *Sufism in the West* (Abingdon: Routledge, 2006), p. 4.

3. See for example, William C. Chittick, 'Part One: Islam in Three Dimensions' in *Faith and Practice of Islam: Three Thirteenth Century Sufi Texts* (Albany: State University of New York Press, 1992).

4. See William C. Chittick, *Sufism: A Short Introduction* (Oxford: Oneworld Publications, 2000).

5. William A. Graham, 'Traditionalism in Islam: An Essay in Interpretation', *Journal of Interdisciplinary History* 23/3 (1993), p. 521.

6. Seyyed Hossein Nasr, *Traditional Islam in the Modern World* (London: John Wiley & Sons, 1990).

7. A good summary of this argument is provided by Elizabeth Sirreyeh in *Sufis and Anti-Sufis: The Defence, Rethinking and Rejection of Sufism in the Modern World* (London: Routledge Curzon Press, 1998).

8. There is a large amount of literature for and against Sufi forms of worship. For a 'pro' view see Nuh Keller's discussion in his article 'How would you respond to the Claim that Sufism is bid'a?', *Cambridge Mosque Project*, n.d., where he explains forms of worship not personally practised by the Messenger are said to have been tacitly approved by him or classed as an acceptable religious innovation and hence cannot be automatically considered *bid'a* at http://www.masud.co.uk/ISLAM/nuh/sufism.htm (accessed 19 May 2015).

9. For more background see, for example, Yossef Rapoport and Shahab Ahmed (eds), *Ibn Taymiyya and his Times* (Pakistan: Open University Press, 2010).

10. Muhammad Abdul Haq Ansari, *Sufism and Shari'ah: A Study of Shaykh Ahmad Sirhindi's Effort to Reform Sufism* (Markfield: Islamic Foundation, 1986), p. 18.

11. Sirreyeh, *Sufis and anti-Sufis*, p. 7.

12. W. Montgomery Watt, *The Faith and Practice of Al-Ghazali* (London: Allen & Unwin, 1953), p. 15.

13. Reynold A. Nicholson, *The Mystics in Islam*, cited in Ron Geaves, *The Sufis of Britain: An Exploration of Muslim Identity* (Cardiff: Cardiff Academic Press. 2000).

14. Ibid.

15. Ibid.

16. For recent analysis of contemporary Sufi trends in Britain, see Geaves and Gabriel, *Sufism in Britain*.

17. For a scholarly biography see Usha Sanyal, *Ahmad Riza Khan Barelwi: In the Path of the Prophet* (Oxford: Oneworld Publications, 2012).

18. His theology focused on the Sufi doctrine of 'Nur-i Muhammadi'. This was based on the idea that the "light of Muhammad" was derived from God's own light and had existed from the beginning of creation.

19. For further background see Lewis, *Islamic Britain*, p. 81.

20. Interview with the author, November 2010.

21. Aftab Malik, *The Broken Chain: Reflections on the Neglect of Tradition* (Bristol: Amal Press, 2002), p. 8.

22. Sirreyeh, *Sufis and Anti-Sufis*, p. 11.

23. Muhammad Qassim Zaman, *The Ulama in Contemporary Islam: Custodians of Change* (New Jersey: Princeton University Press, 2002), p. 4.

24. Interview with the author, July 2009.

25. His popularity among British Muslims was dented after 9/11, when he was invited to attend a meeting with President George W. Bush at the White House, after which they accused him of compromising his previous anti-American position.

26. According to an interview with Ibrahim Osi-Efa, July 2009.

27. Marcia Hermansen, 'Global Sufism "Theirs and Ours"' in M. Dressler, R. Geaves and G. Klinkhammer (eds), *Sufis in Western Society: Global Networking and Locality* (London: Routledge, 2009), p. 36.

28. Keller, 'How would you respond to the Claim that Sufism is Bid'a?'

29. Hamza Yusuf, 'Tasawwuf/Sufism in Islam', *As-Sunnah Foundation of America*, 4 May 1997. Available at http://www.sunnah.org/events/hamza/hamza.htm (accessed 11 May 2015).

30. Abdal-Hakim Murad, 'Understanding the Four Madhhabs: The Problem with Anti-Madhhabism', *Cambridge Mosque Project*, n.d., available at http://www.masud.co.uk/islam/ahm/newmadhh.htm (accessed 11 May 2015).

31. Haifaa A. Jawad, *Towards Building a British Islam: New Muslims' Perspectives* (London: Continuum International Publishing Ltd, 2012), p. 122.

32. Some of these changes are illustrated elsewhere. For example, see Dale Eickelman, 'Mass Higher Education and the Religious Imagination in Contemporary Arab Societies', *American Ethnologist* 19/4 (1992), pp. 643–55 or Ziauddin Sardar, 'Paper, printing and compact disks: The making and unmaking of Islamic culture', *Media, Culture & Society* 15 (1993), pp. 43–59.

33. Malik, *The Broken Chain*, p. 2.

34. Graham, 'Traditionalism in Islam'.

35. Masud Khan, 'Foreword' in Malik, *The Broken Chain*, p. vi.

36. Graham, 'Traditionalism in Islam'.

37. Ibid.

Chapter 5 *Dawah* Discourses: Understanding the Appeal of the Trends

1. Waseef Asghar, 'A Conversation with Ahtesham Ali', *Q-News*, 12–19 August 1994, p. 5. This quote by a former President of YM is reflective of the ways in which discourses of the four trends were recognised within the activist scene at that time.

2. See for example Doug McAdam, Sidney Tarrow and Charles Tilly, *Dynamics of Contention* (Cambridge: Cambridge University Press, 2001) and Suzanne Staggenborg and Bert Klandermans (eds), *Methods of Social Movement Research* (Minneapolis: University of Minnesota Press, 2002).

3. Wiktorowicz, *Radical Islam Rising*, p. 11.

4. For a critical perspective on the limitations of applying SMT to Islamic movements see Roel Meijer, 'Taking the Islamist Movement Seriously: Social Movement Theory and the Islamist Movement', *International Review of Social History* 50/2 (2005), pp. 279–91.

5. See, for example, Jasjit Singh, 'Sikh-ing Online: The role of the internet in the religious lives of young British Sikhs' *Contemporary South Asia* 22/1 (2014), pp. 82–97 and Dhooleka Sarhadi Raj, '"Who the hell do you think you are?" Promoting religious identity among young Hindus in Britain' *Ethnic and Racial Studies* 23/3 (2000), pp. 535–58.

6. For a good summary of the literature see Choudhury, *The Role of Muslim Identity Politics in Radicalisation.* Also see Arun Kundnani *The Muslims are Coming!: Islamophobia, Extremism, and the Domestic War on Terror* (London: Verso, 2014).

7. Justin Gest, *Apart: Alienated and Engaged Muslims in the West* (London: Hurst Publishers, 2010).

8. Wiktorowicz, *Radical Islam Rising*, p. 91.

9. Interview with male respondent 'A', August 2006.

10. Wiktorowicz, *Radical Islam Rising*, p. 99.

11. Ibid., p.100.

12. Alberto Melucci, *Challenging Codes: Collective Action in the Information Age* (Cambridge: Cambridge University Press, 1996).

13. Wiktorowicz, *Radical Islam Rising*, p. 17.

14. Ovamir Anjum, 'Islam as a discursive tradition: Talal Asad and his interlocutors', *Comparative Studies of South Asia, Africa and the Middle East* 27/3 (2007), p. 662.

15. Here I am referring to the large body of literature that discusses the writings of Muslim scholars and thinkers engaged in revivalism, contemporary Islamic thought and its place in the modern world referred to in Chapter 1.

16. Cited in Choudhury, *The Role of Muslim Identity Politics in Radicalisation*, p. 22.

17. See, for example, David A. Snow and Scott C. Byrd, 'Ideology, framing processes, and Islamic terrorist movements' *Mobilization: An International Quarterly Review* 12/1 (2007), pp. 119–36.

18. Quintan Wiktorowicz. 'A new approach to the study of Islamic activism', *International Institute for Asian Studies Newsletter* 33 (2004), p. 13. Available at http://www.iias.nl/sites/default/files/IIAS_NL33_13.pdf (accessed 12 May 2015).

19. Ron Geaves, *Islam in Victorian Britain: The Life and Times of Abdullah Quilliam* (Markfield: Kube Publishing, 2010), p. 312.

20. Benedict Anderson's phrase is one way of understanding the claims of a global Muslim solidarity. See his *Imagined Communities: Reflections on the Origin and Spread of Nationalism* (London: Verso Books, 2006).

21. Sinclair, *The Caliphate as Homeland.*

22. The prevalence of this viewpoint among Muslims can be seen in number of studies, see for example Akbar S. Ahmed, *Islam under Siege: Living Dangerously in a Post-honor World* (Cambridge: Polity Press, 2003) or Peter Oborne and James Jones, *Muslims under Siege: Alienating Vulnerable Communities* (London: Democratic Audit, Human Rights Centre, University of Essex in association with Channel 4 Dispatches, 2008).

23. For more on this viewpoint see Reza Aslan, *How to Win a Cosmic War: Confronting Radical Religion* (London: Arrow Books, 2010).

24. Birt, et al., *Studies into Violent Radicalisation*, p. 19.

25. *Kufr* and *Kaffir* in this sense refers to people and states opposed to Muslim self-determination. Zallum, *How the Khilafah was Destroyed*, p. 1. Cited in Hizb ut-Tahrir, *Hizb ut-Tahrir* (London: Khilafah Publications, 2000), p. 25.

26. Birt, et al., *Studies into Violent Radicalisation*, p. 32.

27. Wali, *Radicalism Unveiled*, p. 49.

28. Mahmud al-Rashid in *Q-News*, 27 August 1993. Cited in Sophie Gilliat, 'A descriptive account of Islamic youth organisations in the UK'.

29. For further background see Jamie Gilham, *Loyal Enemies: British Converts to Islam, 1850–1950* (London: Hurst Publishers, 2014).

30. Extracted from 'British Muslims Monthly Survey for January 1994, Vol. II, No.1'. Available at http://artsweb.bham.ac.uk/bmms/1994/01January94.html (accessed 12 May 2015).

31. Hizb ut-Tahrir, *Dangerous Concepts to Attack Islam and Consolidate the Western Culture* (London: Al-Khilafah Publications, 1997), p. 32. For an exploration of Al-Wasitiya religious thought in Egypt see Raymond William Baker, *Islam without Fear: Egypt and the New Islamists*, (Cambridge MA: Harvard University Press, 2006).

32. Interview with the author, September 2005.

33. Interview with female respondent 'B', August 2006.

34. Interview with male respondent 'C', April 2009.

Chapter 6   Fragmentation and Adaptation:
The Impact of Social Change

1. Quote from the Young Muslims UK Website in 2012. Available at http://www.ymuk.net/index.php?option=com_content&task=view&id=12&Itemid=26 (link not working 12 May 2015).

2. See Olivier Roy, 'The Paradoxes of the re-Islamization of Muslim societies', *10 Years after September 11: A Social Science Research Council Essay Forum*. Available

at http://essays.ssrc.org/10yearsafter911/the-paradoxes-of-the-re-islamization-of-muslim-societies/ (accessed 12 May 2015) and his *Globalised Islam*.

3. For the implications of these developments see Ragui Assaad and Farzaneh Roudi-Fahimi, *Youth in The Middle East and North Africa: Demographic Opportunity or Challenge?* (Washington: Population Reference Bureau, 2007).

4. For recent accounts of youth driving change in Muslim societies see Linda Herrera and Asef Bayat (eds), *Being Young and Muslim: New Cultural Politics in the Global South and North* (Oxford: Oxford University Press, 2010) and Juan Cole, *The New Arabs: How the Millennial Generation is Changing the Middle East* (New York: Simon & Schuster, 2014).

5. For more background see the analysis of the census data in the Muslim Council of Britain Report, *British Muslims in Numbers: A Demographic, Socio-economic and Health Profile of Muslims in Britain Drawing on the 2011 Census* (London: The Muslim Council of Britain, 2015). Available at http://www.mcb.org.uk/wp-content/uploads/2015/02/MCBCensusReport_2015.pdf (accessed 12 May 2015).

6. See for example Philip Lewis, *Young, British and Muslim* (London: Continuum International Publishing, 2007), Anshuman A. Mondal, *Young British Muslim Voices* (Westport: Greenwood World Publishing, 2008), Sughra Ahmed, *Seen and not Heard: Voices of Young British Muslims* (Markfield: Policy Research Centre, Islamic Foundation, 2009), Musab Younis, *Young British Muslims and Relationships* (London: Muslim Youth Helpline, 2010) and Sughra Ahmed and Naved Siddiqi *British by Dissent* (London: Muslim Youth Helpline, 2014).

7. For more on the significance this development see Kate Zebiri, *British Muslim Converts: Choosing Alternative Lives* (Oxford: Oneworld Publishers, 2008), Richard S. Reddie, *Black Muslims in Britain: Why Are a Growing Number of Young Black People converting to Islam* (Oxford: Lion Books, 2009), M.A. Kevin Brice, *A Minority within a Minority: A Report on Converts to Islam in the UK* (London: Faith Matters, 2010). Available at http://faith-matters.org/images/stories/fm-reports/a-minority-within-a-minority-a-report-on-converts-to-islam-in-the-uk.pdf (accessed 20 May 2015) and Yassir Sulieman, *Narratives of Conversion to Islam: Female Perspectives* (Cambridge: University of Cambridge in Association with New Muslims Project, Markfield, 2013). Available at http://www.cis.cam.ac.uk/assets/media/narratives_of_conversion_report.pdf (accessed 20 May 2015).

8. Sean McLoughlin, 'The state, new Muslim leaderships and Islam as a resource for public engagement in Britain', in J.Cesari and S. McLoughlin (eds), *European Muslims and the Secular State* (Farnham: Ashgate Publishing, 2006), pp. 55–69.

9. See the MCB report *British Muslims in Numbers*.

10. This figure is derived from Gavin Berman and Aliyah Dar, *Prison Population Statistics: Note SN/SG/4334* (London: House of Commons Library, Social and General Statistics Section, 2013), p. 11.

11. For background see Paul Thomas, *Responding to the Threat of Violent Extremism: Failing to Prevent* (London: Bloomsbury Academic, 2012) and Derek McGhee, *The End of Multiculturalism? Terrorism, Integration and Human Rights* (Maidenhead: Open University Press, 2008).

12. The shape of early government thinking on how to tackle radicalisation was discussed in the *Draft Report on Young Muslims and Extremism* (UK Foreign and Commonwealth Office/Home Office, 2004). A copy of the report is available at http://www.globalsecurity.org/security/library/report/2004/muslimext-uk. htm (accessed 12 May 2015). Among its candid assessment of the causes of religious extremism are observations about governments engagement with many of the activist organisations discussed in this book.

13. Notable exceptions include HT and most of the Salafi trends.

14. Gerd Baumann, *The Multicultural Riddle: Rethinking National, Ethnic and Religious Identities* (London: Routledge, 1996), p. 126.

15. Extract from a presentation given by Sean McLoughlin, 'Towards a Cosmo-Political Islamism: Generation, Culture, Class', *Liverpool Hope University*, 8 June 2010.

16. Gary R. Bunt explores the impact of the digital age upon Muslim modes of communication and networking in *iMuslims: Rewiring the House of Islam* (Chapel Hill: University of North Carolina Press, 2009).

17. Peter Mandaville, Dilwar Hussain and Maha Azzam, *Muslim Networks and Movements in Western Europe* (Washington: The Pew Forum, 2010). Available at http://www.pewforum.org/Muslim/Muslim-Networks-and-Movements-in-Western-Europe-Event-Transcript.aspx (accessed 13 May 2015).

18. Young Muslims UK, 'About Us'. Available at http://www.ymuk.net/index. php?Itemid=26&id=12&option=com_content&task=view (link not working 20 May 2015).

19. Imtiaz, *Striving for Revival*, pp. 6–7.

20. Interview with the author, November 2011.

21. Interview with the author, November 2011.

22. See also Asef Bayat (ed.), *Post-Islamism: The Changing Faces of Political Islam*, (Oxford: Oxford University Press, 2013), and for a recent commentrary by Peter Mandaville: 'Is the Post-Islamism Thesis Still Valid' for the *Rethinking Islamist Politics* conference 24 January 2014 (Washington: Project on Middle East Political Science. 2014). Available at http://pomeps.org/2014/02/11/rethinking-islamist-politics-brief/ (accessed 13 May 2015).

23. James Brandon and Raffaello Pantucci, 'UK Islamists and the Arab Uprisings', *Current Trends in Islamist Ideology* 13 (2012), p. 38.

24. Ibid., p. 37.

25. Ibid., p. 38.

26. Ibid., p. 39. Also available at http://inayatscorner.wordpress.com/2012/01/21/terror-in-nigeria-why-an-islamic-state-is-not-the-answer/ (accessed 13 May 2015).

27. Shaheen, *The Evolution of Hizb ut-Tahrir*, p. 47.

28. See for example, Choudhury, *The Role of Muslim Identity Politics in Radicalisation* and Richard Norton-Taylor, 'Former MI5 Chief delivers damning verdict on Iraq invasion', *The Guardian*, 20 July 2010. Available at http://www.theguardian. com/uk/2010/jul/20/chilcot-mi5-boss-iraq-war (accessed 13 May 2015).

29. Interview with male respondent 'A', September 2007.

30. Abdul Wahid, 'Hizb-ut-Tahrir's Distinction', *Open Democracy*, 15 August 2005. Available at http://www.opendemocracy.net/conflict-terrorism/criticism_2755.jsp (accessed 13 May 2015).

31. Hizb ut-Tahrir, *Media Information Pack*, Available at http://www.slideshare.net/abusenan/ht-media-pack (accessed 13 May 2015).

32. Ahmed and Stuart, *Hizb ut-Tahrir*, p. 105.

33. See 'A Time for Introspection' by Hamza Yusuf, 'Making the World Safe for Terrorism', by Nuh Keller and 'Recapturing Islam from the Terrorists,' by Abdal-Hakim Murad which were all published in *Q-News* just after the attacks. The articles are available on Masud Khan's website, *Cambridge Mosque Project* at http://www.masud.co.uk/ISLAM/misc/shhamza_sep11.htm, http://www.masud.co.uk/ISLAM/nuh/terrorism.htm and http://masud.co.uk/ISLAM/ahm/recapturing.htm, repetively (accessed 14 May 2015).

34. Usama Hasan, 'Recapturing Islam from the Pacifists', *SunnahOnline.com*, 14 November 2001. Available at http://sunnahonline.com/ilm/contemporary/0031.htm (accessed 14 May 2015).

35. Lewis, *Young, British and Muslim*, p. 139.

36. Interview with the author, September 2007.

37. JIMAS, 'About JIMAS', available at http://www.jimas.org/about-us/ (accessed 14 May 2015).

38. See for example, 'Jimaswatch', *JIMAS and Abu Muntasir: A report on who they are, what they say and which friends they have*. Available at http://www.docstoc.com/docs/95298538/JIMAS-and-Abu-Muntasir (accessed on 14 May 2015).

39. Interview with the author, December 2011.

40. This predatory polygyny of marrying and divorcing women practised by some Salafi men is well known in certain communities. A number of testimonials have circulated on the internet and a website has been designed to expose this behaviour. See for example: http://protectmuslimsisters.com/ (accessed 14 May 2015).

41. Yasir Qadhi is a graduate of Madinah University, Saudi Arabia, and is currently a lecturer in Islamic Studies at Rhodes College, Memphis, US and a high profile speaker in activist circles. He has jettisoned his former hard line viewpoints, no longer describing himself as a Salafi, and has written his own interesting typology of Salafi trends. See 'On Salafi Islam', *Muslim Matters.org*, 22 April 2014. Available at http://muslimmatters.org/2014/04/22/on-salafi-islam-dr-yasir-qadhi/ (accessed 14 May 2015).

42. From the 'About Us' section of the Islam21c.com website. However, these progressive objectives sit uncomfortably with many of his controversial public statements. For example, in an article by al-Haddad after the tsunami in Japan in 2011 he implied that the disaster struck because the Japanese were not Muslims. See 'Reasons Behind the Japanese Tsunami', *Islam21c.com*, 15 March 2011. Available at http://www.islam21c.com/islamic-thought/2387-reasons-behind-the-japanese-tsunami (accessed 14 May 2015).

43. Interview with the author, April 2009.

44. Interview with the author, November 2010.

45. Furthermore, Birt develops his analysis to argue that: 'within the traditionalist movement a liberalising wing was and is manifested in three ways: (1) Firstly the "liberal traditionalists" have put more emphasis upon the critique of political Islamic movements and Wahhabism than on adherence to the rigours of the Sharia in their personal lives [...] Secondly many "liberal traditionalists" seek a personal ethics, a philosophy of Sufism, and have been uncomfortable with what they see as elements of cultishness in Sufi orders [...] Thirdly a critique of (Western) modernity, somewhat imbibed in intellectual quarters within the traditionalist movement and influenced either by perennialist, deconstructionist or conservative Christian analyses has often resolved itself into a personal philosophy.' Yahya Birt, 'Sufis and Salafis of the West: Discord and the Hope of Unity', *The American Muslim*, 26 August 2007. Available at http://theamericanmuslim.org/tam.php/features/articles/sufis_and_salafis_of_the_west_discord_and_the_hope_of_unity (accessed 8 May 2015).

46. According to Aftab Malik, the term 'Super Sunni' refers to some British Barelwis who have decided to question the scholarly authority of these figures after becoming upset with some of the positions they have taken in matters of theology. The accusation by some activists against Hamza Yusuf of being co-opted by the Bush and Blair governments is untrue. However, his public interventions aroused suspicion among some who were disappointed by his advising the American President after 9/11 and by his comments in an interview with the *Guardian* where he stated that young Muslims who rant and rave about the West should emigrate to a Muslim country. Some critics found this ironic given that Yusuf's popularity in his early lectures was earnt in part due to his strident denunciations of the West. Other commentators have suggested these developments are part of a broader strategy by US and UK governments to instrumentalise Sufism against Salafism and Islamism, as suggested in the RAND corporation's 2004 paper *Five Pillars of Democracy: How the West Can Promote an Islamic Reformation*. For futher background see Hisham D. Aidi, *Rebel Music: Race, Empire and New Muslim Youth Culture*, (New York: Pantheon Books, 2014), pp. 71–7.

47. From 'How We Teach', http://www.qibla.com/about/how-we-teach/ (accessed 14 May 2015).

48. Ron Geaves, 'A case of cultural binary fission or transglobal Sufism? The transmigration of Sufism to Britain' in Dressler, Geaves and Klinkhammer (eds), *Sufis in Western Society*, p. 109.

49. Abdal-Hakim Murad, 'Muslim loyalty and belonging: Some reflections on the psychosocial background' in M.S. Seddon, D. Hussain and N. Malik (eds), *British Muslims, Loyalty and Belonging* (Markham: Islamic Foundation, 2002).

Chapter 7   Contemporary British Islamic Activism

1. This is a line from Poet Pilgrimage's lyrics cited in Maruta Herding, *Inventing the Muslim Cool: Islamic Youth Culture in Western Europe* (Bielefeld: Transcript Verlag, 2013), p. 9.
2. Former president Ahtesham Ali conceded this to the author in an interview in November 2011.
3. Interview with the author, November 2011.
4. Interview with the author, May 2009.
5. Coolness of Hind: A Concerned Muslims Blog, *Is ISB Living Islam or Reforming Islam?* The article is a specific critique of a speech given by Ahtesham Ali on the subject of gender segregation at ISB's 'Living Islam' Camp in August 2014. Available at http://coolnessofhind.wordpress.com/2014/08/07/is-isb-living-is lam-or-reforming-islam/#more-1020 (accessed 15 May 2015).
6. His argument can be read in 'The Veil: Between tradition and reason, culture and context', in T. Gabriel and R. Hannan (eds), *Islam and the Veil: Theoretical and Regional Contexts* (London: Continuum International Publishing, 2011), pp. 65–80.
7. Cited in Ahmed and Stuart, *Hizb ut-Tahrir*, p. 89.
8. Interview with the author, December 2011.
9. See Jonathan Birt, 'Wahhabism in the United Kingdom'.
10. Claire Chambers, '"Guantánamo Boy": An interview with Moazzam Begg', *Postcolonial Text* 6/2 (2011), p. 5.
11. Interview with the author, September 2011.
12. This sort of controversy enshrouded the community that was led by Abdal Qadir Murabit in his Norwich community in the late 1970s, were he was alleged to have to become extremely authoritarian.
13. See Shaykh Abdulla Ali, 'Neo-Traditionalism' vs 'Traditionalism', *Lamppost*, 22 January 2012. Available at http://www.lamppostproductions.com/?p=3624 (accessed 15 May 2015). For more background on the experiences of American Muslims seeking sacred knowledge in Muslim cultures see Zareena Grewal, *Islam Is a Foreign Country: American Muslims and the Global Crisis of Authority* (New York: New York University Press, 2014).
14. Interview with the author, September 2009.
15. Interview with the author, November 2010.
16. Abdul Haqq Baker, *Extremists in Our Midst: Confronting Terror* (Basingstoke: Palgrave Macmillian, 2011), p. 80.
17. Interview with the author, July 2010.
18. Robert Bluck, Sophie Gilliat-Ray, David J. Graham, et al., 'Judaism, Sikhism, Islam, Hinduism and Buddhism: Post-war settlements', in L. Woodhead and R. Catto (eds), *Religion and Change in Modern Britain* (Abingdon: Routledge, 2012), p. 120.
19. These ideas are developed further in the recent volume by Amel Boubekeur and Olivier Roy (eds), *Whatever Happened to the Islamists?: Salafis, Heavy Metal*

Muslims and the Lure of Consumerist Islam (London: Hurst Publishers, 2012) and Herding's *Inventing the Muslim Cool.*

20. For further background see Emma Tarlo, *Visibly Muslim: Fashion, Politics, Faith* (Oxford: Berg, 2010).

Conclusion

1. Muhammad Abdul Bari is a member of the Bengali Islamist-oriented IFE and former Secretary General of the MCB. This quote is taken from his analysis paper on the current state of British Islamic Activist organisations in 'Meet the challenge, make the change: A call to action for Muslim civil society in Britain', *Cordoba Papers* 2/1 (2013), p. 21.

2. There is a vast literature on Islamic revivalist movements and social change in Muslim societies. See, for example, Abu-Rabi, *Intellectual Origins of Islamic Resurgence*, Roy, *Globalised Islam* and Baker, *Islam without Fear.*

3. For further background see Tariq Ramadan, *Islam and The Arab Awakening* (New York: Oxford University Press, 2012) and Shadi Hamid, *Temptations of Power: Islamists and Illiberal Democracy in a New Middle East* (New York: Oxford University Press, 2014).

4. Ibid.

5. Mandaville, 'Is The Post-Islamism Thesis Still Valid?, p. 34.

6. To date, I am aware of only five Muslim women who have led prominent organisations: Sughra Ahmed of the ISB, Zareen Roohi Ahmed, former Chief Executive of the British Muslim Forum, Tehmina Kazi, Director of British Muslims for Secular Democracy, and Sara Khan and Kalsoom Bashir, the co-directors of Inspire.

BIBLIOGRAPHY

Abbas, Tahir (ed.), *Islamic Political Radicalism: A European Perspective* (Edinburgh: Edinburgh University Press, 2007).

Abd-Allah, Umar F., *A Muslim in Victorian America: The Life of Alexander Russell Webb* (New York: Oxford University Press, 2006).

Aboulela, Leila, *Minaret* (London: Bloomsbury Publishing, 2006).

Abu-Rabi, Ibrahim M., *Intellectual Origins of Islamic Resurgence in the Modern Arab World* (New York: State of New York Press, 1995).

Ahmad, Irfan, *Islamism and Democracy in India: The Transformation of Jamaat-e-Islami* (Princeton: Princeton University Press, 2009).

Ahmed, Akbar S., *Islam under Siege: Living Dangerously in a Post-honor World* (Cambridge: Polity Press, 2003).

Aidi, Hisham D., *Rebel Music: Race, Empire and New Muslim Youth Culture* (New York: Pantheon Books, 2014).

Algar, Hamid, *Wahhabism: A Critical Essay* (New York: Islamic Publications International, 2002)

Al-Hilali, Muhammad Taqi-ud-Din and Muhammad Mushin Khan (trans.), *The Noble Qur'an* (Riyad: Maktab Darus-Salam, 1993).

Ali, M. M., *A Brief Introduction to the Salafi Da'wah* (Ipswich: Jamiyyah Ihya' Minhaj as Sunnah, 1993).

Allawi, Ali A., *The Crisis of Islamic Civilization* (London: Yale University Press, 2009).

Allen, Chris, *Islamophobia* (Farnham: Ashgate, 2010).

Al-Rasheed, Madawi (ed.), *Transnational Connections and the Arab Gulf* (London: Routledge, 2004).

Ameli, Saied Reza, *Globalization, Americanization and British Muslim Identity* (London: Islamic College for Advanced Studies Publications, 2002).

Andrews, Ahmed Y., 'Sociological analysis of Jamaat-i-Islami in the United Kingdom', in R. Barot (ed.), *Religion and Ethnicity: Minorities and Social Change in the Metropolis* (Kampen: Kok Pharos Publishing House, 1993).

Ansari, Humayun, *'The Infidel Within': Muslims in Britain Since 1800* (London: Hurst Publishers, 2004).

Ansari, Muhammad Abdul Haq, *Sufism and Shari'ah: A Study of Shaykh Ahmad Sirhindi's Effort to Reform Sufism* (Markfield: Islamic Foundation, 1986).

Ayoob, Mohammed, *The Many Faces of Political Islam: Religion and Politics in the Muslim World* (Ann Arbor: University of Michigan Press, 2011).

Baker, Abdul Haqq, *Extremists in Our Midst: Confronting Terror* (Basingstoke: Palgrave Macmillian, 2011).

Baker, Raymond William, *Islam without Fear: Egypt and the New Islamists* (Cambridge MA: Harvard University Press, 2006).

Baran, Zeyno (ed.), *The Challenge of Hizb ut-Tahrir: Deciphering and Combating Radical Islamist Ideology* (Washington: Nixon Centre, 2004).

Bauman, Gerd, *The Multicultural Riddle: Rethinking National, Ethnic and Religious Identities* (London: Routledge, 1996).

Bawer, Bruce, *While Europe Slept: How Radical Islam Is Destroying the West from Within* (New York: Anchor Books, 2007).

Bayat, Asef, *Making Islam Democratic: Social Movements and the Post-Islamist Turn* (Stanford: Stanford University Press, 2007).

——— (ed.), *Post-Islamism: The Changing Faces of Political Islam* (Oxford: Oxford University Press, 2013).

Begg, Moazzam, *Enemy Combatant: A British Muslim's Journey to Guantánamo and Back* (London: Pocket Books, 2007).

Birt, Jonathan, 'Wahhabism in the United Kingdom: Manifestations and reactions', in M. al-Rasheed (ed.), *Transnational Connections and the Arab Gulf* (London: Routledge, 2004).

———, 'Islamophobia in the construction of British Muslim identity politics', in P. Hopkins and R. Gale (eds), *Muslims in Britain: Race, Place and Identities* (Edinburgh: Edinburgh University Press, 2009).

Boubekeur, Amel and Olivier Roy (eds), *Whatever Happened to the Islamists?: Salafis, Heavy Metal Muslims and the Lure of Consumerist Islam* (London: Hurst Publishers, 2012).

Bowen, Innes, *Medina in Birmingham, Najaf in Brent: Inside British Islam* (London: Hurst Publishers, 2014).

Bunt, Gary R., *iMuslims: Rewiring the House of Islam* (Chapel Hill: University of North Carolina Press, 2009).

Bushill-Matthews, Lucy, *Welcome to Islam: A Convert's Tale* (London: Continuum Books, 2008).

Calvert, John, *Sayyid Qutb and the Origins of Radical Islamism* (London: Hurst Publishers, 2010).

Chapra, Muhammad Umer, *Muslim Civilization: The Causes of Decline and the Need for Reform* (Markfield: The Islamic Foundation, 2007).

Chittick, William C., 'Part One: Islam in Three Dimensions' in *Faith and Practice of Islam: Three Thirteenth Century Sufi Texts* (Albany: State University of New York Press, 1992).

———, *Sufism: A Short Introduction* (Oxford: Oneworld Publications, 2000).

Cole, Juan, *The New Arabs: How the Millennial Generation is Changing the Middle East* (New York: Simon & Schuster, 2014).

Commins, David, *The Wahhabi Mission and Saudi Arabia* (London: I.B.Tauris, 2009).

Curtis, Mark, *Secret Affairs: Britain's Collusion with Radical Islam* (London: Serpent's Tail, 2012).

Della Porta, Donatella and Mario Diani, *Social Movements: An Introduction* (New Jersey: Wiley-Blackwell, 1998).

Delong-Bas, Natana J., *Wahhabi Islam: From Revival and Reform to Global Jihad* (Oxford: Oxford University Press, 2004).

El-Affendi, Abdelwahab, *Who needs an Islamic State?* (London: Seal Press, 1991).

El Fadl, Khaled Abou, *The Great Theft: Wrestling Islam from the Extremists* (New York: HarperCollins, 2007).

Esposito, John L., *Islam and Politics* (Syracuse: Syracuse University Press, 1998).

———, *The Islamic Threat: Myth or Reality?* (New York: Oxford University Press, 1999).

Fouad Haddad, Gibril and Sjaad Hussain (eds), *Albani and His Friends: A Concise Guide to the Salafi Movement* (Birmingham: AQSA Publications, 2004).

Fuller, Graham, *The Future of Political Islam* (London: Palgrave Macmillan, 2004).

Garbin, David, 'A diasporic sense of place: dynamics of spatialization and transnational political fields among Bangladeshi Muslims in Britain' in M.P. Smith and J. Eade (eds), *Transnational ties: cities, migrations, and identities. CUCR, vol. 9* (New Brunswick: Transaction Publishers, 2008).

Geaves, Ron, *Sectarian Influences within Islam in Britain: With Special Reference to Community* (Leeds: Department of Theology and Religious Studies, Leeds University. PhD Thesis, 1994).

———, *The Sufis of Britain: An Exploration of Muslim Identity* (Cardiff: Cardiff Academic Press. 2000).

———, 'Learning the lessons from the neo-revivalist and Wahhabi movements: the counterattack of new Sufi movements in the UK', in J. Malik and J. Hinnells (eds), *Sufism in the West* (Abingdon: Routledge, 2006).

———, 'From 9/11 to 7/7: A reassessment of identity strategies amongst British South Asian Muslims' in J. Hinnells (ed.), *From Generation to Generation: South Asians in the West* (London: Palgrave Macmillan, 2007).

———, 'Fieldwork in the study of religion', in G.D. Chryssides and R. Geaves, *The Study of Religion: An Introduction to Key Ideas and Methods.* (London: Continuum Publishing, 2007).

———, 'Transglobal Sufism or a case of cultural binary fission: the transmigration of Sufism to Britain', in R. Geaves, M. Dressler and G. Klinkhammer (eds), *Sufis in Western Society* (London: Routledge, 2009).

———, *Islam in Victorian Britain: The Life and Times of Abdullah Quilliam* (Markfield: Kube Publishing, 2010).

Geaves, Ron, Markus Dressler and Gritt Klinkhammer (eds), *Sufis in Western Society: Global Networking and Locality* (London: Routledge, 2009).

Gerges, Fawaz A., *The Far Enemy: Why Jihad Went Global* (Cambridge: Cambridge University Press, 2009).

Gest, Justin, *Apart: Alienated and Engaged Muslims in the West* (London: Hurst Publishers, 2010).

Ghazali, Abu Hamid and T.J. Winter (trans.), *Remembrance of Death and the Afterlife* (Cambridge: Islamic Texts Society, 1989).

———, and T.J. Winter (trans.), *Disciplining the Soul and on Breaking the Two Desires* (Cambridge: Islamic Texts Society, 1995).

Gilham, Jamie, *Loyal Enemies: British Converts to Islam, 1850–1950* (London: Hurst Publishers, 2014).

Gilliat-Ray, Sophie, *Muslims in Britain: An Introduction* (Cambridge: Cambridge University Press, 2010).

Gove, Michael, *Celsius 7/7* (London: Weidenfeld & Nicolson, 2006).

Graf, Bettina and Jakob Skovgaard-Petersen (eds), *The Global Mufti: The Phenomenon of Yusuf al-Qaradawi* (London: Hurst Publishers, 2009).

Gray, John, *Al Qaeda and What it Means to be Modern* (London: Faber and Faber, 2007).

Grewal, Zareena, *Islam Is a Foreign Country: American Muslims and the Global Crisis of Authority* (New York: New York University Press, 2014).

Halleq, Wael B., *The Impossible State: Islam, Politics, and Modernity's Moral Predicament* (New York: Columbia University Press, 2013).

Hamid, Sadek, 'Islamic political radicalism in Britain: the case of Hizb-ut-Tahrir', in T. Abbas (ed.), *Islamic Political Radicalism: A European Perspective* (Edinburgh: Edinburgh University Press, 2007).

———, 'The attraction of 'authentic Islam': Salafism and British Muslim youth', in R. Meijer (ed.), *Global Salafism: Islam's New Religious Movement* (London: Hurst Publishers, London, 2009).

Hamid, Shadi, *Temptations of Power: Islamists and Illiberal Democracy in a New Middle East* (New York: Oxford University Press, 2014).

Haykel, Bernard, 'On the nature of Salafi thought and action', in R. Meijer (ed.), *Global Salafism: Islam's New Religious Movement* (London: Hurst Publishers, 2009).

Herrera, Linda and Asef Bayat (eds), *Being Young and Muslim: New Cultural Politics in the Global South and North* (Oxford: Oxford University Press, 2010).

Hizb ut-Tahrir, *Dangerous Concepts to Attack Islam and Consolidate the Western Culture* (London: Al-Khilafah Publications, 1997).

———, *Hizb ut-Tahrir* (London: Al-Khilafah Publications, 2000).

———, *The System of Islam* (London: Al-Khilafah Publications, 2002).

Hourani, Albert, *Arabic Thought in the Liberal Age: 1798–1939* (Cambridge: Cambridge University Press, 1983).

Husain, Ed, *The Islamist: Why I Joined Radical Islam in Britain, What I Saw Inside and Why I Left* (London: Penguin Books, 2007).

Imtiaz, Atif, *Striving for Revival* (Markfield: The Young Muslims UK, 1995).

———, *Wandering Lonely in a Crowd: Reflections on the Muslim Condition in the West* (Markfield: Kube Publishing, 2010).

Iqtidar, Humeira, *Secularizing Islamists? Jama'at-e-Islami and Jama'at-ud-Da'wa in Urban Pakistan* (Chicago: University of Chicago Press, 2011).

Ismail, Salwa, *Rethinking Islamist Politics: Culture, the State and Islamism* (London: I.B.Tauris, 2006).

Jawad, Haifaa A., *Towards Building a British Islam: New Muslims' Perspectives* (London: Continuum International Publishing, 2012).

Kabbani, Muhammad Hisham, *Encyclopedia of Islamic Doctrine, vols 1–7* (Chicago: Kazi Publications, 1998).

Karamustafa, Ahmet T., *Sufism: The Formative Period* (Edinburgh: Edinburgh University Press, 2007).

Keller, Nu Ha Mim (ed.), *The Reliance of the Traveller: A Classic Manual of Islamic Sacred Law* (Translation of *'Umdat al-Salik* by Ahmad ibn Naqib al-Misri) (Beltsville: Amana Publications, 1997).

Kepel, Gilles, *The War for Muslim Minds: Islam and the West* (Cambridge MA: Harvard University Press, 2004).

Kundnani, Arun, *The Muslims are Coming!: Islamophobia, Extremism, and the Domestic War on Terror* (London: Verso, 2014).

Jacobson, Jessica, *Islam in Transition: Religion and Identity among British Pakistani Youth* (London: Routledge, 1998).

Janmohamed, Shelina Zahra, *Love in a Headscarf: Muslim Woman seeks The One* (London: Aurum Press, 2009).

Lean, Nathan, *The Islamophobia Industry: How the Right Manufactures Fear of Muslims* (London: Pluto Press, 2012).

Lewis, Philip, *Islamic Britain: Religion, Politics and Identity among British Muslims* (London: I.B.Tauris, 1994).

————, *Young, British and Muslim* (London: Continuum International Publishing, 2007).

Lia, Brynjar, *The Society of the Muslim Brothers in Egypt: The Rise of an Islamic Mass Movement 1928–1942* (New York: Ithaca Press, 1996).

Malik, Aftab, *The Broken Chain: Reflections on the Neglect of Tradition* (Bristol: Amal Press, 2002).

Maréchal, Brigette, *The Muslim Brothers in Europe: Roots and Discourse* (Leiden: Brill, 2008).

Martin, Richard C. and Abbas Barzegar (eds), *Islamism: Contested Perspectives on Political Islam* (Stanford: Stanford University Press, 2009).

McAdam, Doug, John D. McCarthy and Mayer N. Zald (eds), *Comparative Perspectives on Social Movements: Political Opportunities, Mobilizing Structures, and Cultural Framings* (Cambridge: Cambridge University Press, 1998).

McAdam, Doug, Sidney Tarrow and Charles Tilly, *Dynamics of Contention* (Cambridge: Cambridge University Press, 2001).

McGhee, Derek, *The End of Multiculturalism? Terrorism, Integration and Human Rights* (Maidenhead: Open University Press, 2008).

McLoughlin, Sean, 'The state, new Muslim leaderships and Islam as a resource for public engagement in Britain', in J. Cesari and S. McLoughlin (eds), *European Muslims and the Secular State* (Farnham: Ashgate Publishing, 2006).

Meer, Nasar, *Citizenship, Identity and the Politics of Multiculturalism: The Rise of Muslim Consciousness* (London: Palgrave Macmillan, 2010).

Meijer, Roel (ed.), *Global Salafism: Islam's New Religious Movement* (London: Hurst Publishers, 2009).

Melucci, Alberto, *Challenging Codes: Collective Action in the Information Age* (Cambridge: Cambridge University Press, 1996).

Modood, Tariq, *Multicultural Politics: Racism, Ethnicity and Muslims in Britain* (Edinburgh: Edinburgh University Press, 2005).

Mondal, Anshuman A., *Young British Muslim Voices* (Westport: Greenwood World Publishing, 2008).

Murad, Khurram, *Islamic Movement in the West: Reflections on Some Issues* (Markfield: The Islamic Foundation, 1981).

————, *Let us be Muslims: Islamic Movement in the West* (Markfield: The Islamic Foundation, 1985).

————, *Muslim Youth in the West: Towards a New Education Strategy* (Markfield: The Islamic Foundation, 1986).

————, *Da'Wah among non-Muslims in the West: Some Conceptual and Methodological Aspects* (Markfield: The Islamic Foundation, 1986).

————, *The Islamic Movement: Dynamics of Values, Power and Change* (Markfield: The Islamic Foundation, 2007).

Nasr, Seyyed Hossein, *Traditional Islam in the Modern World* (London: John Wiley & Sons, 1990).

———, *The Heart of Islam: Enduring Value for Humanity* (New York: HarperCollins, 2004).

Nasr, Seyyed Vali Reza, *Mawdudi & the Making of Islamic Revivalism* (Oxford: Oxford University Press, 1997).

———, *The Vanguard of the Islamic Revolution: Jama'at-i Islami of Pakistan* (London: I.B.Tauris, 2002).

Nicholson, Reynold A., *The Mystics of Islam* (Sacramento: World Wisdom Books, 2004).

Nielsen, Jorgen S., *Muslims in Western Europe* (Edinburgh: Edinburgh University Press, 1992).

Omaar, Rageh, *Only Half of Me: Being a Muslim in Britain* (London: Penguin Books, 2007).

O'Neill, Sean and Daniel McGrory, *The Suicide Factory: Abu Hamza and the Finsbury Park Mosque* (London: Harper Collins, 2006).

Pankhurst, Reza, *The Inevitable Caliphate?: A History of the Struggle for Global Islamic Union, 1924 to the Present* (London: Hurst Publishers, 2013).

———, *Hizb ut-Tahrir: The Untold History of the Liberation Party* (London: Hurst Publishers, 2015).

Pargeter, Alison, *The Muslim Brotherhood: The Burden of Tradition* (London: Saqi Books, 2010).

Pervez, Zahid, *Building a New Society: An Islamic Approach to Social Change* (Markfield: Revival Publications, 1997).

Phillips, Melanie, *Londonistan: How Britain Created a Terror State Within* (London: Gibson Square, 2008).

Poston, Larry A., *Islamic Da'wah in the West: Muslim Missionary Activity and the Dynamics of Conversion to Islam* (New York: Oxford University Press, 1992).

Ramadan, Tariq, *To be a European Muslim* (Markfield: The Islamic Foundation, 1999).

———, *Western Muslims and the Future of Islam* (Oxford: Oxford University Press, 2004).

———, *Islam and The Arab Awakening* (New York: Oxford University Press, 2012).

Roy, Olivier, *Globalised Islam: The Search for a New Ummah* (London: Hurst Publishers, 2004).

Robert, Na'ima B., *From My Sisters' Lips* (London: Bantam Books, 2005).

Safi, Omid (ed.), *Progressive Muslims: On Gender, Justice and Pluralism* (Oxford: Oneworld Publications, 2002).

Sanyal, Usha, *Ahmad Riza Khan Barelwi: In the Path of the Prophet* (Oxford: Oneworld Publications, 2012).

Sardar, Ziauddin, *Desperately Seeking Paradise: Journeys of a Sceptical Muslim* (London: Granta, 2005).

Seddon, Mohammad Siddique, Dilwar Hussain and Nadeem Malik (eds), *British Muslims, Loyalty and Belonging* (Markham: Islamic Foundation, 2002).

Shaha, Alom, *Young Atheist's Handbook: Lessons for Living a Good Life Without God* (London: Biteback Publishing, 2012).

Shakir, Zaid, *Scattered Pictures: Reflections of an American Muslim* (Hayward: Zaytuna Institute, 2005).

——— (trans.), *Heirs of the Prophets* (Chicago: Starlatch Press, 2006).

———, *Treatise for the Seekers of Guidance* (San Francisco: NID Publishers, 2008).

Siddiqui, Ataullah (ed.), *Ismail Raji al-Faruqi: Islam and Other Faiths* (Markfield: The Islamic Foundation, 2007).

Sinclair, Kirstine, *The Caliphate as Homeland: Hizb ut-Tahrir in Denmark and Britain* (Odense: Centre for Contemporary Middle East Studies Institute for History and Civilization, University of Southern Denmark. Unpublished PhD Dissertation, 2010).

Sirreyeh, Elizabeth, *Sufis and Anti-Sufis: The Defence, Rethinking and Rejection of Sufism in the Modern World* (London: Routledge Curzon Press, 1998).

Stjernholm, Simon, *Lovers of Muhammad: A Study of Naqshbandi-Haqqani Sufis in the Twenty-First Century* (Lund: Centre for Religion and Theology, Lund University. PhD Thesis, 2011).

Tamimi, Azzam S., *Rachid Ghannouchi: A Democrat within Islamism* (Oxford: Oxford University Press, 2001).

Tarlo, Emma, *Visibly Muslim: Fashion, Politics, Faith* (Oxford: Berg, 2010).

Thomas, Paul, *Responding to the Threat of Violent Extremism: Failing to Prevent* (London: Bloomsbury Academic, 2012).

Vidino, Lorenzo, *The New Muslim Brotherhood in the West* (New York: Columbia University Press, 2010).

Voll, John Obert, *Islam: Continuity and Change in the Modern World* (Syracuse: Syracuse University Press, 1994).

Watt, W. Montgomery, *The Faith and Practice of Al-Ghazali* (London: Allen & Unwin, 1953).

Wiktorowicz, Quintan, *The Management of Islamic Activism: Salafis, the Muslim Brotherhood and State Power in Jordan* (Albany: State University of New York Press, 2000).

———— (ed.), *Islamic Activism: A Social Movement Theory Approach* (Bloomington and Indianapolis: Indiana University Press, 2004).

————, *Radical Islam Rising: Muslim Extremism in the West* (Lanham: Rowman & Littlefield, 2005).

————, 'The Salafi Movement: Violence and the fragmentation of community' in M. Cooke and B. Lawrence (eds), *Muslim Networks from Hajj to Hip Hop* (Chapel Hill: University of North Carolina Press, 2005).

Woodhead, Linda and Rebecca Catto (eds), *Religion and Change in Modern Britain* (Abingdon: Routledge, 2012).

Yassin-Kassab, Robin, *The Road from Damascus* (London: Hamish Hamilton, 2008).

Ye'or, Bat, *Eurabia: The Euro-Arab Axis* (Madison: Fairleigh Dickinson University Press, 2005).

Yusuf, Hamza (trans.), *Miracles of the Quran from the Burda of Imam Al-Busiri* (California: Sandala Ltd, 2002).

———— (trans.), *Purification of the Heart Signs: Symptoms and Cures of the Spiritual Diseases of the Heart* (Chicago: Starlatch Press, 2004).

———— (trans.), *The Creed of Imam al-Tahawi* (Chicago: Zaytuna Institute, 2008).

Yusuf, Hamza and Zaid Shakir, *Agenda to Change our Condition* (Chicago: Zaytuna Institute, 2008).

Zallum, Abdul Qadeem, *How the Khilafah was Destroyed* (London: Khilafah Publications, 2000).

Zaman, Muhammad Qassim, *The Ulama in Contemporary Islam: Custodians of Change* (New Jersey: Princeton University Press, 2002).

Journal Articles

Abedin, Mahan, 'Al-Muhajiroun in the UK: An Interview with Sheikh Omar Bakri Mohammed', *Spotlight on Terror* 2/5 (2005).

Allen, Chris, 'The death of multiculturalism: blaming and shaming British Muslims', *Durham Journal of Anthropology* 1/14 (2007).

Al-Rashid, Mahmud, *Q-News*, 27 August 1993.

Anjum, Ovamir, 'Islam as a discursive tradition: Talal Asad and his interlocutors', *Comparative Studies of South Asia, Africa and the Middle East* 27/3 (2007).

Appleton, Michael, 'The political attitudes of Muslims studying at British universities in the post-9/11 world (Part 1)', *Journal of Muslim Minority Affairs* 25/2 (2005), pp. 177–8.

Asghar, Waseef, 'A Conversation with Ahtesham Ali', *Q-News*, 12–19 August 1994.

Bayat, Asef, 'What is post-Islamism?', *ISIM Review* 16 (2005), p. 5.

Bernard, Cheryl, 'Five pillars of democracy: how the west can promote an Islamic reformation', *RAND Corporation* 28/1 (2004), pp. 10–13.

Birt, Yahya, 'Review Article: "Muslims and the Politics of Race and Faith in Britain and Europe"', *The Muslim World Book Review* 26/1 (2005).

Boubekeur, Amel, 'Cool and competitive: Muslim culture in the West', *ISIM Review* 16 (2005) pp. 12–13.

Brandon, James and Raffaello Pantucci, 'UK Islamists and the Arab Uprisings', *Current Trends in Islamist Ideology* 13 (2012).

Chambers, Claire, '"Guantánamo Boy": An interview with Moazzam Begg', *Postcolonial Text* 6/2 (2011).

Commins, David, 'Taqi al-Din al-Nabhani and the Islamic Liberation Party', *The Muslim World* lxxxi/3–4 (1991).

Dumbe, Yunus and Abdulkader Tayob, 'Salafis in Cape Town in Search of Purity, Certainty and Social Impact', *Die Welt des Islams* 51 (2011).

Eickelman, Dale, 'Mass Higher Education and the Religious Imagination in Contemporary Arab Societies', *American Ethnologist* 19/4 (1992), pp. 643–55.

El Fadl, Khaled Abou, 'Islam and the Theology of Power', *Middle East Report* 221 (2001).

———, 'The Orphans of Modernity and the Clash of Civilizations', *Global Dialogue* 4/2 (2002), pp. 1–16.

Geaves, Ron, 'The reproduction of Jamaat-i Islami in Britain', *Islam and Christian–Muslim Relations* 6/2 (1995).

———, 'Tradition, Innovation and Authentication: Replicating the "Ahl as-Sunna wa Jamaat" in Britain', *Comparative Islamic Studies* 1/1 (2005), pp. 1–20.

Gilliat, Sophie, 'A descriptive account of Islamic youth organisations in the UK', *The American Journal of Islamic Social Sciences* 14/1 (1996), pp. 99–111.

Graham, William A., 'Traditionalism in Islam: An Essay in Interpretation', *Journal of Interdisciplinary History* 23/3 (1993).

Hashem, Mazen, 'Contemporary Islamic activism: the shades of praxis', *Sociology of Religion* 67/1 (2006), pp. 23–41.

Hopkins, Peter E., 'Youthful Muslim masculinities: gender and generational relations', *Transactions of the Institute of British Geographers* 31/3 (2006), pp. 337–52.

Kundnani, Arun, 'Islamism and the roots of liberal rage', *Race & Class* 50/2 (2008), pp. 40–68.

Lauzière, Henri, 'The Construction of *Salafiyya*: Reconsidering Salafism from the Perspective of Conceptual History', *International Journal of Middle East Studies* 42/3 (2010), pp. 369–89.

Mayer, Jean-François, 'Hizb ut-Tahrir – The Next Al-Qaida, Really?', *PSIO Occasional Paper* 4 (2004).

Murad, Abdal-Hakim, 'Islamic Spirituality: the forgotten revolution', *Cambridge Mosque Project*, n.d., available at http://www.masud.co.uk/ISLAM/ahm/fgtnrevo. htm.

Murad, Khurram, 'Message to Young Muslims'. Talk given to members of Young Muslims in 1996, reproduced in *Q-News International* 248–50, 27 December 1996–9 January 1997.

Raj, Dhooleka Sarhadi, '"Who the hell do you think you are?" Promoting religious identity among young Hindus in Britain', *Ethnic and Racial Studies* 23/3 (2000), pp. 535–58.

Sardar, Ziauddin, 'Paper, printing and compact disks: the making and unmaking of Islamic culture', *Media, Culture & Society* 15 (1993), pp. 43–59.

Singh, Jasjit, 'Sikh-ing Online: The role of the internet in the religious lives of young British Sikhs', *Contemporary South Asia* 22/1 (2014), pp. 82–97.

Snow, David A. and Scott C. Byrd, 'Ideology, framing processes, and Islamic terrorist movements', *Mobilization: An International Quarterly Review* 12/1 (2007), pp. 119–36.

Svensson, Jonas, 'Mind the beard! Deference, purity and Islamization of everyday life as micro-factors in a Salafi cultural epidemiology', *Comparative Islamic Studies* 8/1–2 (2012).

Taji-Farouki, Suha, 'Islamic Discourse and Modern Political Methods: An Analysis of al-Nabhani's Reading of the Canonical Textual Sources of Islam', *American Journal of Islamic Social Sciences* 11/3 (1994), pp. 365–94.

Wiktorowicz, Quintan, 'Anatomy of the Salafi Movement', *Studies in Conflict & Terrorism* 29/3 (2006), pp. 207–39.

Yawar, Asad, 'Seven years of Q-News', *Q-News* 302–3, March 1999.

Reports

Ahmed, Houriya and Hannah Stuart, *Hizb ut-Tahrir: Ideology and Strategy* (London: The Centre for Social Cohesion, 2009).

Ahmed, Sughra, *Seen and not Heard: Voices of Young British Muslims* (Markfield: Policy Research Centre, Islamic Foundation, 2009).

Ahmed, Sughra and Naved Siddiqi, *British by Dissent* (London: Muslim Youth Helpline, 2014).

Ali, Sundas, et al., *British Muslims in Numbers: A Demographic, Socio-economic and Health Profile of Muslims in Britain Drawing on the 2011 Census* (London: The Muslim Council of Britain, 2015).

Amghar, Sami, 'Salafism and Radicalization of Young European Muslims' in S. Amghar, A. Boubekeur, M. Emerson (eds), *European Islam: Challenges for Public Policy and Society* (Brussels: Center for European Policy, 2007).

Baran, Zeyno (ed.), *The Challenge of Hizb ut-Tahrir: Deciphering and Combating Radical Islamist Ideology* (Washington: Nixon Center, 2004).

Birt, Yahya et al., *Studies into Violent Radicalisation; Lot 2 The Beliefs, Ideologies and Narratives* (London: Change Institute, 2008).

Bright, Martin, *When Progressives Treat with Reactionaries: The British State's Flirtation with Radical Islamism* (London: Policy Exchange, 2006).

Choudhury, Tufayl, *The Role of Muslim Identity Politics in Radicalisation (a study in progress)* (London: Department of Communities and Local Government, 2007).

Hizb ut-Tahrir, *The Future for Muslims in Britain: The British Government's Agenda* (London: Hizb ut-Tahrir, 2011).

Hunter, Shireen T. and Huma Malik (eds), *Islam in Europe and the United States: A Comparative Perspective* (Washington: Center for Strategic and International Studies, 2002).

Institute of Community Cohesion's report, *Understanding and appreciating Muslim diversity: Towards better Engagement and Participation* (London: ICoCo, 2008).

Islamic Society of Britain, *Term Report 2006–2008* (London: Islamic Society of Britain, 2009).

———, *Connected Together: Term Report 2009–2011* (London: Islamic Society of Britain, 2010).

———, *Living Islam 2011: Conference Programme* London: Islamic Society of Britain, 2011).

Khan, Khalida, *Preventing Violent Extremism (PVE) and PREVENT: a Response from the Muslim Community* (London: An-Nisa Society, 2009).

Klausen, Jytte, *A Jihadist census: 'Al Qaeda-Affiliated and 'Homegrown' Jihadism in the UK: 1999–2010* (London: The Institute for Strategic Dialogue, 2010).

Lambert, Robert and Jonathan Githens-Mazer, *Islamophobia and Anti-Muslim Hate Crime: UK Case Studies 2010* (Exeter: European Muslim Research Centre, University of Exeter, 2010).

Mandaville, Peter, 'Europe's Muslim youth: Dynamics of alienation and integration', in S.T. Hunter and H. Malik (eds), *Islam in Europe and the United States: A Comparative Perspective* (Washington: Center for Strategic and International Studies, 2002).

———, 'Is the Post-Islamism Thesis Still Valid' for the *Rethinking Islamist Politics* conference 24 January 2014 (Washington: Project on Middle East Political Science. 2014). Available at http://pomeps.org/2014/02/11/rethinking-islamist-politics-brief/ (accessed 13 May 2015).

Mandaville, Peter, Dilwar Hussain and Maha Azzam, *Muslim Networks and Movements in Western Europe* (Washington: The Pew Forum, 2010). Available at http://www.pewforum.org/Muslim/Muslim-Networks-and-Movements-in-Western-Europe-Event-Transcript.aspx (accessed 13 May 2015).

Oborne, Peter and James Jones, *Muslims under Siege: Alienating Vulnerable Communities* (London: Democratic Audit, Human Rights Centre, University of Essex in association with Channel 4 Dispatches, 2008).

Pew Forum, *Mapping the Global Muslim Population: A Report on the Size and Distribution of the World's Muslim Population* (Washington: Pew Research Center, 2009).

Salafi Publications, *Who are the Salafis? Learn about Islaam on the Methodology of the Prophets* (Birmingham: Salafi Publications, n.d.).

Shaheen, Shaqwir, *The Evolution of Hizb ut-Tahrir in Britain* (London: Muslim College. Unpublished MA thesis, 2008).

Spalek, Basia, Salwa El Awa and Laura Zahra McDonald, *Police-Muslim Engagement and Partnerships for the Purposes of Counter-Terrorism: An Examination* (Birmingham: University of Birmingham, 2009).

Whine, Michael, 'Hizb ut-Tahrir in Open Societies' in Z. Baran (ed.), *The Challenge of Hizb ut-Tahrir: Deciphering and Combating Radical Islamist Ideology* (Washington: Nixon Center, 2004).

Internet articles

Abedin, Mahan, 'Al-Muhajiroun in the UK: An Interview with Sheikh Omar Bakri Mohammed' *Spotlight on Terror* 2/5 (2005), p. 5. Also available at http://www.jamestown.org/single/?tx_ttnews%5Btt_news%5D=290&no_cache=1#.VUuH_vlViko (accessed 7 May 2015).

Ahmed, Nafeez, 'How Violent Extremists Hijacked London-Based "Counter-Extremism" Think Tank', *AlterNet*, 28 April 2015. Available at http://www.alternet.org/world/how-violent-extremists-hijacked-london-based-counter-extremism-think-tank (accessed 18 May 2015).

'Al-Waie', June 2001. Available at http://www.alwaie.org/home/issue/170/doc/170w02doc.zip (link not working, 21 May 2015).

Baksh, Nazim, 'In the Spirit of Tradition', *Cambridge Mosque Project*, n.d. Available at http://masud.co.uk/ISLAM/misc/tradition.htm (accessed 8 May 2015).

Githens-Mazer, Jonathan and Robert Lambert, 'Quilliam on Prevent: the Wrong Diagnosis', *The Guardian*, 19 October 2009. Available at http://www.theguardian.com/commentisfree/belief/2009/oct/19/prevent-quilliam-foundation-extremism (accessed 18 May 2015).

Godlas, Alan, 'Sufism, the West, and Modernity', Islam and Islamic Studies Resources, n.d. Available at http://www.uga.edu/islam/sufismwest.html (accessed 21 May 2015).

Hanson, Hamza Yusuf (trans.), 'Shaykh Murabtal Hajji's Fatwa on Following One of the Four Accepted Madhabs', *Cambridge Mosque Project*, n.d. Available at http://www.masud.co.uk/ISLAM/misc/mhfatwa.htm (accessed 21 May 2015).

Hizb ut-Tahrir, 'Adopting Secularism in Government is Apostasy from Islam', *Hizb ut-Tahrir Leaflet*, 2 July 1996. Available at http://www.islammuslims.com/article/discussion_q_a/discussion_forums/adopting_secularism_in_government_is_apostasy_from_islam (accessed 19 May 2015).

'Jimaswatch', *JIMAS and Abu Muntasir: A report on who they are, what they say and which friends they have*. Available at http://www.docstoc.com/docs/95298538/JIMAS-and-Abu-Muntasir (accessed on 14 May 2015).

Keller, Nuh Ha Mim, 'How would you respond to the Claim that Sufism is bid'a?', *Cambridge Mosque Project*, n.d. Available at http://www.masud.co.uk/ISLAM/nuh/sufism.htm (accessed 19 May 2015).

———, 'The Place of Tasawwuf in Traditional Islamic Sciences', *Cambridge Mosque Project*, 1995. Available at http://www.masud.co.uk/ISLAM/nuh/sufitlk.htm (accessed 21 May 2015).

Khilafah.com, 'The Muslim Ummah will never submit to the Jews', *Hizb ut-Tahrir Leaflet*, 3 November 1999. Available at http://web.archive.org/web/20041118022619/www.khilafah.com/home/category.php?DocumentID=94&TagID=3 (accessed 21 May 2015).

———, 'The Arab and Muslim rulers' betrayal of the issue of Palestine and its people', *Hizb ut-Tahrir Leaflet*, 25 March 2001. Available at http://web.archive.org/web/20010617234537/www.khilafah.com/1421/category.php?DocumentID=1621&TagID=3 (accessed 21 May 2015).

Lee, Umar, *The Rise and Fall of the Salafi Dawah in North America* (Kindle Edition, 2014). Available at http://www.amazon.com/Rise-Fall-Salafi-Dawah-America-ebook/dp/B00I1AEYL2 (accessed 19 May 2015).

Malik, Shiv, 'Youth wing of UK Muslim group calls for jihad', *The Independent*, 31 July 2005. Available at http://www.independent.co.uk/news/uk/this-britain/youth-wing-of-uk-muslim-group-calls-for-jihad-302698.html (accessed 19 May 2015).

————, 'The attacks on London, part three: Conflict within Islam', *The Independent*, 31 July 2005. Available at http://www.independent.co.uk/news/uk/crime/the-attacks-on-london-part-three-conflict-within-islam-302702.html (accessed 19 May 2015).

Morris, Steven, 'Muslim group holds "anti-terrorism" summer camp', *The Guardian*, 8 August 2010. Available at http://www.theguardian.com/world/2010/aug/08/muslim-anti-terrorism-camp (accessed 21 May 2015).

Murad, Abdal-Hakim, 'Understanding the four madhabs: the problem with anti-madhhabism', *Cambridge Mosque Project*, n.d. Available at http://www.masud.co.uk/ISLAM/ahm/newmadhh.htm (accessed 21 May 2015).

MuslimHipHop.com, 'Hip-Hop – Poetic Pilgrimage', n.d. Available at http://www.muslimhiphop.com/index.php?p=Hip-Hop/Poetic_Pilgrimage (accessed 21 May 2015).

Norton-Taylor, Richard, 'Former MI5 Chief delivers damning verdict on Iraq invasion', *The Guardian*, 20 July 2010. Available at http://www.theguardian.com/uk/2010/jul/20/chilcot-mi5-boss-iraq-war (accessed 13 May 2015).

Oliver, Haneef James, 'The Wahhabi Myth'. Available from http://www.islamdaily.org/Media/Documents/EN-thewahhabimyth.pdf (accessed 19 May 2015).

Salafi Publications, 'Historical Development of the Methodologies of al-Ikhwaan al-Muslimeen and Their Effect and Influence upon Contemporary Salafee Dawah', *Salafi Publications*, March 2003. Available at http://www.salafipublications.com/sps/downloads/pdf/MNJ180001.pdf (accessed 19 May 2015).

Uwais, Abu, 'Story of an ex-Hizbi', *Indigo Jo Blogs: Politics, tech and media issues from a Muslim perspective*, n.d. Available at http://www.blogistan.co.uk/blog/articles/story_of_an_ex-hizbi (accessed 21 May 2015).

Wahid, Abdul, 'Hizb-ut-Tahrir's distinction', *Open Democracy.net*, 15 August 2005. Available at www.opendemocracy.net/conflictterrorism/criticism_2755.jsp (accessed 13 May 2015).

Yusuf, Hamza, 'Tasawwuf/Sufism in Islam', *As-Sunnah Foundation of America*, 4 May 1997. Available at http://www.sunnah.org/events/hamza/hamza.htm (accessed 11 May 2015).

Websites consulted

Allaahu Akbar: http://www.allaahuakbar.net/ (website no longer working, 21 May 2015).

Al Kawthar Academy, Birmingham: http://www.akacademy.eu/ (accessed 21 May 2015).

Al Muntada Al-Islami Trust: http://www.almuntadatrust.org/ (accessed 21 May 2015).

Association for British Muslims: http://members.tripod.com/british_muslims_assn/contents.html (accessed 21 May 2015).

British Muslim Forum: http://www.thebmf.org.uk/ (website no longer working, 21 May 2015).

Cambridge Mosque Project: http://www.masud.co.uk/ (accessed 21 May 2015).

City Circle: http://www.thecitycircle.com/ (accessed 21 May 2015).

Council of Ex-Muslims of Britain: http://www.ex-muslim.org.uk/ (accessed 21 May 2015).

Darul Iftaa (Institute of Islamic Jurisprudence): http://www.daruliftaa.com/ (accessed 21 May 2015).

Deenport: www.deenport.com (accessed 21 May 2015).

East London Mosque & London Muslim Centre: http://www.eastlondonmosque.org.uk/ (accessed 21 May 2015).

emel magazine: www.emel.com (accessed 21 May 2015).

Eye on Gay Muslims: http://gaymuslims.org/ (accessed 21 May 2015).

Federation of Student Islamic Societies: http://www.fosis.org.uk/ (accessed 21 May 2015).

Islam Channel: http://www.islamchannel.tv/ (accessed 21 May 2015).

Islam For Today: http://www.islamfortoday.com (website no longer working, 21 May 2015).

Islam Online: http://www.islamonline.net/ (accessed 21 May 2015).

Islamic Awakening: http://www.islamicawakening.com/ (website no longer working, 21 May 2015).

Islamic College: http://www.islamic-college.ac.uk/ (accessed 21 May 2015).

Islamic Education and Research Academy (iERA): http://www.iera.org.uk/ (accessed 21 May 2015).

Islamic Forum of Europe: http://www.islamicforumeurope.com/ (accessed 21 May 2015).

Islamic Foundation: http://www.islamic-foundation.org.uk/ (accessed 21 May 2015).

Islamic Human Rights Commission: http://www.ihrc.org/ (accessed 21 May 2015).

Islamic Society of Baltimore: http://www.isb.org/ (accessed 21 May 2015).

Jamiat Ulama-e-Britain: http://www.jamiat.co.uk/ (accessed 21 May 2015).

JIMAS: http://www.jimas.org/ (accessed 21 May 2015).

Karima Institute: http://www.karimia.com/ (accessed 21 May 2015).

Lamppost Productions: http://www.lamppostproductions.com/ (accessed 21 May 2015).

Lancashire Council of Mosques: http://www.lancashiremosques.com/ (accessed 21 May 2015).

Minhaj-ul-Quran International UK: http://www.minhajuk.org/ (accessed 21 May 2015).

Muslim Association of Britain: http://www.mabonline.net/ (accessed 21 May 2015).

Muslim Council of Britain: http://www.mcb.org.uk/ (accessed 21 May 2015).

Muslim Directory: http://www.muslimdirectory.co.uk/ (website under construction, 21 May 2015).

Muslim Engagement and Development: http://www.mend.org.uk/ (accessed 21 May 2015).

MuslimHeritage.com: http://www.muslimheritage.com/ (accessed 21 May 2015).

Muslim Public Affairs Committee UK: http://www.mpacuk.org/ (accessed 21 May 2015).

Muslim Student Society: http://www.mssuk.net (website no longer working, 21 May 2015).

Muslim Youth Helpline (MYH): www.myh.org.uk/ (accessed 21 May 2015).

Nawawi Foundation: http://www.nawawi.org/ (accessed 21 May 2015).

New Islamic Directions: http://www.newislamicdirections.com/ (accessed 21 May 2015).

Peace TV: http://www.peacetv.tv/ (accessed 21 May 2015).

Website of Dr Bilal Philips: http://www.bilalphilips.com/ (accessed 21 May 2015).

Qibla – Islamic Sciences Online: http://www.qibla.com/ (accessed 21 May 2015).

The Revival: http://www.therevival.co.uk/ (accessed 21 May 2015).

Salaam: http://www.salaam.co.uk/ (accessed 21 May 2015).

SalafiTalk.net: http://salafitalk.net/ (accessed 21 May 2015).

Sandala: http://sandala.org/blog/ (accessed 21 May 2015).

The Seekers Path: http://theseekerspath.com/ (accessed 21 May 2015).

Shadhili Tariqa: http://shadhilitariqa.com/ (website no longer working, 21 May 2015).

Spirit 21: http://www.spirit21.co.uk/ (accessed 21 May 2015).

Sufi Muslim Council: http://www.sufimuslimcouncil.org.uk/ (accessed 21 May 2015).

As-Sunnah Foundation of America: http://sunnah.org/ (accessed 21 May 2015).

Ummah.com – The Online Muslim Community: http://www.Ummah.com/forum (accessed 21 May 2015).

Unto The One: http://untotheone.com/ (accessed 21 May 2015).

World Assembly of Muslim Youth UK: http://www.wamy.co.uk/ (accessed 21 May 2015).

Yanabi.com – Reviving the Spirit of Islam: http://www.yanabi.com/ (accessed 21 May 2015).

Young Muslim Organisation: http://www.ymouk.com/ (website no longer working, 21 May 2015).

Young Muslims UK: http://www.ymuk.net/ (website no longer working, 21 May 2015).

Zhikr.org (website no longer working, 21 May 2015).

INDEX